Distributive Institutions

The crisis of distribution is one of the longest standing and most complicated issues facing human society. Imbued with social, political, historic, and cultural elements, it varies significantly across different countries as a result of all these factors. As an emerging economy which transferred from a planned to a market economy, China has experienced large distribution gaps since it implemented the Reform and Opening-up Policy in the early 1980s, requiring stronger economic law to mitigate and regulate the crisis of distribution.

In this second volume, the author analyzes crises of distribution from a theoretical perspective and proposes law and policy solutions. Believing that such crises are a collective result of systematic limitations, the author proposes a theoretical framework of "system–distribution–development" in order to resolve distribution problems and promote economic development. He argues that a crisis of distribution cannot be avoided without coordinated development of economic law and relevant constitutional, civil, and commercial law systems. In addition, it is necessary to differentiate the territories, industries, enterprises, and individuals that constitute such diverse systems.

The book should be of keen interest to researchers and students of law, economics, and political science.

Shouwen Zhang is a professor at Peking University Law School. His research interests include economic law, social law, information law, and more.

China Perspectives

The *China Perspectives* series focuses on translating and publishing works by leading Chinese scholars, writing about both global topics and China-related themes. It covers humanities and social sciences, education, media and psychology, as well as many interdisciplinary themes.

This is the first time any of these books have been published in English for international readers. The series aims to put forward a Chinese perspective, give insights into cutting-edge academic thinking in China, and inspire researchers globally.

To submit proposals, please contact the Taylor & Francis Publisher for China Publishing Programme, Lian Sun (Lian.Sun@informa.com).

Titles in law currently include:

Building the Rule of Law in China
Procedure, Discourse and Hermeneutic Community
Weidong Ji

Deciphering Intellectual Property Law and its Conflict/Reconciliation with Competition Law
Kongzhong Liu

The Crisis of Distribution (Set: The Crisis of Distribution and the Regulation of Economic Law)
Theoretical Analysis from Economic Law
Shouwen Zhang

Distributive Institutions (Set: The Crisis of Distribution and the Regulation of Economic Law)
The View of Economic Law
Shouwen Zhang

For more information, please visit https://www.routledge.com/China-Perspect ives/book-series/CPH

Distributive Institutions
The View of Economic Law

Shouwen Zhang

LONDON AND NEW YORK

This book is published with financial support from the Chinese Fund for the Humanities and Social Sciences.

First published in English 2021
by Routledge
2 Park Square, Milton Park, Abingdon, Oxon, OX14 4RN

and by Routledge
52 Vanderbilt Avenue, New York, NY 10017

Routledge is an imprint of the Taylor & Francis Group, an Informa business

© 2021 Shouwen Zhang
Translated by Xu Yan and Zhang Dong

The right of Shouwen Zhang to be identified as the author of this work has been asserted by him in accordance with sections 77 and 78 of the Copyright, Designs and Patents Act 1988.

All rights reserved. No part of this book may be reprinted or reproduced or utilised in any form or by any electronic, mechanical, or other means, now known or hereafter invented, including photocopying and recording, or in any information storage or retrieval system, without permission in writing from the publishers.

Trademark notice: Product or corporate names may be trademarks or registered trademarks, and are used only for identification and explanation without intent to infringe.

English version by permission of Peking University Press.

British Library Cataloguing-in-Publication Data
A catalogue record for this book is available from the British Library

Library of Congress Cataloging-in-Publication Data
A catalog record has been requested for this book

ISBN: 978-0-367-67670-4 (hbk)
ISBN: 978-1-003-13229-5 (ebk)

Typeset in Times New Roman
by Deanta Global Publishing Services, Chennai, India

Contents

List of tables	vi
Preface	vii

1	Introduction	1
2	The consistency of key distribution systems	6
3	Unification and difference of distribution systems	49
4	The legal protection of distribution rights and interests	100
5	Legal response to distribution crises	149
6	Conclusion	178

Bibliography	181
Index	194

Tables

2.1	The shift of the taxation law system and taxation administration	38
2.2	The approach, area, and entity of tax reduction	40

Preface

Problems concerning distribution are global. Unbalanced distribution caused by large distribution gaps and unequal distribution has existed in varying degrees throughout different historical periods around the world. These problems have been highly intertwined with elements of society, economy, politics, law, history, and culture. They have close links to issues like economic crises such as the Great Depression in the 1930s and the global financial crisis in 2008, as well as social crises such as the Ebola outbreak and the COVID-19 pandemic.

Distribution problems induce distribution risks which, when accumulated and concentrated, will trigger distribution crises. In essence, every economic crisis is a distribution crisis. Unbalanced distribution causes an unbalanced economy overall, disturbing the proper functioning of the economic and social system. Thus, distribution problems must be addressed on an ongoing basis, and distribution risks must be mitigated in a timely manner to prevent severe distribution crises.

Distribution problems are not limited to economic and social problems, and they affect those of politics and law as well. Legal measures are required to efficiently solve these problems. Within the framework of the rule of law, many kinds of values should be balanced: efficiency, fairness, freedom, and order. Related rights and obligations should be reasonably distributed across multiple legal systems. The efficient enforcement of laws protects the interests of relevant entities and achieves distributive justice. Although differences exist among legal systems in different countries, these systems share common ground in their basic values, which form the common denominator for international and domestic governance in solving distribution problems.

Comprehensive adjustments to numerous legal systems, especially those regarding economic law, are needed to solve distribution problems and guard against distribution risks. Economic law is mainly a concept in countries with civil law. Even so, in the common law system, economic law exists in other forms, such as fiscal law, tax law, financial law, and antitrust law. Although the names of these legal systems vary, in practice they all address distribution problems. Thus, solving distribution problems and defusing distribution crises should be regarded through the theoretical and systematic lens of economic law. Distribution crises should be effectively controlled and addressed by strengthening the regulation of economic law.

viii *Preface*

China, the largest developing country in the world, is a transitioning country (or an "emerging economy") that shifted from a planned economy to a market economy. Thus, China has a special distribution system: its planned economy period stressed "equalitarianism". Its early period of reform and opening up emphasized "prioritizing efficiency with due consideration to fairness". Afterwards, concepts such as "harmonious society" and "scientific development" were proposed, which show an evolution of the understanding of distribution. Needless to say, during its rapid economic development, China, like many other countries, had relatively large differences in the distribution ratios of factors such as labour, capital, and technology, as well as problems such as large distribution gaps and unfair distribution, which are caused by many factors. For this, a policy system and a legal framework had to be established to solve these distribution problems. Of particular necessity was a synergy among legal systems ranging from constitutional law to economic law. In fact, the theme of solving distribution problems has run through the whole process of China's reform and opening-up. Thus, studying distribution can help shed light on the course of China's reform and opening-up and the development of the rule of law. It can also help us gain a comprehensive understanding of the problems in China's economy, society, rule of law, and development.

The successful solution of its distribution problems will determine whether China achieves its modernization goals, which is vital for China's future. Therefore, it is essential that we study distribution problems to figure out how to guard against and mitigate distribution risks and crises through strengthening regulations over economic law. To do this, we need to analyze distribution problems and crises from the perspective of theories on economic law, and we must address the improvement of distribution systems through the lens of economic law.

These problems inspired me to write *Distribution Crisis and Economic Law Regulation*, which was published by Peking University Press in 2014. In 2017, the book was included in the "Translating Chinese Books Project" supported by the National Social Science Fund of China. At the same time, the book was translated into English and published at the invitation of Routledge. During the translation process, I added new ideas to the book based on new theories and practices, and the book is presented in two volumes: *The Crisis of Distribution: Theoretical Analysis from Economic Law* and *Distributive Institutions: The View of Economic Law*. I believe readers from different backgrounds will now find it easier to grasp the ideas in these books from both theoretical and systematic perspectives.

I would like to take the opportunity to extend my most sincere gratitude to the following individuals and institutions (in chronological order): First, I would like to thank the National Social Science Fund of China for including the book in the "Excellent Works in the Social Science Series" and for supporting the publishing efforts of Peking University Press. Second, I would like to thank Mrs Wang Jing, the editor at Peking University Press, for her detailed and efficient work in publishing the Chinese edition and in translating it into English. Third, I would like to thank the National Social Science Fund of China for including the book in the "Translating Chinese Books Project" and for supporting its translation. Fourth,

I would like to thank Routledge and its staff members for their invitation and all their hard work and commitment. Last but not least, I would like to especially thank Dr Xu Yan and Dr Zhang Dong, the translators of the book, both graduates of economic law from the Peking University Law School, now teaching at China University of Political Science and Law. They devoted considerable energy to the translation of the book and demonstrated a high level of professionalism and English proficiency, which guaranteed the quality of this translation. Finally, many thanks to all the diligent "unsung heroes" whose names are not listed here!

Distribution is an extremely complicated topic. Since economic and law systems vary greatly from country to country, each country has its specific problems, which further causes variation in terms of solutions and public opinion. Nevertheless, distribution problems, which have long been a focal point in history, are still significant today, and this calls for investigation by and discussion among colleagues in relevant fields across the world. I am humbly open to criticism and opinions about this book.

Shouwen Zhang
Peking University Law School

1 Introduction

1.1 Issue and theoretical framework

Distribution is a real issue that has huge significance, given that each and every state is striving to deal with it. Distribution risks, and sometimes even distribution crises, may occur if states fail to solve distribution problems. In fact, all kinds of economic crises are, in essence, distribution crises. Therefore, for the purpose of preventing and solving distribution risks and overcoming distribution crises, distribution problems need to be resolved.

The solving of distribution problems is a systematic project which requires comprehensive measures including policy and law. Among the various legal instruments, constitutional law, civil and commercial law, and economic law are of huge importance with regard to solving distribution problems. Economic law, as a typical "distribution law", consists of the state's macro-control laws (including financial laws, taxation laws, monetary laws, and industry laws) and market regulatory laws (including antitrust laws, anti-unfair competition laws, and consumer protection laws), which are all indispensable in preventing and solving distribution risks as well as dealing with distribution crises. Therefore, it is necessary to analyze the distribution system from the perspective of economic law in the discussion of how various institutions aim to resolve distribution problems. This is vital to the adequate establishment of distribution institutions of a state.

The reality that distribution systems are dispersed in economic law requires that attention be paid to the relationship among various types of distribution systems in the analysis of distribution systems from an economic law perspective. This is to enable mutual coordination among these systems and the systematic protection of various distribution rights and interests during the process of distribution problems. Based on that, distribution risks would be prevented and resolved, distribution crises would be effectively resolved, and the development of various agents would be enhanced through the resolution of distribution problems.

The above thinking may constitute an important framework for theoretical analysis – a framework of "system–distribution–development" that is more helpful in analyzing the distribution system from the perspective of economic law.

First, from the perspective of the system, both economic and legal systems are key components to the overall social system. Even though the distribution

2 Introduction

problem is often considered an economic and legal problem, it is a social and political problem as well. This means its resolution needs to be a systematic project. However, an analysis of the various distribution systems that aim to resolve distribution problems solely from the legal angle also constitutes a system, given that the priorities, types, and essence of such systems are substantially different. Because constitutional law, economic law, and civil and commercial law are all involved with distribution systems, it is crucial for there to be mutual coordination and mutual completion among these systems. As a system, the entire distribution institution can function well only when consistency and unity are achieved. Therefore, the consistent and coordinated development of constitutional law and economic law, as well as the internal distribution system within the two kinds of laws, are valuable topics that deserve our attention.

Second, from a distribution perspective, it is important to underscore that of among the various sorts of distribution institutions, the distribution institution in economic law remains the most vital. Therefore, understanding the whole distribution system from the perspective of economic law becomes necessary. Meanwhile, due to the differences among distribution institutions within economic law, the unity and difference of distribution institutions shall be addressed.

In addition, from the perspective of economic law, the core issue of the distribution institution is to provide legal protection of distribution rights. Distribution crises may occur if the distribution problem is not adequately resolved and distribution rights are not effectively protected.

Finally, from the perspective of development, the systematic resolution of distribution problems and comprehensive adjustments to the distribution system are both for the purpose of enhancing development.

1.2 Logical framework and basic contents

The aforementioned theoretical framework based on "system–distribution–development" could form the logical framework for this book. First, it views the distribution system, among various legal systems, as one thing in the system of legal institutions that examines the relations between the systems of distribution in economic law and other legal areas as well as the relations among various distribution systems in economic law. Second, based on such "relations", it emphasizes the key factors that influence distribution systems in economic law in order to understand relevant elements that affect distribution systems in economic law. This makes it possible to comprehend the balance between the unity and diversity of these distribution systems, as well as the embedded legal values. Third, on the foundation of focusing on the realistic differences among agents and distribution systems, it further analyzes the protection of the distribution rights of different objects implicated in the different distribution systems, thereby revealing the defects in formulating and implementing laws and regulations and approaches to resolving such defects. At last, it discusses the main functions of different distribution systems in dealing with distribution issues and overcoming distribution crises. Such an analysis illustrates how distribution systems may facilitate the

Introduction 3

development process which remains crucial to the existence of the distribution systems.

This outline is formed on the basis of the theoretical framework of "system–distribution–development", from which a clue of "internal/external relation-distribution difference-distribution rights-crisis response" could be extracted. This is because from systematic analyses to the distribution system, the main focuses are the external and internal relations of distribution institutions in the area of economic law. The aim is to identify agent differences in terms of the reality and resolution of relevant and diversified distribution problems by balancing the unity and differences of distribution institutions as well as reflected legal values. Meanwhile, the divergence in distribution is the prerequisite and foundation for the legal protection of the distribution rights of relevant agents. Only through the protection of the distribution rights of relevant agents can distribution problems be settled and distribution risks be prevented and solved. This means distribution crises could be effectively resolved while various agents comprehensively develop.

Based on such an outline, the contents of this book are made up of the following sections:

- A comprehensive and synthetic application of various distribution systems with a view to reaching a systematic solution to distribution problems through which the unity, compatibility, and relevant differences shall be addressed for the purpose of better enhancing the development of the economy and society.
- An analysis of complicated distribution institutions where a multi-dimensional approach from the perspective of economic law is required. This includes an analysis from different disciplines and types of laws, including economic law and constitutional law, as well as an analysis of relevant distribution institutions within economic law.

Therefore, from the systematic dimension of legal systems, the coordination of economic law and other legal institutions is important, especially the coordination of constitutional law and civil/commercial law through which the function to comprehensively adjust the distribution relations of different laws could be better exercised. Meanwhile, from the perspective of economic law, the unity and difference of norms of economic law should be addressed thereby realizing distribution justice, guaranteeing genuine fairness and resolving overall distribution problems. Besides, the construction of economic law institutions shall ensure the protection of distribution rights of relevant agents. This is an essential institutional protection with regard to the resolution of distribution problems.

Besides, if economic law and other laws are not adequately regulated and they cannot resolve distribution problems, then distribution crises may emerge. Regulating economic law may be useful in dealing with distribution crises but it is important to underscore the fact that regulations should be carefully applied given that multiple factors contribute to the occurrence and development of distribution crises. In particular, the legality of the regulations should be addressed.

4   *Introduction*

Even in the time of crisis, such regulations shall comply with the rule of law in economic areas.

1.3 The structure and main points of this book

Based on the outline and the aims of the research, the basic structure of this book, aside from the introduction and conclusion, is the perspective of economic law which explores the distribution system, and in four chapters, attempts to resolve distribution problems.

The first chapter proposes the issue of coordinated development between economic law systems that aims to resolve distribution problems and constitutional, civil, commercial law systems that are related to distribution. The second chapter discusses the unity and differences between distribution systems that are within the territory of economic law, and it emphasizes that such systems should comply with relevant principles that govern the rule of law. The third chapter specifically analyzes the protection of distribution rights by distribution institutions in economic law and emphasizes that the continuous completion of the relevant distribution system is indispensable in solving multiple distribution problems. These chapters attempt to reveal existing, realistic issues concerning distribution and strive to complete the distribution system in economic law. The fourth chapter analyzes the existing problems of relevant distribution systems in dealing with distribution crises, revealing the importance and limitation of distribution systems in economic law when faced with a crisis and emphasizing the legality of distribution regulation.

Through the exploration of these chapters, this book presents the following views.

First, despite the importance of the distribution system in economic law, the resolution of distribution problems should take into consideration the importance of the distribution system in constitutional law and civil/commercial law. Therefore, in establishing and completing various distribution systems, attention should be paid not only to the consistency and coordinated development of economic law and constitutional law but also to the coordination of economic law and civil/commercial law regulations. At the same time, the internal coordination of various distribution systems is worth noting for only through this can the functions of different distribution systems be effectively exercised, distribution problems better solved, and distribution risks and crises adequately prevented and resolved.

In addition, when focusing on the coordination and unity of the distribution institutions, we should also admit that it is relevant to emphasize the unity of distribution institutions, given the unity of laws and regulations. However, there are differences among various agents that make it necessary to differentiate distribution institutions in various ways. Such differences may exist among different territories, industries, enterprises, and individuals at the same time. In reality, the trial legislation, the internal differences within one law (i.e. the Corporate Income Tax Law), along with the differences in the implementation of one system (i.e. the accumulative tax-paying system) tend to trigger a conflict between unity and difference and further affect the distribution of interests among relevant agents. Therefore, the issue of conflict should be correctly recognized and effectively dealt with.

Also, it is necessary to resort to the distribution system embedded in various legal systems, including in economic law, to prevent different kinds of distribution problems, especially distribution risks resulting from distribution pressure, distribution divergence, and unfairness. Hence, the protection of the distribution rights of relevant agents, especially the distribution rights to economic development, and distribution rights reflected in specific systems (i.e. the deduction rights in the value-added tax system and the right to income in the income tax system) should be strengthened with the knowledge that this is the only way to better prevent and solve distribution crises.

Lastly, if the distribution problems are not properly resolved, the emergence of distribution crises will become the reality. To deal with distribution crises, there is a need to take note of the indispensable function of the distribution system within economic law (especially specific financial/taxation law) in resolving crises. At the same time, emphasis should be placed on the limitation and legality of relevant macro-control measures on distribution. Furthermore, the completion of the distribution theory and system should be enhanced during the process of dealing with crises.

Another book of mine, *The Crisis of Distribution: Theoretical Analysis from Economic Law* is a sister treatise to this book. It focuses on the analysis of distribution problems, distribution risks, and relevant distribution crises from the perspective of economic law theory. The book, however, analyzes the solution to distribution problems and the distribution system aimed at solving distribution crises from the perspective of economic law. Reading these two books together may enable readers to better understand distribution problems and economic law solutions to distribution crisis in a systematic way. Also, it could help readers to better comprehend the theory and system of economic law from the perspective of distribution.

2 The consistency of key distribution systems

The strengthening of economic law regulation is necessary both to resolve distribution problems and to prevent and resolve distribution crises. During the process of economic law regulation, the relationship between the distribution systems within economic law and other laws inevitably poses challenges. It is only by maintaining consistency in the various systems that disputes can be avoided and adjustments among the various distribution systems can be achieved. Among various distribution systems, constitutional law and economic law are the most dominant. As a law to divide power, constitutional law is relevant to the distribution of important rights and powers as well as to specific distribution systems. While economic law is the typical "distributional law" directly relevant to the distribution of income, wealth, and interests. The consistency of constitutional law and economic law, which are key sources of the distribution system, directly affects the protection of rights of relevant distribution agents and also the actual performance of the whole distribution system. For this purpose, this chapter emphasizes the consistency and coordination of these two laws and further illustrates the importance of the consistency of key distribution systems based on different hierarchies and types. Besides, civil and commercial law are indispensable to the confining of property rights of relevant agents and are instrumental to the distribution system. Studying the coordination of economic law and civil and commercial law also contributes to resolving distribution problems and preventing distribution crises. For this purpose, this chapter will, taking taxation law among economic laws as an instance, explore how taxation and private law orders are coordinated and also study how different distribution systems are regulated in a coordinated manner.

In addition, the coordination of different internal components is also extremely important, even for the same types of distribution systems. Therefore, this chapter discusses the coordination of internal systems, taking taxation law, which is very important for distribution, as an example.

2.1 The consistency of distribution systems in the legal system

In the entire legal system, the hierarchy or legal effect of various distribution systems is different. For such systems, the internal consistency or coherence must be guaranteed so that a fair distribution is assured and distribution justice is achieved,

Consistency of key distribution systems 7

and distribution risks and crises are prevented and resolved. In different distribution systems of the hierarchical structure, the systems in constitutional law and economic law are most typical. The following section will illustrate the issue of consistency in distribution systems based on different hierarchical positions.

2.1.1 The internal consistency of the system from the economic nature of distribution

The development of the market economy has benefited from the optimization of the economic system which has, in turn, been affected by the institutional arrangement of constitutional law and economic law concerning power distribution. The consistency of the relationship between constitutional law and economic law profoundly affects the effective implementation and protection of institutional economic reform, the rational management for distribution relations, the solving of distribution problems, and the further promotion of economic development. Therefore, the relationship between constitutional law and economic law is not only a vital theoretical issue but also a key realistic issue that deserves our special attention.

Researchers have often developed an important approach based on hierarchy and nature in their analysis to establish the connection and differences between constitutional law. This book follows the same approach to transfer the perspective and analyze the relationship of constitutional law and economic law from the "economic" latitude of distribution and to discuss the issue of consistency among distribution systems that belong to different hierarchies. In fact, though scholars have explored the economic nature of constitutional law and economic law, insufficient research has been undertaken to establish the internal links between the economic nature of these two laws as well as the connection and consistency of the economic nature of distribution systems in the domains of constitutional law and economic law. Thus, it is necessary to search for the similarities of distribution systems of constitutional law and economic law in the aspect of economic nature to deepen the study of the relationship between constitutional law and economic law, and to exercise the joint power of adjustment in distribution area of constitutional law and economic law with a view to better solving distribution problems, preventing crises, and facilitating economic and social development and the rule of law.

From existing research, we could see that by focusing on the "economic dimension of constitutional law" and "economic constitutional law", the academia is increasingly associating "economic analysis to the constitutional law" while enhancing research in "economic constitutional norms" (Pingxue Zhou 1995).[1] In addition, there has been the extension of such research to areas including "constitutional law economics" (or constitutionalist economics) (Brennan and Buchanan 2004)[2] and "economic constitutional law" (Yue Wu 2007)[3] in states with different legal systems. The results generated from the above areas may contribute to the discussion on the "economic dimension" of the distribution system in constitutional law, as well as the constitutional law issues of economic law with

8 *Consistency of key distribution systems*

regard to distribution. The results can further promote the interaction and fusion of constitutional law and economic law and the construction of specific distribution systems.

However, neither "constitutional economics" nor "economic constitutional law" could sufficiently reveal the internal relations between economic and social development of constitutional law and economic law concerning distribution systems, nor could they reveal the function to promote such developments, regardless of the perspectives they take (economic or legal). It is due to the fact that the objective or area is still concentrated on constitutional law.[4] Therefore, it is necessary to find the intersection of constitutional law and economic law and choose an appropriate entry point to initiate the analysis.

The interrelation between economic law and constitutional law is reflected in various aspects, especially how they both originate and develop in distribution systems. This relationship is worthy of our attention and has been examined accordingly. If we take the link or basis of this interaction and integration as the perspective and breakthrough point, it is undoubtedly helpful to study the relationship among various distribution systems of constitutional law and economic law, as well as distribution systems within these two laws.

An important intersection point between the distribution systems of constitutional and economic law is that they are both economic. That is, the economy is the bond that exists between them, enables them to coexist, and serves as the foundation for them to interact. Also, both are directly linked to the adjustment to distribution relations. To analyze through an "economic" analysis of the relationship between constitutional law and economic law would not only help us to comprehend the characteristics of modern constitutional laws and basic features of economic laws but also assist us to understand the reason for which constitutional law amendment by modern states is concentrated in the economic area, especially the economic distribution area. Meanwhile, such an analysis from the economic perspective would facilitate the discovery of institutional deficits of constitutional law and economic law systems, including deficits existing in distribution systems, thereby enabling us to better coordinate the relationship between these two laws and to achieve adjustment goals.

Besides, the fact that the economic dimension has a profound influence on the source and development of both constitutional law and economic law plays a vital role in linking these two laws. Understanding both laws from an economic standpoint would foster research in the theories underlying the origin and transformation of constitutional law and economic law; make it possible to better understand the importance of distribution issues and distribution systems; and explore the specific approach to complete the coordination and interaction system of constitutional law and economic law to facilitate the consistency of the distribution system.

Based on the above factors, the following parts attempt to illustrate that the distribution system of constitutional law and economic law has an economic dimension and that the economic dimensions of both constitutional law and economic law are internally consistent. The economic dimension is the common basis for the existence of the close link and the effective interaction between constitutional law and economic law. It is solely through the facilitation of institutional interaction and mutual consistency between constitutional law and economic law that the benign interaction between constitutional law and economic law be constructed, including the coordination in distribution systems within these two laws. It would be hugely beneficial to the effective resolution of distribution issues and to the development of the economy, society, and rule of law.

2.1.2 The economic dimension shared by constitutional law and economic law

The discussion on the relationship between constitutional law and economic law is not rare in academia. From the perspective of economic analysis, the close link between constitutional law and economic law has resulted from the fact that both have far-reaching economic attributes. The economic dimension shared by these two laws is the bond and foundation for their connection and also reflects their similarities. Because of the economic dimension, distribution systems contained in constitutional law and economic law could affect each other and co-exist.

In economic law research, most scholars agree that economic law has an important economic dimension and that constitutional law also has an economic dimension. However, currently, there is a lack of consensus as to the existence of "economic constitution". Public choice schools, represented by US scholars such as Buchanan and Tullock, have already conducted in-depth research regarding the economic dimension of constitutional law and they tend to explore the economic functions of constitutional law, the impact of constitutional law on the change of economy, the impact of the economy on constitutional law, etc. from the perspective of economics and they also promote economic studies such as "constitutional economics", "economics of constitutionalism", or "constitutional governmental economics" through economic analysis of constitutional law.[5] Besides, the Freiburg School, represented by German scholars including Euchen and Böhm, has paid attention to "economic constitutional law" or "constitutional law with economic dimension", through which they focus on constitutional norms related to the economic domain. In particular, they emphasize studying the state limitation to economic freedom and to the states' power of intervention from a legal perspective, thereby carving the research area of "economic constitutional law" and promoting research in constitutional law as well as related economic law.[6] The above research is based on the premise that the constitutional law is economic or there exists an "economic constitutional law", regardless of differences in emphasis, on economics or law, or of their focus on ideal or regulation. Hence, the economic dimension of constitutional law has become a subject of extensive research. The attention of Chinese constitutional law research to the "political dimension", "legal dimension", or "normative dimension" seems to be excessive while, comparatively, there is less of a focus on the economic dimension. However, since the law is responsive, there will always be changes in the content of constitutional law that corresponds to different eras. Especially in

10 *Consistency of key distribution systems*

modern society, based on the demand of economic development, numerous economic legislations and norms related to the economic system will be merged into constitutional law thereby increasing the relevance of the economic dimension of constitutional law.

Therefore, considering the response to the demands of this era, and also the reflection of the economic function of the state with regard to constitutional law, the economic dimension of modern constitutional law continues to expand in a way that influences the formation of the economic law system and also makes the economic dimension of economic law more imposing. In fact, the economic dimensions of constitutional law and economic law are closely interrelated and share many common features. Specifically, their similarities are reflected in the following aspects.

First, no matter the definition of constitutional law with regard to property rights, division of state power and civil rights, specifications by economic law to relevant stipulations of the constitutional law, and specific regulations to the "right-obligation structure" of various economic law agents, the overall aim is to settle disputes through fair and effective distribution thereby attempting to lower the cost of operating the economy, reducing conflicts, increasing efficiency, and finally, promoting the overall economic outcome. It can, therefore, be concluded that both constitutional law and economic law should protect and promote a more "economical" development of the national economy through effective right-obligation configuration and make relevant distribution fairer and more reasonable.

Second, in order to achieve these goals, constitutional law and economic law should both reflect the "laws of the economy". For example, the stipulations concerning the economic system and the influence of specific institutions of economic law to constitutional law are directly related to the legislators' understanding and comprehension of the laws of the economy. In fact, the choice of economic institutions by a state is not only a political decision[7]. It is also affected by the understanding of laws of the economy and of the effective distribution system. Therefore, Article 15, Clause 1 of the Constitution of the People's Republic of China (PRC) stipulates that "the State practices socialist market economy" – an economic system that reflects their understanding of economic law. Meanwhile, announcing the implementation of a market economic system means to explicitly admit the function of market institutions in resource allocation and in the basic distribution system. Also, in order to ensure the effective application of market institutions, and to promote fair distribution, the state must exercise macro-regulation and control, and undertake market regulation in key areas where economic law plays a vital role.

Article 15 Clause 2 of the Constitution of PRC stipulates that "the State strengthens economic legislation and improves macro-regulation and control". This article and clause embody the "laws of economy" under market economy circumstances. China, as a huge country that has developed rapidly, requires the continuous completion and strengthening of macro-regulation and control. At the same time, the market economy requires fair competition and regulation against monopoly and unjust competition while maintaining a healthy market order.

Therefore, Article 15 Clause 3 of the Constitution of PRC stipulates that "the State prohibits in accordance with [the] law any organization or individual from disturbing the social and economic order". Besides the "inter-state trade articles" of the US Constitution,[8] the stipulation of the Russian Constitution concerning monopoly and unjust competition[9] also reflects their understanding of economic law with regard to market regulation. The macro-regulation and control, as well as market regulation systems of various states mentioned above, contain significant distribution systems which have made economic systems an essential system in resolving distribution crises.

Third, the above macro-regulation and control and market regulation require the effective division of power, a primary task of constitutional law. Neither the power of macro-regulation and control nor market regulation is different from traditional "political" power that has its own characteristics and is sometimes known as "the fourth type of power" (Yunliang Chen 2007).[10] Because of the fact that they are important powers with an influence on the basic rights of citizens, the "distribution" at the constitutional level has to be done appropriately. For this purpose, the constitutional laws of many states try to make explicit stipulations on public finance, taxation, finance, industry adjustment powers that are related to macro-regulation and control, anti-monopoly, and anti-unfair competition powers that are related to market regulation. Such efforts generate constitutional norms with regard to economic institutions and constitute the basis for "institutional law" attributes of economic law. This is a vital internal relationship between constitutional law and economic law.

At last, the economic dimension of constitutional law and economic law is reflected not only through stipulations on basic power of macro-regulation and control and market regulation but also through the legalization of such "economic policies". It should be understood that both macro-regulation and control and market control require legal measures to regulate and control, therefore the legalization of regulatory measures including budget, taxation, national bond, currency, and monopoly constitute part of an expanding economic law system. Meanwhile, the purpose of exercising such legal economic measures is to protect the smooth functioning of the market order and the distribution order and to realize the overall benefit of the macro-economy. All these factors make the "economic dimension" of economic law more outstanding and further promote the development of constitutional law economic norms.

In conclusion, as an economic law, constitutional law should respond to the economic demands of the time and with an obvious economic dimension visible via the following aspects: both of them should reflect the economic function as well as economic activities of the state. In addition, both should follow the laws of the economy and should define the economic power of the state as macro-regulation and control and market regulation. Furthermore, both economic law and constitutional law should reflect the legalized economic measures to effectively solve distribution problems and facilitate the healthy functioning of the economy as a way of achieving overall economic benefit. Such similarities shared by constitutional law and economic law constitute the foundation for

12 Consistency of key distribution systems

their interrelation and the bond that connects distribution systems that are part of the two laws.

Based on the requirements of the economic dimension of constitutional law, the constitutional laws of different countries should help in the development of economies and systems while institutions which are laid out in the constitution and which fail to facilitate or even hinder development should be changed. Improving constitutional law economic norms is undoubtedly an important direction for the achievement of Pareto improvement.

2.1.3 The mutual influence of constitutional law and economic law from the perspective of the economic dimension

The relationship between constitutional law and economic law is reflected by the increasing importance of the economic dimension, and also by the fact that they mutually affect each other based on the economic dimension. For this purpose, the following part will respectively discuss the important influence of constitutional law on economic law and the implementation/promoting effect of economic law on constitutional law from the perspective of the economic dimension.

2.1.3.1 The important influence of constitutional law on economic law

The constitutional law economic norms of various states, or the economic norms of the constitutional law, mainly contain the structure for the division of power in the economic area of constitution law. This is especially true for stipulations regarding basic economic systems with regard to economic institutions, to the property right system, and distribution system, as well as to stipulations concerning economic functions. The above norms viewed as typical "economic constitution" or "economic dimension of the constitution" have direct and vital effects on the economic law, which are discussed below.

First, from the structure of the division of power in the economic domain, constitutional law, as the "general bylaw" of a state, implies the political and economic existence of a state. From an economic perspective, the operation of any organization requires financial support. The state is obliged to exercise an increasing number of functions which require a more robust financial basis. Therefore, constitutional law has to make huge amounts of stipulations concerning the economy to clearly divide the public economy and private economy, and identify the property rights and economic rights of different agents which all constitute "distribution issues" on the constitutional level. Therefore, at the constitutional level, the "binary structure of the property rights" for "state's financial power" and "citizens' property rights" will be formed. This is the basic structure for the division of economic power between state and citizens at the constitutional level. It is also the foundation for the extension of various systems of the economic law thereby constituting a tremendous influence on the formation of economic law systems (Yushi Gui 2005).[11]

Besides, with regard to the state-citizen property rights structure, the constitutional law of one state has to directly stipulate or indirectly reflect its basic economic system. Irrespective of the differences from one state to another of the legislation style of such stipulations, the underlying inclusions are the general basic ownership system, the distribution system, and the economic institutions implicated. For example, in terms of the ownership system, constitutional law stipulates whether public or private ownership is applied. With regard to the vital land system, the constitution stipulates what land ownership system, i.e. public or private,[12] is implemented by the state. As for the economic system, there will be stipulations as to whether the state applies a market economy or a planned economy. In terms of the specific distribution system, there will also be stipulations as to whether the state applies a system of distribution based on labour or based on other factors. For the property protection rights, there are stipulations on how the state protects such rights, both private and public. The Constitution of PRC has comparatively explicit stipulations concerning all the above aspects. The stipulations concerning economic systems and the protection of economic freedom rights of market agents constitute the core content of "economic constitution". Furthermore, the constitution stipulates that the formation and development of the economic law system have been built around the abovementioned systems, especially the protection of the distribution rights of market agents.

In addition, the "economic function and power" of national institutions should also be formulated in constitutional norms. The function and power include fiscal power, budgetary power, taxation power, bond and currency-issuing power, and antimonopoly power, all of which fall within the realm of distribution. It is essential to identify the distribution of economic function and power that some states define as the distribution of income among different levels of government.[13] For this reason, constitutional law makes stipulations not only from apolitical view but also from an economic or distributional aspect. To put it differently, constitutional law is not only a political/legal scripture but also an economic scripture. For instance, the "no taxation without representation" spirit of the Magna Carta of the UK emphasizes the division of taxation power between parliament and the government. In essence, this refers to the allocation of function and power based on economic considerations given that they directly affect the distribution of interests of relevant agents. Constitutional law is the result of political conflict or competition among many parties and is also "the concentrated reflection of the economy", directly linked to the economic interest of various agents. The famous scholar Beard especially emphasized that "the Constitution is basically an economic scripture"[14] based on the fact that the US Constitution allocates interests among different groups out of economic consideration. The economic functions and power, including fiscal power stipulated by the above constitutional laws, require special economic law stipulations. It can be concluded that the stipulations or distributions of the above economic functions and power by constitutional law have laid the foundation for the establishment of the economic law system.

At last, the agent structure and relevant right structure established by constitutional law have a significant influence on economic law. Based on the "agent

14 *Consistency of key distribution systems*

binary structure" between state and citizen, the core content of constitutional law consists of stipulations regarding the state governance structure and the civil right structure. From the division of power perspective, the right to distribute power and the structure between state and citizens, on the one hand, forms the basic rights of nationals or citizens as contained in the so-called civil right bills (or "right constitution"). On the other hand, state power needs to be distributed among national institutions, both horizontally and longitudinally, because they are both crucial to state governance. Such contents form the constitutional stipulations that define the relevant function and power of national institutions (which contain relevant contents of "economic constitution").

The above agent structure and relevant rights structure set in constitutional law directly affect the theory and system establishment of economic law and could contribute to the understanding of the "binary structures" in economic theories including state intervention and economic freedom, state regulation, and market reaction. In addition, it provides an important analytical framework for us to study various issues of economic law.

In general, if we view the influence of constitutional law on economic law from the economic dimension perspective, it is not difficult to see that the division and definition provided for in constitutional law regarding the state's fiscal power and citizens' property rights set up the necessary framework for "economic property right" based on which one state needs the fiscal system and taxation system to influence the public and private economy (which constitute important foundations for many distributive activities), the financial system to support the effective functioning of the economy, the bond system, the industry policies and the industry organization system to play increasingly useful roles, and all these above systems to solve the complicated distribution problems. The above framework is the constitutional basis for fiscal, taxation, financial, industry, and competition systems, and it is also the basis for the entire economic law given that all systems outlined above are indispensable for the formation of an economic law system.

Besides, the economic system established by constitutional law directly affects the choice of a state between public and private ownership, state-operated and private-operated systems, and state-owned and publicly owned land property systems. These choices are very basic and impose important restrictions and they directly affect the distribution of interests of relevant agents as well as an effect on the goals that economic law adjustments seek to achieve, i.e. the steady growth of the economy. Meanwhile, the economic and distributive systems set up via constitutional law are also vital to the systemic establishment of economic law. Without the market economy system stipulated in constitutional law, state macro-regulation and control and market regulation would be unnecessary. Therefore, the income distribution of relevant agents would be affected. In fact, the incident that the "market economy" was written into the Constitution of PRC in 1993 has strongly promoted the overall development of economic law and has also facilitated the development of distribution systems in different areas.

In addition, when discussing the influence of constitutional law in economic law, it is necessary to distinguish economic norms in constitutional law from norms in economic law that are relevant to the constitutional law. This would reveal the connection and differences between constitutional law and economic law, and also illustrate that economic constitution research cannot substitute economic law norms research. In particular, the independent existence of economic law should not be denied through the simple division of economic law norms to economic constitution law and economic administrative law.[15]

2.1.3.2 Economic law fulfils and promotes constitutional law

The interaction between constitutional law and economic law is reflected by the profound influence on economic law by constitutional law, and also by the fact that the implementation and fulfilment of constitutional law need economic law which, in turn, promotes the development of constitutional law.

The implementation of constitutional law in all states relies on ordinary laws. The economic norms in constitutional law, including norms concerning distribution, need economic law for their implementation. Therefore, the rule of law construction in economic law directly affects the fulfilment of constitutional law. Without realistic implementation by economic law, economic constitutional law, including constitutional norms relating to distribution, would be hollow words that have no impact.

Economic law and constitutional law would benefit each other in a mutual influential process. When implementing constitutional law, economic law may also propel the development of the constitutional law given that both of them are vital components for the whole legal system. A comparison with constitutional law leads to the conclusion that economic law and economic life are directly and closely related. Certain requirements brought out by the development of the economy and society, including the resolution of distribution problems and the prevention of distribution crises, may initially be reflected in economic law. In addition, relevant economic law systems may be further formed, and such influence may further be transferred, directly or indirectly, to constitutional law thereby facilitating the development, by economic law, of constitutional law.

The promotion of constitutional law by economic law is not just a contemporary phenomenon. In fact, it was clearly visible in the era when economic law did not constitute a system yet. For instance, the emergence of taxation law norms was comparatively earlier and as an important distribution system, it was directly connected to the protection of the basic property rights of citizens. The link between constitutional law and constitutional government is very close, therefore the promotion of constitutional law is significant. The Magna Carta and the ensuing constitutionalism and legislation were all connected to budget and taxation, areas where economic law should make specific stipulations. It is the realistic need to solve distribution issues, such as the distribution of the power of the budget and taxation, which continuously propels the diversification and development of constitutional law in different states. Also, during the reform and opening-up of China, the occurrence and maturity of the exploration and system transformation preceded specific stipulations on constitutional law. Some amendments to

16 *Consistency of key distribution systems*

the Constitution obviously reflect the systematic transformation of economic law, especially the influence of the distribution system on the transformation of constitutional law. With the further development of economic law, voices demanding that vital legal principles such as "taxation according to the rule of law" and "currency according to the rule of law" shall be written into the constitution. If such principles would finally be included in constitutional law, it would become another instance proving that economic law propels the development of constitutional law.

In general, based on the economic dimension they share and on the common focus on distribution issues, the constitutional law and economic law mutually affect each other: on one hand, constitutional law, based on its fundamental status, could lay tremendous influence on economic law; while on the other hand, as the state economic function as well as the actual requirements of economic law rise in importance, especially pertaining to the need to resolve distribution problems and prevent distribution crisis, the principles and systems concerning distribution in economic law continue to be written into constitutional law thereby vigorously promoting the development of constitutional law. It is solely through a benign interaction and co-existence that the economy, society, and rule of law can be better facilitated. And the "consistency" issue of these two types of law must be solved first in order to achieve the benign interaction between constitutional law and economic law.

2.1.4 Exploring the "consistency" of constitutional law and economic law

Based on the common economic dimension and a common focus on the issue of distribution, as well as the mutual influence resulting from the above two points, constitutional law and economic law should have an internal "consistency" with each other. First, from the common economic dimension, constitutional law and economic law are consistent in the following aspects: both of them guarantee the benign operation and the coordinated development of the economy; both comply to the laws of economy, mutually facilitate the resolution of distribution issues, and prevent distribution crises; and both promote the "economical" level of economic operation. Meanwhile, they are consistent in that both of them emphasize the legality and constitutionality of macro-regulation and control as well as market regulations. Second, based on their mutual influence and given that constitutional law has a direct and important influence on economic law, and that economic law tends to conform to constitutional law, it goes without saying that in terms of constitutionality, economic law should be consistent with constitutional law. Also, the promotion of constitutional law by economic law while implementing constitutional law would achieve consistency by making constitutional law more in line with actual needs and by making it more responsive to distribution problems.

As outlined before, the economic norms (including norms concerning distribution) laid out in constitutional law are important reasons for economic law legislation and are vital for economic law system construction and theoretical research.

Consistency of key distribution systems 17

Meanwhile, because of the fact that "economic norms" in the constitutional law have a fundamental value for economic law, economic law should be consistent with constitutional law. According to normal legal theories, stipulations in constitutional law, the fundamental and basic law, have "fundamental" meanings, while economic law has to make the "fundamental norms" of constitutional law practice through a specific system arrangement during the implementation of constitutional law. Hence, the potential guarantee of the effective execution of constitutional norms.

Emphasizing the consistency between constitutional law and economic law is extremely important with regard to enhancing their interaction and their continuous development. Since the economic norms of constitutional law demand the actual implementation of economic law, while many basic systems of economic law need a constitutional basis, they may, therefore, target the same issue, stipulate relative principles, and more specific clauses respectively. For instance, in terms of protecting fair distribution, many states not only make stipulations about principles of constitutional law but also layout specific stipulations with regard to specific economic laws. Such speculations are highly consistent and concern areas including currency issuing, budget, taxation, and bond issuing. Though the political system, economic system, and historical tradition differ among states in countries like the US, Germany, and Russia, the various constitutions of these countries make such stipulations and specify such norms in specific economic law[16] in a way that reflects the consistency of constitutional law and economic law. Of course, the status of constitutional law, as well as its influence in economic law, are also factors that contribute to the abovementioned fact.

Apart from emphasizing consistency between the constitutional law and economic law based on norms, there is a need to solve the existing "inconsistency" issue. In practice, the inconsistency between constitutional law and economic law would bring enormous problems demanding quick "dynamic coordination" to constitutional law and economic law to keep their "dynamic consistency".

Looking back at history, we can see that since the economic law of China is closely linked to the reality of reform and opening-up and could quickly reflect the results of system reform. In contrast, we can see that constitutional law amendment has been comparatively left behind. Therefore, during the reform process of the economic system, the phenomenon that constitutional law is inconsistent with economic law has emerged with the result that some types of specific economic legislation do not comply with the stipulations of constitutional law. For instance, some economic legislation reflecting the market-oriented reform spirit is contrary to the planned economy system prescribed in the constitution and this phenomenon has caused scholars to discuss and debate the issue of the "benign violation to the Constitution".[17] It is from the sole requirement of the rule of law through emphasis on the consistency between constitutional law and economic law, and through scientific design and quick improvement, that the issue of violation to constitutional law can be better prevented.

China is still in the process of continuously deepening its reform and opening-up. During this period, some vital institutions have not been completely

18 *Consistency of key distribution systems*

established. This directly affects the formation of relevant laws concerning such institutions. Currently, stipulations on "institutional law" are still weak and the stipulations on the duties and powers of many government agencies are lacking. Therefore, the authority has applied a "flexible" method (for example, the "Three Determination Program" and decisions made by the Standing Committee of the National People's Congress) to determine them. Besides, some vital economic system reforms are undertaken by the State Council, for instance, the fiscal management system that deals with the tax division system, tax sharing, financial, and investment systems. These are important systems that are connected to distribution and they are managed by the State Council.[18] The legislation concerning institutions has considerable lacunas resulting from the fact that institutional reforms are not completed and that interest groups are not willing to comply with strict legal restrictions based on their own interests. These factors seriously hinder the effective resolution of problems.

Since the institution of the Constitution of 1982, China has emphasized the promotion of reform and opening-up and the development of a market economy under the framework of the rule of law. Based on the rule of law, all the above-mentioned institutions and systems should, from a legislation standpoint, be relatively stable and established. For after the declaration that the legal system has already formed,[19] the stability and predictability of the law become important, and the bar for consistency between constitutional law and economic law is higher. It is necessary to examine whether there is violation of the Constitution in the area of economic law from the perspective of "consistency", and whether the Constitution does not fit the requirement of actual economic activities. Through institutional interaction between constitutional law and economic law and their consistency within the framework of constitutional law, the following questions arise: Could the overall construction of a benign interaction between constitutional law and economic law be established, and can the development of the economy, society, and the rule of law be better promoted?

2.1.5 Summary

From the perspective of the distribution system, the relationship between constitutional law and economic law is central to resolving distribution problems, distribution risks, and crises. This book discusses the "common dimension of the economy" of constitutional law and economic law and their common focus on distribution problems from an economic dimension perspective with the aim of revealing the foundation and link on which constitutional law and economic law build their close connections. In addition, it analyzes the influence of constitutional law on economic law and the implementation and promotion by economic law to constitutional law in order to illustrate their mutual influence. On this basis, it brings about the issue of "consistency" between constitutional law and economic law and emphasizes that the issue of "inconsistency" in practice should be addressed based on the requirement of the common economic dimension and consistency. Also, the benign interaction between constitutional law

Consistency of key distribution systems   19

and economic law should be built under the framework of constitutionalism. All these are vital to the development of the economy, society, and rule of law, especially to solving dominant distribution problems and the prevention of distribution crises.

Determining the relationship between constitutional law and economic law is of huge theoretical value to the study of "economic constitution" or "constitutional economy", of "constitutional issues in economic law", as well as distribution problems and distribution crisis. Meanwhile, it would be of great help to solve the issue of constitutional law violation in the domain of economic law during the practice of rule of law, or the issue of the incoherence between constitutional law and economic law. The prior analysis from the perspective of the economic dimension involves the consideration of basic goals of constitutional law and economic law adjustment, and the basic contradictions and issues that many countries currently face are incorporated, including obvious distribution problems (the contradiction between individual preference for profit and the public interests inevitably results to distribution problems. Various "market failure" issues are, in fact, involved with distribution problems). Therefore, this augurs well for the future development of the rule of law.

With the increased acceptance of economic civilization and the rule of law, more issues in constitutional law concerning the economy (including the distribution issue on the constitutional level) can be settled through specific economic law. Also, many economic law issues (including relevant distribution issues) are fundamental constitutional issues and should be settled through the completion of constitutional law. Economic law is closely and directly linked to not only the actual economy, but also to constitutional law, and therefore could constitute the bridge that links constitutional law and actual economic activities. The economic dimension shared by constitutional law and economic law, their mutual influence, and their co-existence bring out a higher requirement for their consistency. This is of significant importance to assuring the consistency of constitutional and economic law distribution systems respectively.

2.2 The coordinated development of different types of distribution systems

In the legal system of a state, various types of distribution systems exist at different levels and are distinct in nature. It is only through coordinated development that the distribution system can become improved. For instance, both constitutional law and economic law contain a series of important distribution systems with different precedences or effectiveness. Or, both economic law and civil and commercial law contain many distribution systems which have different legal natures. However, coordinated development should be guaranteed regardless of the types of each distribution system. Based on this perspective, the following takes constitutional law and economic law as examples and illustrates the issue of coordinated development among distribution systems with different precedences. Then it uses economic law and civil and commercial law as examples to explain

20 *Consistency of key distribution systems*

the coordination and regulation issues of distribution systems with different legal nature.

Based on the discussion on the consistency of constitutional law and economic law, it could be concluded that constitutional law and economic law should be coordinated and should develop coordinately with each other thereby ensuring a necessary requirement of the rule of law. If the development of constitutional law and economic law is not in conformity, the development of the rule of law then would be problematic, the resolution of distribution problems and the prevention of distribution risks and crises would be difficult and, finally, a legality crisis would appear. Therefore, based on the consistency and conformity of constitutional law and economic law, it is necessary to discuss the coordinated development of constitutional law and economic law in view to illustrating the coordinated development of distribution systems with different precedences.

2.2.1 *Explaining the focus on the coordinated development of constitutional law and economic law*

As the law to foster development, economic law deeply affects the fate of a country and the living conditions of the people. It is directly related to distribution pressure. The development of economic law, therefore, is not only related to the resolution of distribution problems and the development of the economy and society, but also to the development of different sector laws as well as the overall construction of the rule of law. Thus, besides the "origination", emphasis should be further placed on the "development" of economic law, especially the issue of coordinated development between distribution systems in economic law and constitutional law.[20]

Considering the fact that the development of economic law involves undertaking structural adjustments and institutional changes in the legal system,[21] as well as adjusting the overall distribution structure and institutional evolution from the perspective of structure-function analysis, there is no doubt that it is necessary to review the specific functions of each sector law in the legal system in order to facilitate the whole "coordinated development" of the legal system and to promote the optimization of distribution structure. In fact, though the areas and approaches of adjustment vary in various sector laws, all the laws have their own roles and should not be neglected. Hence the construction of the rule of law in China should not only be rule-of-law-oriented but it should also emphasize systematic thinking through which the coordinated development of different elements of the legal system, especially relevant to distribution systems, can be achieved.

Research toward the development of the entire economic law or distribution or the distribution system within economic law could be conducted from many different angles. Among these, it is extremely important to examine the relationship between economic law and other sector laws and analyze the interrelations between the distribution systems in different sector laws in order to promote the coordinated development of economic law and other sector laws. In the past, academia focused more on analyzing the relationship between economic law and one specific sector law, whereas a "triangle-relationship" comprehensive investigative research approach should be adopted for various factors including politics, economy, society, and culture. For example, based on the government-market relationship which is of fundamental importance in economic law (Shouwen Zhang 2014),[22] it is necessary to investigate the "triangle-relationship" among economic law, civil and commercial law, and administrative law. It is through this "triangle-relationship" that the relations among important distribution systems can be directly discerned.

Whether the research target is the binary relationship or "triangle-relationship", the promotion of the coordinated development between economic law and relevant sector laws should be considered. The coordinated development of distribution systems in different sectors should also be encouraged. After all, the "historical background" and "multi-foundation" of the origin of each sector law or distribution system are different and so are different missions and functions. Yet, continuous development is required under the contemporary context. Meanwhile, each sector law or distribution system is often faced with many common or related issues.

Economic law and constitutional law play a vital role in contemporary economic and social development as well as in the correlated political and legal development process, especially with regard to the resolution of distribution problems. Distribution systems within these laws, which have various precedences, are fundamental to solving distribution issues. Therefore, the "coordinated development" of economic law and constitutional law is vital, and correspondingly, the distribution systems in these two sector laws should also develop coordinately.

Considering that each sector law should develop "coordinately" with other sector laws, and the development of constitutional law and economic law is exceedingly significant, the following part is based on the perspective of the relationship between economic law and constitutional law, analyzes economic law and the constitutional foundation for the distribution system that is contained in economic law, and, at the same time, discusses the promotion of constitutional law by the development of economic law. This is to highlight the necessity to develop economic law and to explain why different states choose to develop economic law and to solve distribution problems through the strengthening of economic law regulation. Based on this, this book further discusses the coordination problems of economic law and constitutional law in development, focusing on the approach to achieve coordinated development between them and to better solve the distribution problems.

2.2.2 The constitutional foundation for the development of economic law

The development of economic law has a solid constitutional foundation. Currently, many states are developing economic law and substantially promoting the stipulation and implementation of economic law not because they necessarily share the same preference for legislation but because economic law plays a predominant

22 Consistency of key distribution systems

role in facilitating the development of the economy and society, especially with regard to solving distribution problems. The development of economic law therefore reflects the requirement of constitutional norms and contributes to the fulfilment of legal system functions.

The development of economic law is a reflection of constitutional norms. Under the current circumstance where many states are increasing economic norms which constitute an "economic constitution",[23] if economic stipulations and implementation are absent, large amounts of constitutional provisions will not be implemented and this could result in the "invalidity of the Constitution". This would be against the stipulations and spirit of the constitution, and would severely affect the whole practical functions of the legal system triggering many other issues such as distribution imbalance.

According to the legal precedency theory, constitutional law is the foundation of other laws and the development of economic law should comply with the constitutional law requirements.[24] In the literal context, the majority of economy-related clauses in the constitutional law of many countries are directly related to economic law. These economic constitutional norms involve many basic economic institutions including the economic institutions, the ownership system, and the distribution system which all form the "economic constitution" of these countries and which all lay the constitutional foundation that is vital for the development of economic law.

For example, Article 15 of the Constitution of PRC is an article that has a fundamental influence on the development of economic law.[25] In the current constitution, all three clauses of Article 15 are directly related to economic law, with fundamental meaning, which not only lay the foundation for the economic system and reveal the necessity for the origination and development of economic law, but also establish the adjustment area, basic structure, or system for economic law.

Specifically: Clause 1 stipulates that "the State practices socialist market economy".[26] This was the first time in the history of China to adopt a market economy system in its Constitution. It has been of tremendous significance toward the development of economic law because the modern market economy is the premise and foundation for the origin and development of economic law. Besides, once a market economy system is practised, macro-regulation and control and market regulation require to be strengthened, and that requires macro-regulation and control laws as well as market regulation laws – both of which are economic laws. Without a market economy system, the regulation and control of the market economy would not exist. Therefore, the existence of modern economic law is not necessary. In addition, as long as the market economy system exists, the corresponding distribution system is indispensable. This includes the fiscal distribution of the state and the profit distribution of enterprises which require protection by economic law. Thus, stipulations regarding the market economy system are directly related to the origination and development of economic law as well as the foundation or necessity of the existence of economic law. Though not all states choose to explicitly incorporate the market economy system in their constitutions,[27] as long as a market economy system is practised, economic law would be developed through which the distribution system in economic law would be improved.

Clause 2, which stipulates that "the State strengthens economic legislation, and improves macro-regulation and control",[28] is directly related to Clause 1. As long as the market economy system is adopted, the state has to strengthen economic legislation, especially economic law legislation. Meanwhile, it is only by strengthening economic legislation that macro-regulation and control can be improved. In the Chinese economic legislation, laws relating to macro-regulation and control are the most significant. These relate to the characteristics of China as a "huge nation" and to the fact that the duration during which China has implemented a market economy system is relatively short. Through the increasing application of the rule of law, the stipulation and implementation of laws of macro-regulation and control are required if the state intends to "improve macro-regulation and control" through "strengthening economic legislation". Besides, the formation of the whole social distribution structure is directly linked to macro-regulation and control whereas macro-regulation and control, itself, is an important method to promote the fairness of distribution and to solve distribution imbalance. For the issue of macro-regulation and control, though some states may not directly stipulate relevant contents in their constitutions, the interpretation of the constitution involves a large number of identical issues. For instance, the Commerce Clause in the US Constitution is considered to be related to the federal power in issues of macro-regulation and control. From the era of Marshall to the present, the Supreme Court of the US has made many important verdicts which not only confirm the federal power to regulate and control trade but also to expand that power through interpretation (Qianfan Zhang 2001)[29] which involves the distribution and balance of the interests of relevant agents.

Clause 3, which stipulates that "the state prohibits in accordance with law any organizations or individuals from disturbing the social and economic order", is important for the protection, by the constitution, of the healthy development of a market economy. In the market economy system, the effective regulation of the market economy order in accordance with the law is vital to the protection of the relevant distribution order and the overall social and economic order. For such purposes, the legislation and implementation of market regulation law must be strengthened. German scholar Böhm views economic constitutional law as the public choice or the whole decision on the order of civil economic life. For him, this is also the reflection of the common emphasis on an economic or market order by constitutional law. In fact, it is for the protection of the social and economic order emphasized by constitutional law that forms the requirement for the strengthening of market regulation or supervision, as well as specific power and law of market regulation.

Therefore, the three clauses of Article 15 of the Constitution of PRC emphasize the economic system basis for economic law and the adjustment sphere of economic law (namely, macro-regulation and control and market regulation), and explicitly spell out the dichotomy system and target field of economic law. They also reveal the constitutional basis for the promotion of economic law and lay the

24   *Consistency of key distribution systems*

vital constitutional framework for the system construction of economic law and the study of economic law.

The above part takes the provisions of the Constitution of PRC as an example to illustrate the constitutional basis for the development of economic law and the requirement of constitutional law toward the development of economic law. In fact, with the development of constitutional law in different states, economic norms are increasing especially norms pertaining to provisions in the fiscal, taxation, finance, and competition fields, confirming the framework for the dichotomous structure between state and citizens, government and market, central government and local government, etc., and specifying the distribution boundary of relevant agents in power, income, right, etc. Thus, it provides a significant constitutional basis for the development of economic law and the corresponding distribution system.[30]

Certainly, the constitutional foundation of economic law is not only reflected by the explicit provisions of constitutional law. The ideals and values embodied in constitutional law, including equality, liberty, fairness, effectiveness, justice, security, etc., are also indications for it.[31] Therefore, though some states do not make explicit provisions in relevant articles of their constitutional law, the ideal, value, and overall design of constitutional laws could also lay the foundation for the development of economic law. Correspondingly, the arrangement system to fulfil distribution justice and fairness in economic law is connected with the ideals and values of fairness and justice emphasized in constitutional law. To solve distribution problems and prevent distribution imbalance and crises through economic law regulations, there is an intrinsic requirement of constitutional law and an effort to promote the implementation of constitutional law.

2.2.3 *Promotion of constitutional law development through the development of economic law*

The development of economic law would contribute to the fulfilment and improvement of constitutional law and further promote the development of constitutional law. For instance, many "institutional laws" of economic law involve constitutional issues and during the process to solve institutional issues related to the constitution, there is the natural promotion of constitutional law. In particular, the institutional arrangement of fiscal policy, taxation, finance, industry, competition, foreign trade, etc., in economic law involves many distribution systems. This means the rule of law with regard to the abovementioned aspects would affect the development of constitutional law.

From the history of the development of economic law in the early stage and for the purpose of enhancing market regulation, the US Congress promulgated the Interstate Commerce Act and the Sherman Anti-trust Act in 1887 and 1890 respectively and further established independent regulatory institutions such as the Interstate Commerce Commission and Federal Commerce Commission, through which a set of special regulatory institutions and systems were established. These appear as milestones with regard to the development of economic law. The origination and development of the abovementioned economic law system promote the change of relevant regulations and control systems, solve the distribution problems in relevant areas, form specific distribution systems, and promote the development of constitutional law.

For example, the Interstate Commerce Act, according to the US Constitution, reflects the power of Congress to regulate and control the economy. Yet, with the development of trade and the emergence of various disputes, for the purpose of defining the scope of the federal power to regulate and control trade and commerce as well as the exercising of such power, the Supreme Court had been making complicated interpretations for a long period of time. Through the process of interpretation, the power to regulate and control trade and commerce expanded, thereby promoting the development of economic law. Also, during the process of economic development, constitutional law itself is fulfilled and improved (Qianfan Zhang 2011).[32]

The contemporary economic law of China originated and developed from the transformation from a planned market system to a market economy system. The practice of a market economy system and the enhancement of macro-regulation and control gradually became consensus due to the reform and opening-up. There has also been the continuous improvement of a relevant distribution system. At the beginning of the reform and opening-up, China had already realized the deficits of government's direct management of the micro-economy, and had started to emphasize "macro-adjustment" which, in essence, constitutes "macro-regulation and control".[33] The system reform and practice of the economic law system in the fiscal sector, taxation, finance, and prices in the 1980s, especially "the decentralization of power and relinquishing the profits" and "loosening regulation", deepened the construction of a market-oriented system of reform (Shouwen Zhang 2009).[34] The essence of such a process is that the state uses legalized economic measures to improve macro-regulation and control while completing various distribution systems and releasing distribution pressure. At that time, the abovementioned system reforms resolved distribution problems to a large extent, sharply increased the level of productive forces, and further promoted the origination and development of economic law. It propelled the final establishment of a market economy system and macro-regulation and control in the Constitution.

"Macro-regulation and control" was written into the Constitution and has become an extremely important legal concept for the development of macro-regulation and control in economic law. With the deepening, completion, and stabilization of the economic system reform, the vital results of the system transformation in China, including the outcomes from completing the distribution system, will not only be established in economic law but will also be reflected in future amendments of the Constitution, including the promotion from economic law to constitutional law.

During the process of reform and opening-up in China, because of the fact that the National Congress as well as its Standing Committee had conducted too much "authorized legislation" which made "trial legislation pattern" popular (Shouwen Zhang 2013),[35] many systems, including the taxation system with

26 *Consistency of key distribution systems*

regard to distribution, were "trialled" in advance in the domain of economic law. Sometimes there were issues of "benign violation against the Constitution" (which involved the consistency of economic law and constitutional law). Meanwhile, because the violation was "benign" and was reasonable economically, it promoted the amendment and improvement of constitutional law. It also led to the promotion of constitutional law by economic law.

The format for the promotion of constitutional law via economic law would naturally be different from state to state and in different epochs. Because the Constitution of PRC is comparatively concise and composed of abstract principles, the change in the "form" of the Constitution due to the development of sector laws would be less significant. In states where constitutional law stipulations are more specific and complicated, the promotion of the constitutional law by sector laws, such as economic law, would be more pronounced.

The above part takes the market regulation laws of the US and the macroregulation and control laws of China as examples to illustrate how economic law fosters constitutional law, through which it is evident that both economic and constitutional laws in different states at different eras have had dissimilar characteristics. However, the consistency between economic law and constitutional law and the coordination of distribution systems embodied in economic and constitutional laws should be emphasized during the process of development, irrespective of the differences of systems.

2.2.4 *Coordination between economic law and constitutional law in the development process*

Based on the initial conclusion, it is worth noting that economic law and constitutional law interact with each other. On the one hand, the development of economic law is based on constitutional law given the fact that both stipulation and constitutional law implementation are required to establish economic law. On the other hand, the development of economic law may contribute to the completion and fulfilment of constitutional law, and would further promote the development of constitutional law. Therefore, the mutual interaction between constitutional law and economic law in the development process should be considered, especially from an economic and normative dimension perspective, to enhance their consistency and coordination and to realize "coordinated development".

As mentioned above, the "economic dimension" shared by constitutional law and economic law (Shouwen Zhang 2009)[36] is the vital premise for the coordinated development of the distribution systems embodied in economic law and constitutional law. With increasing economic norms in constitutional law, the "economic dimension" of constitutional law becomes increasingly predominant. The continuous fulfilment of the economic constitution, especially with regard to distribution issues, is a reflection of contemporary requirement and of the demand to develop. To implement the economic constitution, economic law, as well as the affiliated distribution systems, should be developed. If economic law cannot be

Consistency of key distribution systems 27

effectively developed, then constitutional law stipulations cannot be fulfilled and economic development may equally be substantially jeopardized.

The normative dimension shared by constitutional law and economic law provides the foundation for the coordinated development of the distribution system within constitutional law and economic law. As a vital component of the legal system, both constitutional law and economic law have the regulation function, sharing norms in common.[37] Besides, the norms of constitutional law and economic law, which have different hierarchies or orders of precedence, point to two different types of orders. Therefore, the distribution system in economic law cannot violate the distribution system in constitutional law which has higher precedence. On the contrary, they should be based on the distribution norms in constitutional law and keep consistency to it. It is worth noting that clarifying the precedency of different distribution systems is vital to their coordinated development.

Based on the abovementioned economic and normative dimensions, it is worth noting the consistency between distribution systems within constitutional law and economic law. From the legal effect perspective, economic law norms should comply with constitutional law norms to avoid the risk of violation of constitutional law. Meanwhile, from the perspective of the development of law, constitutional law shall absorb the benefits of the development of economic law during its own development process and make appropriate adjustments to maintain consistency between them. Only consistency on the basis of economic and normative dimensions can achieve coordinated development between constitutional and economic laws.

The consistency or coordination between economic law and constitutional law should be examined judicially or non-judicially. The "judicial verdict" by the court through judicial review is one-dimensional and, during certain periods, the legislation concerning economic law norms may be considered a "violation against the constitution".[38] However, as the perception of the court deepens with regard to the function and control of the state, the interpretation of the constitutional law also changes. For example, some specific economic law systems that had been considered as being inconsistent to constitutional law (i.e. the income tax system, which is also an important distribution system) had, for a long time, not been deemed as a "violation against the constitution". Some states even integrate the income tax system into the constitution to form a distribution system at the level of constitutional law.[39] The changes of the judicial verdicts or constitutional interpretations, as well as the development of relevant systems, reflect the mutual influence and adjustment between constitutional law and economic law.

Besides, non-judicial agents such as scholars and the general public may provide "non-judicial verdicts" for the consistency or coordination between economic law and constitutional law. As legal awareness rises, especially people's awareness of constitutional law, the attention to legality and constitutionality increases, thereby promoting constitutional law and economic law in the development process. On the one hand, based on the vital influence of macro-regulation and control and market regulation to the basic rights of citizens, including property rights and economic liberty rights, the compliance, stipulation, and implementation of an

28 Consistency of key distribution systems

economic law system to constitutional law is increasingly important. Therefore, economic law has to be consistent and coordinated with the provisions of constitutional law. On the other hand, based on economic constitution requirements, the stipulation and implementation of macro-regulation and control law and market regulation law should be enhanced in order to limit the state's power according to the law, and to protect economic development rights of market agents (Shouwen Zhang 2012),[40] instead of being held captive by interest groups who intentionally hinder the development of economic law. Currently, comprehensive and profound reform is required in order to facilitate the development of China. Also, many institutional "bottlenecks", such as the fiscal and taxation system and financial system, should be broken. Barriers that obstruct fair competition should be removed, and various distribution issues should be resolved. The solution to all these problems demands coordinated reform in various systems including the economy, politics, and society; the coordinated development of various distribution systems; and the common protection provided by economic law and constitutional law.

When constitutional law develops simultaneously with economic law, on whatever level, norm, or value, distribution systems in all precedences must maintain their consistency in dynamic adjustment, otherwise many negative effects would emerge due to inconsistencies. The backwardness of the development of either constitutional law or economic law would bring negative effects on the solution to relevant distribution problems and to the overall construction of the rule of law.

2.2.5 Conclusion

Economic law is "the law to promote the [sic] development". The coordinated development between economic law and other sector laws, as well as the cooperation among distribution systems of different types and precedency directly involve the "adjacency" of economic law in the legal system and the quality and effectiveness of the development of economic law. Specifically, the coordinated development of economic law and constitutional law affects a wide range of affairs and may contribute to the long-term development of distribution systems of different types. Therefore, investigating economic law becomes a necessity.

In the previous part, the emphasis was on the constitutional basis for the development of economic law and the promotion of the development of constitutional law by economic law. It is not difficult to conclude that economic law development and improvement of the distribution system cannot be realized without the support and protection of constitutional law. Enhancing economic law regulation and effectively solving distribution issues are both the prerogative of constitutional norms and the need to exercise the constitutional law. Meanwhile, the development of economic law and the improvement of various distribution systems embodied in it would, to some extent, fulfil and complete constitutional law and foster the development of constitutional law. The above discussion may contribute to illustrating why various countries promote the development of economic law, and why they promote the coordinated development of distribution systems in economic law and constitutional law. Based on the above discussion, the interaction and coordination of economic law and constitutional law in development should also be explored, especially by targeting and resolving questions of the inconsistency of different distribution systems through judicial verdict and non-judicial judgement and based on the common economic and normative dimensions shared by economic law and constitutional law. Such efforts may enhance the consistency and coordination between them as well as ensure their coordinated development.

Maintaining the dynamic and coordinated development of the distribution system in economic law and constitutional law may contribute to the rule of good laws and resolve the issue of (benign) violation against constitutional law in distribution systems. Also, it is vital for the benign development of the economy and the resolution of distribution issues to focus on the dynamic transformation of various distribution systems and institutional adjustments and to substantially enhance judicial review.

The economic law area involves a considerable number of constitutional law issues, and the economic constitutional law area also involves a considerable number of economic law issues. Both of these, along with distribution issues in these two areas, require further research. It is increasingly important to focus on the relationship between economic law and constitutional law and to promote the coordinated development of distribution systems of different types. Correspondingly, future economic law research should not only focus on research results generated from interdisciplinary research such as "constitutional economics", but also on interdisciplinary economic law research, constitutional law, and other legal disciplines. This would significantly contribute to the prosperity of law research, the development of the rule of law, and the resolution of distribution issues.

2.3 Mutual completion among distribution systems of different natures

In the area of distribution, both public and private laws have a profound influence, especially economic law and civil and commercial law, which a have a more profound influence on the distribution of interests of various agents. Therefore, except for research on the consistency and coordination between distribution systems and the nature of public law such as constitutional law and economic law, attention should also be paid to the coordination and mutual completion of economic law and civil and commercial law – two types of important distribution systems with different natures.

Considering the fact that both economic law and civil and commercial law involve distribution systems, and that both are concerned with the nature of public law and private law at the same time, the following part intends to discuss the coordination between the transformation of taxation law system and the private law order generated from the adjustment of the civil and commercial law taking taxation, which with regard to economic law has a tremendous influence on distribution, further revealing the coordination and mutual completion between the

30 *Consistency of key distribution systems*

distribution systems from the perspectives of economic law and civil and commercial law.

As it is well known, the transformation of taxation law has continued to attract attention due to the fact that it directly affects the distribution of interests of relevant agents. Far-reaching reforms, both in ancient and contemporary times, in China or in foreign countries are directly or indirectly implicated in this. At the same time, private law and order are deeply affected thereby making the issue of conflict and coordination between taxation law transformation and private law order a vital issue worthy of continuous research.

Taxation law transformation and ordinary private law adjustment both involve the establishment and protection of property rights. They are directly linked to the distribution issue and are likely to invoke conflicts. Meanwhile, during the Chinese constitutional amendment process, though the protection of property rights has been discussed, such discussion has been mainly from the perspective of taxation law or constitutional law. There are still many issues that are worthy of studying from the perspective of the coordination between public law and order and private law and order, through which the necessity and the important approach to strengthen the coordination between economic law and civil and commercial law in solving distribution issues could be found.

2.3.1 The inevitability of conflict and the necessity for coordination

The adjustment of taxation law mutually influences private law and order generated from the adjustment of private law. As a law with higher precedence, taxation law is based on the adjustment of private law. For instance, the goods tax depends on the circulation of goods, while the circulation of goods is regulated primarily by private law. Income tax depends on the confirmation of income, while the confirmation of income is primarily regulated by private law. It is also true for the property tax area. Thus, it can be concluded that private law adjustment establishes the goods, income, and properties that are associated with "object" characteristics (Shouwen Zhang 2012),[41] and also establishes the amount and sphere of such "objects", though the "objects" established by private law adjustment are only "potential" objects of taxation. The real object of taxation, as well as its sphere and amount, ultimately need to be determined by the stipulations for the taxation elements in taxation law. Hence, the taxation law would profoundly affect the final distribution.

In fact, the "objects" established by private law[42] do not strictly correspond to the object of taxation stipulated in taxation law, because taxation law adjustment in any state makes compromises which account for the difference between private law adjustment and taxation law adjustment. Taxation law cannot, at least in form, affect the final ownership of the "object" established by private law if it is not an object of taxation. On the contrary, if the "object" established by private law is also the object of taxation, then taxation law adjustment may directly affect its final destiny. In this sense, the private law and order generated from private law adjustment often may not be the stable "final situation". At least for the final ownership of the "object", taxation law adjustment may still affect it (causing, to some extent, a change in quantity). This reflects the role played by law in participating in the distribution and redistribution of social products. Therefore, though adjustments by private law and the resulting private law order are the basis for adjustments by taxation law, adjustments by taxation law, as a "higher law", would still have a vital influence on the final formation and stabilization of private law order. The interaction between such two factors will seem increasingly important with the development of the market economy.

The issue of the ownership and extent of completion of "material" adjusted by private law would normally be deemed as the issue of property rights as well as the protection of it. How the property right is protected would directly affect relevant private law orders. While the adjustment by taxation law is seen as a "violation" against individual property rights and therefore formulating the conflict between the adjustment of taxation law and private law between taxation law order and private law order. Such conflicts are directly linked to the target that taxation law and private law intend to protect and to the mechanism of them; thus the emergence of these conflicts are inevitable.[43]

Since the adjustment by private law involves the formation of wealth and the determination of the ownership of private property rights, while the adjustment by taxation law may "deny" or "reduce" the confirmation of private property right, therefore private law is generally deemed to emphasize the protection of private property rights, while taxation law may constitute the "violation" against private property rights. Private law and taxation law conflict with each other on the protection of private property right in terms of legal adjustment, which reflects the conflict between state and citizen, government and market, and public power and private right. If such conflicts cannot be effectively resolved, the steady development of the economy and society could be hampered, and many aspects of public and civil life could be negatively affected. It may even affect the rise or fall of a state (Douglass North 1994).[44] For this reason, they have to be coordinated effectively.

Normally, the necessity to coordinate arose from the perspective of the importance of steady and harmonious legal order for the steady development of economy and society. Historically, only those countries that can effectively protect private property rights while providing public goods could fully develop economically and socially and could gain advantageous positions in international competition. From the perspective of the law, taxation law and private law, with their respective functions, are both vital secondary systems to the whole legal system, and they cannot effectively exercise their functions without the effective integration of the legal system. For this purpose, the legal system needs to be internally coordinated to eliminate the conflict between taxation law and private law, and the conflict between taxation law, private law, and other laws.

As an open system, each secondary system of the legal system needs to make adjustments regarding the development of the economy and society. Because of the fact that taxation law is more easily affected by public policies, including economic and social policy, the change of some regulatory norms is more frequent

32 *Consistency of key distribution systems*

(Shouwen Zhang 2001).[45] Therefore, it would inevitably affect private law and order. The questions that require further discussion are whether it is plausible to coordinate the conflict between the said change of taxation law and private law order, and if plausible, what would be the basis for such coordination?

2.3.2 Reason for the separation of "two kinds of right" and possibility for coordination

In the past, people focused on the separation of "two kinds of right", that is, the separation of ownership and the right to operate. Yet the separation we mention here refers to another type of "separation of right", which has existed for a long time but has not received sufficient attention. Here we are referring to "the separation of private property rights and public property rights" or, in the narrow sense, if we understand property rights as private property rights, the separation of "property rights and fiscal power".

The reason for the separation is that the satisfaction of human desire is considered justice and it is directly related to the distribution of interests between state and citizens. From the perspective of basic human rights, basic human needs should be satisfied through relevant channels. To satisfy individual desires by individual objects requires private law to determine private property rights. Likewise, to satisfy the desire of the public by public objects requires public law to determine and protect public property rights. Each type of desire and object corresponds to two different types of rights, which are a reflection of the separation between private property right and public property right.[46]

In the era when a family owned the whole state, the space for the existence of such "separation", in the modern sense, was absent, and the property of the royal family was not separated from the public treasury. Also, emperors or kings could impose taxation arbitrarily to meet their own needs, meaning that the private property rights of the public naturally could not be protected steadily. The establishment of principles such as legitimate budget and taxation according to law, which reflect the spirit of modern rule of law, is consistent with the separation and legitimization of these rights and makes fiscal and taxation law an important system for the protection of these rights.

According to past research, there exists a divergence in the perception of the nature of property right regarding whether property rights include only the right to objects and claims to debt, or they include rights other than those. Still, when talking about the protection of property rights, people tend to emphasize private property rights. From the perspective of private law, it is indeed important and necessary, yet from the perspective beyond private and public law and from the overall satisfaction of human desires, it is not sufficient to only focus on private property rights. The protection of public property rights is also indispensable given that without such protection, the provision of public goods may be severely affected, as evidence from history and reality have continuously indicated.

It is generally believed that private law emphasizes the protection of private property rights while public law, especially taxation law emphasizes the protection of public property rights. Also, the formation of public property rights is based on private property rights and it results from the transfer of private property. Therefore, the adjustment by taxation law and private law would necessarily bring conflict to the protection of private property rights. This is justifiable given that the separation of the two rights is related to the satisfaction of public and private desires, and corresponds to the provision of public and private goods. In addition, the correlating conflict between public law (especially taxation law) and private law may potentially be coordinated.

In fact, the separation would first appear at the constitutional level. All the states need to specifically address the distribution of income or wealth and set or differentiate the property rights of citizens and the fiscal power of the state. This means that separation requires coordination during constitutional legislation and it forms a "balance". For the division and configuration of "two types of rights", coordination in constitutional law is primary while the relevant laws and regulations should reflect such an arrangement and should constitute the foundation of the rule of law with regard to the separation and protection of these rights.

The adjustment of both taxation law and private law cannot exist without such a foundation that provides institutional plausibility for the change of taxation law and coordination of private law order. From the perspective of the entire system of the rule of law, taxation law and private law are both the specification of constitutional law and they both protect public and private property rights despite the different emphasis on specific systems. Due to the fact that the two types of rights are separated and their protection justifiable, when the relevant provisions of taxation law and private law are inconsistent, coordination should be contemplated from the perspective of constitutional stipulations and a constitutional spirit based on the comprehensive protection of these rights.

2.3.3 External effects of the change of taxation law and institutional coordination

Changes in taxation law are frequent and sometimes occur periodically. The influence of changes in taxation law on individual behaviour, private interests, and private law order is a kind of external effect of the change of taxation law. The negative external effects of the taxation law deserve further examination, for they directly involve the protection of private property rights and the stability of private interests and private law order.

Changes to taxation law in various countries from around the world are conducted through the following ways: change of taxation elements including the taxation agent, specific tax denominations, tax rate, etc.; or the initiation and suspension of specific denominations that are all specific reflections of changes in taxation law and directly affect private law order. For example, taxation system reforms in China in 1994 initiated new types of tax (consumer tax and land VAT), adjusted the target of some types of tax (VAT and business tax), and combined some types of tax (corporate income tax and individual income tax), all of which influenced existing private law orders.

34 *Consistency of key distribution systems*

As is widely known, private law order generated by adjusting private law needs to be relatively stable especially with regard to property rights. Only when the state law provides comprehensive and effective protection of the ownership right of citizens and forms stable private law order can the development of the economy and society be better promoted. North has explained this phenomenon in his study on constitutional economics where the impact of the protection of property rights to the rise and fall of nations in the history of economic development is clearly presented. Therefore, the coordination with private law orders needs to be considered during the transformation process of taxation law to avoid the excessive interference and influence of the formation of a sturdy private law and order. The transformation of taxation law is continuously needed given the development of the economy and society. Focusing on the coordination between taxation law reform and private law order intends to emphasize that the transformation of taxation law shall consider the expectations of individuals and equally reduce its impact on individual economic activities. In areas where market adjustment plays a dominant role, the "neutrality of taxation" should be advocated while in areas where macro-regulation and control plays a dominant role, it is important to reduce the burden of individuals. For this reason, the allocation of private property rights and public property rights needs to be conducted effectively to enhance the fair distribution of social wealth.

However, in real economic life, the conflict between private property rights and public property rights is an eternal issue which requires constant efforts. The relevant legislation in China has evolved from partially focusing on one certain type of power or right to focus on the coordinated protection of different types of powers and rights. For instance, the previous *Law on Taxation Regulation* focused on the interest of the public treasury or the obtention of public property. Therefore, stipulations on taxpayer obligations were plenty while stipulations on their rights were insufficient. In the 21st century, through the amendment to the law, the rights of taxpayers have been incorporated in many parts[47] which primarily deal with private property rights. It is undoubtedly evident that progress through greater efforts is still required in the achievement of effective coordination between the adjustment of taxation law and private law.

Taxation law involves broad areas and could hugely influence private law order. Each reform on taxation law would generate shockwaves on private law order which was steady before. Also, the expectations, behaviour, and interest of individuals would be affected leading to the destabilization of the entire private law order. For instance, each reform of the export tax rebate system in China would directly affect the division and allocation of public property rights and private property rights, and may even generate different influences on public property rights in different layers (for example, the public property right of the central and local governments), as well as the private property rights of different agents (for example, the private property right of enterprises that export/do not export goods). From the legal perspective, one of the central issues is to protect the claim to taxpayer rebate, or in other words, how to balance private and public property rights and to coordinate the taxation law reform and private law order.

Consistency of key distribution systems 35

The external effects of taxation law reform on private law areas should be estimated properly and corresponding systematic coordination should be undertaken in the form of specific arrangement in taxation law or private law. At the same time, coordination with constitutional law and other laws, especially the stipulations on the allocation of power or right usually would be of tremendous value to taxation law reform which may bring instability to private law order.

Because of the fact that the taxation law system is immense and involves broad areas, certain taxation law systems should be relatively stable, judging from the maintenance of the stability of private law order and effectively coordinating the protection of private and public property right. Taxation law is important to macro-regulation and control and to the allocation of resources, yet "governing a great nation is like cooking a small fish", indicating that the reform to taxation law should be discrete. This is vital to maintain a stable private law order. Such efforts would constitute another form of "coordination" with private law order.

Besides, the reason for reforming taxation law sometimes is that the adjustment of private law is not sufficient to effectively protect public property right, nor could it comprehensively protect the private property right of various agents. Under such circumstances, private law reform is also needed to coordinate taxation law reform. The coordination of taxation law and private law at the institutional level could be unidirectional or bidirectional and some higher-level legal theories or principles may act as the link for their coordination. For example, the principle of honesty is a vital principle that is applicable to both private law and taxation law and it serves as an important bridge that connects the two. In fact, to establish, develop, and terminate the economic relationship between individuals based on the principle of honesty constitutes a vital foundation on which the state may gain tax. Meanwhile, individuals should also act honestly and when they attempt to evade taxes through illegal activities, the state may also take action to regain such taxation through the confirmation of reality. Besides, when individuals try to abrogate taxation laws by abusing rights in private law, the state may deny the effectiveness of such rights in private law through taxation law and gain substantial taxation.[48]

In fact, active coordination in the domain of private law is significantly important. For instance, civil law stipulates that civil acts that violate the law are null and void, so private transactions violating taxation law are naturally null and void. It is of the same importance to both stabilize private law order and protect public and private property rights. In this sense, even though emphasis has been placed on the protection of public and private property rights, taxation law, and private law, both laws have the important function to protect "two rights" and to comprehensively solve distribution problems which constitute a crucial foundation for coordination.

2.3.4 Conclusion

From the basic principle of taxation law and private law adjustment, the coordination between changes in taxation law and private law order originating from

36 *Consistency of key distribution systems*

private law adjustment is required. Coordination is necessary to satisfy different human needs and enhance fair and effective distribution. Such coordination is directly linked to the separation of private and public property rights. For the external effects generated from the change of taxation law, especially the negative external effects to the private law order, special attention is required and a specific systematic arrangement is needed in addition to institutional coordination conducted respectively from the aspects of taxation law, private law, or other laws and regulations. Only through this can distribution problems be better solved and distribution crises prevented.

The separation of public and private property rights has its internal rationality, and both taxation law and private law have significant value in protecting both and in establishing a benign distribution order. Therefore, resolving the negative effects of taxation law transformation to private law order through institutional coordination among taxation law, private law, and constitutional law is both necessary and plausible. However, these problems may appear occasionally and they require constant efforts to solve. Solving these problems is a process to constantly regulate distribution activities using the law and constitutes a process that requires the constant coordination of economic law and civil and commercial law.

2.4 Internal coordination among identical distribution systems

Coordination among the abovementioned important distribution systems of different types (different precedences and different natures), including constitutional law and economic law, and civil and commercial law, needs to be enhanced. Besides, coordination among distribution systems of the same type needs to be addressed particularly with regard to the target and legal basis of regulation. For instance, one of the important targets of Chinese taxation system reform after 2008 has been "structural taxation reduction". As an important measure to reduce the burden of market agents and trigger energy in the market, the reduction of taxes should be reflected in various taxation law systems. Therefore, specific taxation law systems, as distribution systems of the same type, should remain consistent concerning their legal basis and their aim to reduce taxation. For this purpose, the following parts illustrate the issue of internal coordination among distribution systems of the same time, taking structural taxation reduction as an example.

2.4.1 Proposal for structural taxation reduction

As an important measure to deal with the distribution crisis, taxation reduction is applied frequently and widely and would generate significantly influence relevant agents with regard to the distribution of income.[49] After the 2008 financial crisis, China faced the problem of high costs while, at the same time, the people faced enormous pressure. The burden of enterprises was heavy and this affected their

Consistency of key distribution systems 37

growth and competitiveness (Shouwen Zhang 2012).[50] Under such circumstance, it was necessary to adjust the economic structure, reduce the burden of the people, and activate the energy of the market thereby making "moderate taxation reduction" a consensus.

To implement such reduction in taxation, China advocated for "structural taxation reduction" (Tifu An and Haiyong Wang 2004)[51] which meant "to implement the taxation reduction of specific agents in specific areas in order to achieve specific purposes". It was not overall taxation reduction but a moderate reduction that discriminated against different agents. The summarized description of the "structural taxation reduction" emphasizes the "specification" or "particularization" of the reduction and does not pay attention to its "structural" characteristics. In fact, every taxation reduction involves the structure, for it relies on the current taxation law structure and affects the structural optimization of taxation law. If the unified target for taxation reduction could be maintained and relevant legal basis could be defended, the internal coordination among distribution systems in taxation law system would also be facilitated. In other words, the "structural taxation reduction" would bring "structural change" to taxation law and would promote a level of coordination among relevant taxation systems. At the same time, it would generate positive effects on economic, fiscal, taxation, and distribution structures at the macro level. Therefore, it is indeed necessary to deeply investigate the "structural" issues resulting from "structural taxation reduction" (Tifu An 2012).[52]

"Structural taxation reduction" is not only an issue of policy or economy, rather it is much more a legal issue and it calls for the enhancement of internal coordination among different taxation law systems and the optimization of the taxation law structure based on a unified legal target and basis only through which a "good governance" under the structure of the rule of law could be realized(Brennan and Buchanan 2004).[53]

Though "structural taxation reduction" is an important measure in dealing with the crisis, when emphasizing the close connection between "structural taxation reduction" and the adjustment of fiscal income and spending structure, the taxation law structure and taxation law system, it could be concluded that China has implemented a "structural taxation reduction" since 2004. From the change of taxation law structure and the emphasis on the "particularity" of "structural taxation reduction", such a conclusion is consistent with reality.

Judging from the actual conditions, the specific approaches for "structural taxation reduction" mainly include: 1) the adjustment of overall taxation types through the abolition, suspension, and merging various taxes to change relevant taxation systems, and 2) the adjustment of elements of one specific tax type, i.e. the realization of taxation law system through the change of type, basis, and rate of taxation. These two specific approaches directly affect the coordination of taxation law systems because of the fact that they all involve shifting the taxation law system and they further affect the realization of the overall function of the taxation law system. These changes are discussed in the section that follows.

38 *Consistency of key distribution systems*

2.4.2 Coordination of the taxation law system from the perspective of overall taxation adjustment

Based on the types of taxation, the Chinese taxation law system had long been composed of three types of norms, namely industrial and commercial taxation law, agricultural taxation law, and custom taxation law. The formation of such a structure is relevant to the taxation system where taxation, finance, and customs share the power to impose taxes (especially the power to levy and regulate the tax) and to the multiple standards (industry/commerce and agriculture; domestic and foreign) according to which taxation is divided. Yet, such standards and systems had significant problems. For instance, the identification of power was ambiguous, the taxation law structure was unreasonable, and the taxation law system was inconsistent. Through the constant implementation of "structural taxation reduction" these problems, to a certain extent, were solved.

For example, agricultural tax was domestic and in the system of "broad" agricultural taxation, agricultural and husbandry taxes were already abolished. The existing agricultural taxes, namely occupation of cultivated land tax and deed tax, were levied by the taxation administration rather than fiscal administration[54] and, by that token, "agricultural tax" was eliminated. Therefore, a more precise "binary" division to the taxation law system for "domestic taxation law" and "foreign taxation law" could be done. Through the "structural taxation reduction" and the adjustment to the levy of taxation, the taxation law system and the governing body in China became a "binary" structure and the relevant taxation law system and configuration of power to taxation became more coordinated (see Table 2.1).

It was vital to abolish agriculture tax through "structural taxation reduction" for the transformation process of the Chinese taxation law system. As early as 2004, the central government announced that agriculture taxation would be abolished in two provinces, Heilongjiang and Jilin, and soon after, other provinces took the same measure. This situation made the Standing Committee of the National People's Congress to formally pass the decision to rescind the Regulation on Agriculture Taxation. The decision became effective at the beginning of 2006.[55] It is a significant step of the "structural taxation deduction" and it facilitated the adjustment and optimization of the taxation law structure, through which various specific taxation law systems may produce better results with the overall goal to solve three agricultural issues – agriculture, village, and farmers.

Table 2.1 The shift of the taxation law system and taxation administration.

Original structure of taxation law system	Current binary structure of taxation law system	Current binary structure of taxation administration
Industry and commerce taxation law	Domestic taxation law	Taxation administration
Agriculture taxation law		
Custom taxation law	Foreign taxation law	Customs

Consistency of key distribution systems 39

Of course, under the unified goal of taxation reduction, it is not only agriculture taxation that has been abolished; the influential butcher tax and feast tax were also abolished. After the rescinding of Interim Regulation on Butcher Tax in 2006, the Interim Regulation on Feast Tax was also abolished in 2008. Economic and social factors, as well as considerations regarding the efficiency of taxation, jointly contributed to the abolition of these taxes. For the specific agents that were involved in the abolished taxes, the effect of taxation reduction was obvious and could better contribute to resolving distribution issues in relevant areas.

Besides, with regard to the specific approach to "structural taxation reduction", China once applied the method of "suspension" which consists of reducing tax through the suspension of certain taxes. For instance, the tax for guiding investments on fixed assets was "suspended" in 2000. Though the suspension of certain taxes increased the efficiency of taxation and fostered socio-economic development in different phases, the stipulations of laws or administrative regulations did not provide any legal grounds for such measures and such decisions were based merely on "the permission of the State Council" or "the State Council decides". Whether such sentences are with the same effect as "administrative regulation" remains to be determined given that it is a much stricter process to make administrative regulations. If a department or affiliated institution of the State Council could add a sentence such as "with the permission of the State Council" into a document, then such a document could be effective throughout the whole nation, which is both against the current rules and against the basic requirements of rule of law. According to the theory of the power of taxation, to commence and to abolish a tax are both important elements of the taxation legislation and they should be exercised as taxation legislation. Meanwhile, in accordance with current laws, the suspension of taxes should also abide by the laws. Even with the authorization of laws, the stipulations of administrative regulations are still required.[56] Therefore, according to the requirements of current laws, regulations concerning the suspension of taxes should not be inferior to the level of administrative regulations. The suspension of a tax for guiding investment on fixed assets is problematic. Without the unification of the agent which exercises the power to suspend the tax, the inconsistency of the taxation law system permanently exists and the coordination among taxation law systems can only be enhanced through the strict implementation of statutory taxation.

Apart from the aforementioned abolition or suspension of certain taxes, China also "merged" certain taxes. Merging was directly associated with abolishing and was achieved by abolishing relevant taxes and rescinding relevant taxation laws or regulations, aiming mainly at solving the inconsistency of the taxation law system generated from the parallel "two types of taxation laws" which discriminated between domestic and foreign agents. For instance, the current enterprise income tax originated from the merging of two types of income taxes that were respectively applied to domestic and foreign enterprises,[57] Meanwhile, the current real property tax and vehicle and vessel tax also originated from the merging of two taxes applied to domestic and foreign agents. However, because of the fact that they maintain the name and relevant institution of the prior taxes, such change

40 *Consistency of key distribution systems*

is akin to merging through absorbing.[58] The merging also directly influenced the structure of taxation law and is likely to increase the consistency of the taxation law system. Besides, although the extent of tax reduction generated from merging is not as sharp as "abolition" or "suspension", it still produces the result of a tax reduction. After all, under the previous taxation system that discriminated domestic and foreign agents, the unification of taxation law and merging of taxes could reduce the number of tax types. Also, the adjustment followed the principle of "applying the lower rate when merging two taxes with different rates", which essentially reduces the burden of relevant agents. For example, in terms of enterprise income tax, though originally the rate had been 33% for both domestic and foreign agents, the actual rate for domestic enterprises is higher than for foreign agents. Through the unification of taxation law and "merging" of taxes, the rate for domestic enterprises could reduce at least to 25%, or even lower for some enterprises. This is the tax reduction effect generated from the "merging" of taxes.

The above three specific approaches correspond to different areas of tax reduction, and the agents that exercise the power to reduce taxes are different. An illustration is provided in Table 2.2.

The "abolition", "suspension", and "merging" are specific approaches to "structural tax reduction" in China and the respective effect to tax reduction is as the consequence. "Abolition" has the most significant effect because it directly cancels a tax in one specific area. "Suspension" is next because it indicates the temporary suspension of a tax, and not totally abolish it, within a certain period of time abolition. While "merging" means to abolish a tax while creating a new one.[59] The tax reduction effect depends on the elements of the newly created tax. Since the general trend declines, it goes without saying that the actual rate would decline as well.

Besides, when analyzing the tax reduction effect, it is important not only to consider a specific type of tax but also to determine whether to reduce the overall tax. For instance, the tax reduction measures through all the above-mentioned approaches contribute to the coordination of different taxation systems and would

Table 2.2 The approach, area, and entity of tax reduction.

Specific approach	*Area*	*Entity*
Taxes abolished	2006: Agricultural Tax	Standing Committee of the
	2006: Butcher tax	National People's Congress
	2008: Feast tax	State Council
	2013: Tax on investment in	State Council
	fixed assets	State Council
Taxes suspended	2000: Tax on investment in	Department of Finance, State
	fixed assets (Abolished in	Administration of Taxation,
	2013 by the State Council)	National Development and
		Reform Commission
Taxes merged	2007: Vehicle and vessel tax	State Council
	2008: Enterprise income tax	National People's Congress
	2009: Real property tax	State Council

Consistency of key distribution systems   41

reveal the issue of "systematic duplicate taxation". After all, the possibility of duplicate taxation for one specific entity would be tremendously increased when multiple taxes are simultaneously put forward. The abolishing and merging of taxes would reduce the number of tax, further reduce the "systematic duplicate taxation", and finally decrease the overall tax burden.

It is worth noting that the approaches to "structural tax reduction" are different, so are the agents that exercise the power to reduce taxes. Mainly there are three types of agents, namely the National People's Congress as well as its standing committee, the State Council, and the relevant departments, committees, and bureaus affiliated to the State Council. The abolition of taxes (including abolishing through merging) is mainly conducted by the National People's Congress as well as its standing committee and the State Council. As for the suspension of taxes, the legislative authority mainly rests with the State Council and its departments to reduce taxes. The difference is relevant to the degree of influence on the structure of taxation law. After all, "abolition" and "merging" are important and would directly affect the system and structure of taxation law and would generate greater influence, while "suspension" is a temporary measure which maintains the existence of the relevant tax and is therefore relatively less important.[60]

Does the State Council exercise the power to tax deduction too frequently? Do the affiliated, eligible departments/committees have the legality to sufficiently exercise such power? These questions are realistic issues worth our attention, for they would affect the coordination of the taxation law system to different extents, especially the coordination between the legislation of the National People's Congress and the State Council, and the "taxation legislation" by the departments/committees of the State Council and the National People's Congress/State Council.

2.4.3 Coordination of the taxation law system from the perspective of tax elements

Coordination among taxation law systems is not only reflected through overall adjustment of types of tax but also through the adjustment of the item, rate, tax base, and incentives of one specific tax. Reducing taxes by adjusting tax incentives is an approach that is commonly followed by the market and is familiar to the public. However, public attention is lessened with regard to the approach to tax reduction through adjusting the item, rate, and tax base.

In fact, there have already been large quantities of institutional practices of tax reduction through the adjustment of tax items. Commonly, the adjustment of tax items would appear as the cancellation or change of certain tax items of the same type of tax. For instance, in the area of consumer tax, "vehicle tyre" was a taxable item which, since 2006, has been cancelled in order to establish the "structural tax reduction". Besides, the adjustment of tax items sometimes appears as changes in multiple types of tax. For instance, since January 1, 2012, China has instituted an experimental project of "business tax to VAT" in Shanghai as a "structural tax reduction" which serves to transfer tax items of business tax into VAT, through

42 *Consistency of key distribution systems*

which relevant industries no longer bear the original tax burden that was relatively higher and through which the purpose of "substantial tax reduction" could be achieved. All the above approaches to "structural tax reduction" are relevant to the coordination among taxation law systems. Specifically, "business tax to VAT" involves the coordination between the two most important goods tax systems which would produce a direct influence on the distribution of incomes of relevant market agents and between central and local governments.

The adjustment of tax items within one type of tax would affect its "width" and while the width of taxation is limited, or the original tax item is cancelled or replaced by tax items with a lower rate, the effect of tax reduction would be produced. On the other hand, the adjustment of tax items across different types of taxes would maintain the width of taxation while affecting the distribution of income because of the influence of the rate, tax base, etc., of the other tax. Thus, it could be concluded that when a tax item is adjusted, the changes in the tax rate and base should also be analyzed, without which a comprehensive examination of the "tax reduction effect" is impossible.

Normally, the adjustment of the tax rate directly affects the "depth" of tax. Lowering the rate could directly generate a tax reduction effect; therefore, reducing the tax rate is an important instrument for "structural tax reduction". For example, the Law of Corporate Income Tax which came into effect in 2008 in China reduced the tax rate that was applicable to both domestic and foreign enterprises from 33% to 25% (special enterprises may enjoy lower rate).[61] This action not only produced an obvious tax reduction rate but was also consistent with the worldwide trend of increasing the competitiveness of corporations through decreasing the tax burden of income tax. Besides, multiple amendments of the Law for Individual Income Tax have produced the lowest tax rate applicable to salary from 5% to 3% and greatly increased the deduction amount. Through such measures, the number of individual income taxpayers has decreased considerably meaning that there is a need to focus on the effects of tax reduction. Such adjustments in income tax areas are relevant to the amount of direct tax and have a more direct effect on tax reduction. This contributes to the protection and improvement of the life of ordinary citizens and to the rising of working-class income, to the increasing of corporate competitiveness, and to the fulfilling of fair competition. In fact, similar tax rate adjustment measures are employed commonly and widely in every tax area and are not just limited to income tax.

Apart from the adjustment to the tax item and tax rate, the adjustment to the tax base is also vital for tax reduction. For example, in the area of indirect tax, to deal with financial crises, to make VAT more "neutral", to reduce and prevent duplicate taxation, and to facilitate the shift from "productive VAT" to "consumptive VAT", on January 1, 2009, China began to expand VAT deductions to decrease the tax base and to comprehensively promote the tax reduction in the domain of VAT. Also, in the area of direct tax, the approach China applied to improve the Law for Individual Income Tax is to constantly increase the standard of salary deduction to achieve the aim of tax reduction through lowering the tax base. All these changes require coordination under the common target of tax reduction.

Consistency of key distribution systems 43

2.4.4 Summary

Structural tax reduction is a vital measure that would influence the income distribution of relevant agents and would have significant outcomes to the state and to the citizens. As an important distribution method, the implementation of structural tax reduction affects the change of the taxation law system and change of specific tax systems and enhances internal coordination within the taxation law systems under the unified goal of tax reduction.

As an important distribution system, the internal coordination of taxation law systems is directly connected to achieving the overall goal of distribution. Therefore, it is necessary to maintain consistency and coordination between the goal and specific measures among different systems of the taxation law system. Therefore, during the process of implementing structural tax reduction measures, the maintaining/abolition of specific tax systems and the adjustment to relevant tax systems should be coordinated under the same goal.

As is mentioned before, both overall tax type adjustments and partial change to specific tax types or tax elements are important approaches to "structural tax reduction". The overall adjustment to tax types through "abolition", "suspension", "merging", and adjustment to tax elements through name change, rates, and foundations of one specific type of tax is relevant to the comprehensive taxation law structure and to the internal structure of specific taxation laws, as well as to the coordination among different types of taxation law systems. As similar types of distribution systems, the various taxation law systems require a unified design of institution for their coordination. The steady and gradual completion of such systems is also needed for the better achievement of unified distribution goals and to provide a better solution to relevant issues in the area of distribution.

Notes

1 See Pingxue Zhou. (1995). Attention shall be Paid to the Research to the Economic Attributes of the Constitutional Law. *Law Science*, (12), pp. 16–17.
2 For the discussion on "Constitutional Economics", see Brennan and Buchanan.(2004). *Constitutional Economics*, translated by Feng Keli, *et al*. Beijing: China Social Science Press, p. 2. preface by Feng Xingyuan.
3 Some scholars believe that the emphasis of constitutional economics is the influence on economic growth by different types of systems, while economic constitutional law, when focusing on the institutional protection of economic growth, pays more attention to the just position of fundamental individual human rights and freedoms in economic systems. See Yue Wu. (2007). *An Introduction to Economic Constitutional Law: The Game between Economic Right and Power in China during Transformation*, the Law Press, Preface,p. 4.
4 Though the concept of "economic constitution" originates from economic law research in Germany, Linke, the German scholar, still positions economic constitution as a constitutional norm. See Shiyi Zhao. (2001). Basic Questions on Economic Constitutionalism. *Chinese Journal of Law*, (4), pp. 32–41.
5 For efforts and results in this area, See Buchanan and Tullock. (2000). *The Calculus of Consent: Logical Foundations of Constitutional Democracy*, translated by Chen Guangjin, Beijing: China Social Science Press; Brennan and Buchanan (2004). *Constitutional Economics*, translated by Feng Keli, *et al*. Beijing: China Social Science Press.

44 Consistency of key distribution systems

6 Famous economists such as Böhm and Rink emphasize the research on the relationship between constitutional law and economic law. Along with economist Okun, they value the close interrelation between economic constitution and "order", and emphasize that economic constitution is the comprehensive choice to the order of civil economic life.

7 In the opening words for the *Economic Order,* edited by Böhm and Okun, they emphasized that "the economic constitution should be understood as the comprehensive choice to the order of civil economic life". Though such choice is definitely political, it is also directly related to the perception to objective economic regulations.

8 Article 1, Clause 8 of the US Constitution defines interstate trade, and emphasizes that Congress owns the legislative power to regulate interstate trade. Based on this clause, the US published a series of important economic legislations such as *Interstate Commerce Act* and *Sherman Antitrust Act.*

9 Article 23, Clause 2 of the Constitution of the Russian Federation stipulates that "the economic activity aimed at monopolization and unfair competition shall not be allowed", which represents the constitutional basis for anti-monopolization and anti-unfair competition legislation.

10 Some scholars call it "the power of the state to regulate" and believe that it belongs to the fourth form of power. See Yunliang Chen. (2007). State's Regulatory Power: The Fourth Power. *Modern Law Science,* 29(6), pp.15–21.

11 Some scholars reckon that the ownership institution is the core to the fundamental economic institution (i.e. market economy or planned economy institution) established by the constitution. See Yushi Gui (2005). *Economic Institution in Chinese Constitutional Law.* Wu Han: Wuhan University Press, pp. 20–21.

12 For example, Article 8 of the Constitution of the Russian Federation stipulates that "in the Russian Federation, recognition and equal protection shall be given to the private, state, municipal and other forms of ownership", and Article 9 stipulates that "land and other natural resources may be in private, state, municipal and other forms of ownership".

13 For example, the Constitution of the Federative Republic of Brazil (published on October 5, 1988) makes specific stipulations to the distribution of taxation income of different levels of government in Article 157 and 158 in Chapter 6.

14 This conclusion was made by famous American historian Charles A. Beard based on the economic analysis of the US Constitution, employing the economic historic perspective to interpret the US Constitution. See Charles A. Beard. (2011). *An Economic Interpretation of the Constitution of the United States,* translated by Xiqi He. Beijing: Commercial Press.

15 Academia has significant discourse concerning the issue of economic administrative law. For example, Rolf Stober. (2008). *Allgemeines Wirtschaftsverwaltungsrecht: Grundlagen des Wirtschaftsverfassungs- und Wirtschaftsverwaltungsrechts, des Weltwirtschafts- und Binnenmarktrechts,* translated by Libin Xie. Beijing: Commercial Press. However, in China, many scholars oppose the idea of equating economic law with economic administrative law. See Kepeng Xue. (2013). Investigation to the Origin of Economic Administrative Law Theory: Economic Administrative Law in the Context of Economic Law. *Contemporary Law Review,* (5), pp. 123–130.

16 For example, Article 71 of the Constitution of the Russian Federation stipulates that "the jurisdiction of the Russian Federation includes: …g. establishment of legal groups for a single market; financial, currency, credit, and customs regulation, money issue, the principles of pricing policy; h. federal economic services, including federal banks; federal budget, federal taxes and dues, federal funds of regional development". These are all important areas in economic law.

17 For earlier discussion and dispute, see Tiechuan Hao. (1996).On Benign Violation against the Constitution.*Chinese Journal of Law,* (4), pp. 89–91; Zhiwei Tong. (1996). "Benign Violation against the Constitution" Should not be Recognized. *Chinese Journal*

of Law, (6), pp. 19–22. With the improvement of rule of law, various issues of violation against the constitution should be avoided, regardless of whether it is "benign" or not.

18 See *The Decision to Implement the Binary Taxation Fiscal Management Institution* (1993); *The Notice to Distribute the Reform Scheme of Income Tax Revenue Sharing* (2001); *The Decision concerning Financial Institution Reform* (1993); *The Decision concerning the Reform to Investment Institution* (2004), etc.

19 Though China announced that the socialist legal system, with Chinese characteristics having been established as early as January 2011, many legal systems concerning distribution are far from being complete, and the task for legislation in the field of distribution is still heavy.

20 For the vertical development process of economic law, the scholars have already achieved certain results, i.e. Xinhe Cheng. (2008). Research to the 30-years Development of the Economic Law in China. *Journal of Chongqing University* (Social Science Edition), 14(4), pp. 104–108. Yet in general, deeper research is still required.

21 The emergence and development of economic law change the fundamental structure of the legal system in various states, and generate essential influence to the protection of property rights, which is consistent with the institutional change theory of North. See Douglass North. (1994). *Structure and Change in Economic History*, translated by Yu Chen, Huaping Luo. Shanghai: SDX Joint Publishing Company, Shanghai People's Press, p. 24.

22 The relationship between the government and market has always been fundamental during the process of reform and opening-up, and it is important to the solution to distribution issues. See Shouwen Zhang. (2014). "Decision to Reform" and the Consensus for Economic Law. *Law Review*, 184(2), pp. 18–29; Shouwen Zhang. (2014). Legal Adjustment to the Relationship between the Government and Market. *China Legal Science*, (5), pp. 60–74.

23 Economic constitution is the vital foundation for economic law. Famous economic law expert Böhm focused on "economic constitution" in a comparatively earlier time and promoted the research in "economic constitution" along with Okun. Buchanan initiated the research to constitution economics and paid attention to the issue of economic law institutions. Therefore, the close interrelationship among the previous institutions and theories should be noticed when studying the development of economic law.

24 The theory of precedency emphasizes more on the hierarchy among constitutional law and other laws. Therefore, economic law should submit to the requirement of constitutional law. See Dieter Grimms. (2010). *Ursprung, Wandel und Zukunft der Verfassung*, translated by Liu Gang. Beijing: China Law Press, p.14.

25 This article is crucial to the development of the economic law institution and the economic law study. In terms of constitutional interpretation, its function should be emphasized so that it could provide important constitutional support to the institutional construction and legal discussion of economic law.

26 The original stipulation is "the State implements planned economy on the basis of socialist public ownership". Such tremendous change in the economic institution involves many important theoretical and institutional problems in constitutional law and economic law and directly affects the development of economic law.

27 The difference in the conception to "economic Constitution" in Germany, see Hui Huang. (2009). The Application of Economic Institution Clauses in the Constitution: The Dispute Concerning German Economic Constitution. *Peking University Law Journal*, 21(4), pp. 559–573.

28 The original stipulation is "the State guarantees the coordinated development of civil economic in proportion, through combining the comprehensive balance of economic planning and the assistive function of market adjustment". There exist similarities between the original and new stipulations with regard to the issue of comprehensive balance and coordinated development.

46 *Consistency of key distribution systems*

29 See Qianfan Zhang. (2001). Regulation and Control to Interstate Trades by the Federal Government of USA. *Journal of Nalnjing University (Philosophy, Humanities and Social Sciences)*, 38(2), pp. 141–150.

30 The stipulations concerning the economy or economic law in the constitutions of relevant states are numerous, for example, the stipulations to fiscal institutions in Basic Law for the Federal Republic of Germany, stipulations to macro regulation and control institutions including budget, taxation, and monetary institutions in The Constitution of the Bolivarian Republic of Venezuela.

31 For instance, Article 151 of the Weimar Constitution stipulated that "the economy must be regulated according to the principles of justice with the goal of assuring humane living conditions for everyone. Within these boundaries the economic liberty of the individual is guaranteed". Article 217 of the Constitution of the Dominican Republic stipulates that "the economic regime is oriented towards the search for human development. It is based on economic growth, redistribution of wealth, social justice, equity, social, and territorial cohesion and environmental sustainability". These stipulations reflect the value and spirit of constitutional law.

32 See Qianfan Zhang. (2011). *US Federal Constitution*. Beijing: China Law Press, pp. 98–100.

33 The *Decision concerning Economic Institution Reform* passed by the Central Committee of CPC in October 1984 brought forward the "macro-regulation and control", having emphasized that through comprehensive employment to economic leverage including price, taxation, and loan, the total amount of supply and demand of the society should be adjusted, and the industry structure and allocation of productive forces should be regulated. It roughly equals the later definition of "macro regulation and control".

34 See Shouwen Zhang. (2009). The Meridian that Runs through the Research of Economic Law in China: From the Perspective of Distribution. *Tribune of Political Science and Law*, 27(6), pp. 122–135.

35 See Shouwen Zhang. (2013). The "Experiment Mode" of Taxation Legislation in China: Taking VAT Legislation Experiment as Example. *Law Science*, (4), pp. 61–68.

36 See Shouwen Zhang. (2009). *General Introduction to Economic Law*. Beijing: Renmin University Press, p. 48, 59.

37 The function of constitutional law to regulate could be understood as the function to regulate or restrict, which is not entirely the same to the regulation function of economic law. See H. Th J. F. van Maarseveen. (2007). *Written Constitutions: A Computerized Comparative Study*, translated by Chen Yunsheng. Peking University Press, p. 315.

38 For example, the US once announced in 1895 that the imposition of income taxation was against the Constitution (and the imposition of income tax was resumed till 1913), and that the National Industrial Recovery Act was against the Constitution in 1935.

39 The US does not deem the income tax institution as violation against the Constitution. In the constitutional laws of Germany, Brazil, etc., specific stipulations concerning income tax institution are made, and stipulations regarding macro regulation, control systems, and market regulation systems, including finance and taxation, are also included.

40 See Shouwen Zhang. (2012). Economic Law: Thinking on the Right to Economic Development. *Modern Law Science*, 27(2), pp. 3–9.

41 Commodity, income, and property as wealth in dynamic or static form is normally the object of taxation. See Shouwen Zhang. (2012). *Principles of Taxation Law*, 6th ed. Peking University Press, pp. 54–55.

42 The "objects" being discussed in a broader sense, from the perspective of normal legal research (especially the taxation law research). The "objects" in the context of private law are also not limited to "objects" in the sense of property law.

43 This issue could also be investigated from the perspective of "the paradox of Douglass North". North once believed that the existence of the state is the key to economic growth, and also the source of recession. The state should define and protect prop-

Consistency of key distribution systems 47

erty rights, and meanwhile increase its income, and such two aims are intrinsically contradictory with each other. In fact, the contradiction in "the paradox of Douglass North" is consistent with the contradiction between taxation law and private law, which would contribute to illustrating the necessity of conflict between taxation law and private law.

44 See Douglass North. (1994). *Structure and Change in Economic History*, translated by Chen Yu. Shanghai: SDX Joint Publishing Company, Shanghai People's Press, pp. 166–177.

45 See Shouwen Zhang. (2001). The Universal Applicability of Taxation Law and its Limitations. *Peking University Law Journal*, 13(5), pp. 554–566.

46 Adam Smith once pointed out that political economics has two goals: to make the state prosperous and to make the people wealthy. See Adam Smith (2003). *The Nature and Causes of the Wealth of Nations*, translated by Guo Dali and Wang Yanan. Beijing: Commercial Press, p. 1. To make the state prosperous, the public property right should be established. While in order to make the people wealthy, the private property right should be protected. Therefore, the separation of the two rights is justified.

47 The State Administration of Taxation organized and published the *Announcement Concerning the Right and Obligation of Taxpayers* in November 2009, and the number of the rights concerning taxpayers is 14.

48 Article 42 of German Taxation Law makes specific stipulations concerning activities aiming at avoiding tax, emphasizing that substantial taxation shall be imposed on taxpayers who abuse their rights. It is widely acknowledged as a typical illustration to the principle of substantial taxation.

49 When the 2008 financial crisis occurred, states such as the US, Germany, UK, Japan, and Australia began to institute the tax reduction. The *Emergency Economic Stabilization Act* of 2008 and the *Energy Improvement and Extension Act* of 2008 had a huge influence as they involved over hundreds of billions of dollars.

50 Tax reduction is directly relevant to the right to economic development of market agents. See Shouwen Zhang. (2012). Economic Law: Thinking on the Right to Economic Development. *Modern Law Science*, 34(2), pp. 4–10.

51 "Structural tax reduction" is a vital tool to solve economic and social problems and should become a strategic choice. See Tifu An and Haiyong Wang. (2004). Structural Tax Reduction: Choice for Taxation Policy under the Limitation of Macro-economy. *International Taxation in China*, (11), pp. 7–12.

52 See Tifu An. (2012). On Several Issues concerning Structural Tax Reduction. *Taxation Research*, (5), p. 3.

53 See Geoffrey Brennan and James M. Buchanan. (2004). *Constitutional Economics*, translated by Feng Keli, *et al.* Beijing: China Social Science Press, pp. 6–10.

54 According to the requirement of Department of Finance and State Administration of Taxation, before December 31, 2009, the function of levying of the two types of tax should be transferred from local fiscal departments to local taxation administrations.

55 The *Decision to Rescind the Regulation on Agriculture Taxation* was passed by the Standing Committee of the National People's Congress in December 2005, thus the *Regulation on Agriculture Taxation* that passed in 1958 was rescinded from January 1, 2006.

56 Article 3 of the *Law on Taxation Administration* has made explicit stipulations on this and it shall be discussed in subsequent sections.

57 One of the taxes is "corporate income tax", and the other is "income tax of foreign invested company and foreign company". The unified *Law on Corporate Income Tax* was passed by the National People's Congress and has been implemented since Jan 1, 2008.

58 Originally, foreign companies and individuals were subject to urban real estate tax and vehicle and vessel license tax. After the reformation, such agents are subject to the same real estate tax (from Jan 1, 2009) and vehicle and vessel tax (since Jan 1, 2007)

48 *Consistency of key distribution systems*

as domestic companies thereby achieving the unification of real estate tax and vehicle and vessel tax.

59 For example, the "income tax for foreign invested and foreign companies" is now abolished, yet a new "corporate income tax" has been imposed. The "urban real estate tax" for foreign companies has been abolished, yet a new "real estate tax" has been levied. The "vehicle and vessel license tax" imposed on foreign companies has been abolished, yet a new "vehicle and vessel tax" has been imposed.

60 In China, the suspension of tax must result from the fact that the levying of such tax is inconsistent with the social and economic policy, therefore the influence of such suspension would be minor. Apart from the tax for guiding the investment on fixed assets, the suspension of the "interest tax" is another instance.

61 For example, according to Article 28 of the *Law on Corporate Income Tax*, the rate for micro-scale companies is 20%, while the rate for high and new tech companies supported by the state is 15%. In addition, during particular periods, the State Council may grant micro-scale companies more taxation preferential measures.

3 Unification and difference of distribution systems

The governance of laws, especially economic laws, is indispensable to the solving of distribution issues. Based on the unification of the legal system, distribution systems that are relevant to each other should also be unified to a certain degree. This is essential to solving essential and common distribution issues. However, the unification of the distribution system can only be relative. Because of the fact that the specific situations of various types of agents are different, the violation or exception to a unified distribution system always exist, and new differences in the system are generated. These differences constitute a violation of the unified distribution system. Whether such violations are legal and comply with the principles of the rule of law are worthy of serious research and discussion. Therefore, when focusing on the unification of the distribution systems, existing differences should also be addressed. The relationship between unification and difference shall also be resolved in order to better realize the comprehensive aim of the distribution system.

In fact, arrangements with regard to discrimination in distribution systems are very common. For instance, the "experiment" for taxation legislation is a discriminated arrangement outside the unified system. At the same time, the focus should be on the realization of distribution goals and the unification of the legal ground during such a process, given that it is especially important during the implementation of structural tax reduction measures. Besides, the differences existing in the unified law of corporate income tax, under some circumstances, for example, the very special collection taxation system, partly resulting from the consideration to factors relating to the state. For such purposes, it is necessary to illustrate the dialectical relation between the unification and differences of distribution systems with the institutional practice in the aforementioned areas, as well as the existing issues' different distribution systems.

3.1 Difference outside the unified distribution system

To solve the complicated distribution problems, selective arrangements are made outside the unified distribution system because of the practice of "experimentation" during the establishment of the distribution system, which is, to some extent, against the requirement of the law. In the area of taxation, the legislative

50 *Unification of distribution systems*

"experiment" is more common and it directly affects the distribution of interest of relevant agents, especially the distribution between the state and the citizen. For example, the experiment on the reform of real estate tax once drew a lot of attention. In fact, besides the real estate tax, there have been many "experiments", some of which are ongoing. Analyzing the merits and flaws of the mode of the experiment would assist us to analyze the existing problems of the Chinese distribution system from another perspective.

Since the start of China's reform and opening-up, economic legislation has received an increasing focus among which taxation legislation is centrally important and is predominantly typical.[1] After all, the income tax legislation in international areas, as the earliest economic legislation after the reform and opening-up, has laid an important foundation for the rule of law of taxation and for the comprehensive rule of law of the economy.[2] Meanwhile, massive economic legislation in every cycle has been led by taxation legislation. Although currently, the basic framework of taxation legislation has been established, the taxation system is still flawed and the structure is still not completed.[3] Thus, it is still necessary to profoundly explore the issues in taxation legislation.

From the legislative process since the reform and opening-up, one important characteristic of Chinese taxation legislation is to emphasize the legislative "experiment". For example, in the first stage of reform and opening-up, the State Council announced a series of taxation regulations (draft) within the framework of the "experiment".[4] With the deepening of reform and opening-up, though many taxation legislations are not in an "experimental period", they still remain "interim".[5] In recent years the "experiment for taxation reform" has been conducted in areas including VAT, real estate property, and resource property, while reforms regarding the adjustment of taxation elements or taxation levying are implemented at the legislative level. Therefore, the aforementioned "experiment for taxation reform" is, in essence, a "legislative experiment". The long-term, quantitative, and frequent legislative experiments as a common and significant phenomenon in Chinese taxation legislation deserve attention and deserve to be researched.

In fact, the legislative pattern to "to experiment first" has been widely applied to many areas and has formed a model. The legislative institution prefers the "experiment" for many reasons: to accumulate legislative experiences through such experiments, to find out the flaws of the original institution, to improve the institution, and to lower costs. It is reasonable to apply such a method based on the abovementioned factors given that it corresponds to the "trial and error" method proposed by Karl Popper. Therefore, "first experiment, then popularize" has become the approach of many institutions in China.

However, to conduct the legislative "experiment" requires that it is necessary to identify factors that need or could be "experimented", to find out whether such experiments could solve the abovementioned issues, genuinely improve the flaws of the institution, and reduce the cost associated with the rule of law. If a legislative "experiment" increases instead of reduces the cost and brings chaos rather than facilitate the improvement of the institutions, then such "experiment" is not preferable.

Unification of distribution systems 51

Besides, the "experiment" should also take the legal ground, feasibility, necessity, and reasonableness into account, and should focus on the achievement of values through justice and efficiency. If the experiment lacks sufficient legal ground or may have a negative impact on justice among relevant agents or the efficiency of the operation of the system, then such an experiment should not be conducted. Thus, a specific taxation legislative "experiment" should comply with the principles of law, justice, and efficiency, which are standards set to verify legality, reasonableness, and necessity. Meanwhile, such principles or standards are important parameters for assessing the "experiment model" for taxation legislation.

Considering that VAT is the biggest tax in China and that it is likely to significantly impact the distribution of interests for various kinds of agents, the following part, taking the legislative experiment of VAT as an example, intends to discuss the legality and reasonableness of the "experiment model" and bring out its merits and demerits. We intend to promote the improvement of comprehensive taxation legislation and economic legislation and to enhance the understanding of the unification/difference of the distribution system as well as relevant issues pertaining to the rule of law.

3.1.1 The VAT system under a long-term "experiment" state

VAT covers wide areas including sales of goods, provision of labour, import/export, and areas which continue to expand through "experiment". The completion and relative stability of the VAT system are vital given that VAT constitutes one third to half of the entire taxation income and generates enormous influence to the distribution of the taxation interest and wealth of the state and citizens. Yet the VAT system in China has always been under "experiment". The following part will observe and analyze the underlying legal issues through the process of the legislative experimentation of VAT as a way of investigating the common issues existing in the "experiment model" of taxation legislation.

During the early stage of reform and opening-up, the economy was mainly a product economy and industry/commerce tax or product tax was once in a predominant position. VAT appeared at the time as the replacement of product tax to solve the issue of repeated levying, and finance and taxation administrations initiated the "experiment" of VAT in relevant industries. Considering the fact that the State Council was not eligible to make taxation legislation, the Standing Committee of the National People's Congress decided on September 18, 1984 to authorize the State Council "to formulate relevant taxation regulations and publish in the form of draft during the process of implementing the reform of 'profit to tax' for state-owned enterprise income and the reform of industry/commerce tax. The State Council was also authorized to amendments to such drafts according to experiences generated from practice and submit to the Standing Committee of National People's Congress' reviewing" (The Standing Committee of the National People's Congress 1984).[6] The State Council, on the same day, published Regulations for VAT (draft) and it was "experimented" for ten years, till the publishing of the *Interim Regulation on VAT*. Although the following "Interim

52 *Unification of distribution systems*

Regulation" was not "experimented" in the form of a "draft", the VAT institution has, in essence, constantly changed. The Department of Finance and the State Administration of Taxation have promulgated numerous normative documents to fix the loopholes which have made the *Interim Regulation on VAT* different from its original form. Many nominally valid stipulations have been made void. By the beginning of the 21st century, the VAT institution became relatively mature but from 2004, having started in the northeast region of China, the "experiment for transformation" which changes VAT from "productive" to "consumptive", was initiated and gradually spread to central areas and finally to the entire nation in 2009 forced by pressure resulting from the financial crisis. At that time, the appeal to upgrade the *Interim Regulation on VAT* to law continued to grow. Yet, before the realization of the effort to upgrade the level of VAT regulations, a new experiment began in 2012 starting from Shanghai then spreading to the whole nation. The experiment, of "business tax to VAT" has become the emphasis of the whole taxation reform in the new era.

The VAT system in China has been constantly in an "experiment" phase. This has resulted from various reasons including the diversity and complicity of social-economic relations, the shift from a planned economy to a commodity economy with plans, and to the market economy all of which call for a corresponding change of the taxation law system. Also, some objective elements contribute to such change, for example, the legislators' lack of acknowledgement of the principles of VAT and VAT systems, the lack of comprehension to the speed of development of the national economy and society, the lack of legislative technology and capacity, etc. Nevertheless, from the normative perspective, VAT needs to be "a complete chain", which requires that the VAT system should be commonly applied throughout the nation. Therefore, the VAT system in a constant "experiment period" needs to be stable and needs to become a vital system that is applicable to the whole nation and which directly affects economic development.

A stable VAT system is somehow problematic from the perspectives of both the stability of laws and the applicability of taxation laws (Shouwen Zhang 2001).[7] It is vitally important for the rule of law in taxation to make the appropriate balance and coordination between stability and flexibility.

As discussed earlier, China has conducted experiments for system transformation in areas like real property tax and resource tax.[8] "Experiment before full-scale application" is a common economic reform and economic legislation practice in China. Such an "experiment model" is advisable for human reasons especially the lack of experience of the government with regard to economic management, as well as the lack of understanding by legislators of principles, techniques, and results of economic legislation. In the early stages of the reform, because of the lack of understanding and experience in shifting the economy, implementing institutional reforms, undertaking upper construction or top-level design, and because of the relative absence of a strong economy and the rule of law, it is necessary to emphasize "prior experimentation". However, the market economy and the construction of the legal system have developed, and experience from mature market-economy states and emerging market-economy states has been accumulated by

Unification of distribution systems 53

China. The question now is whether the "experiment model" should be applied and whether continuous, quantitative legislative "experimentation" is necessary. Is the "experiment model" legal and how does it affect equality and efficiency? Such issues are worth studying. The following part discusses these issues, taking the legislative "experiment" of VAT as an example.

3.1.2 Legality of legislative "experimentation"

Legislative "experimentation" in any field should have its legal ground. It is directly linked to the legality of the legislative "experiment" and the effectiveness of relevant legislations. In the case of legislation that is authorized, it involves the issues of the legality and effectiveness of authorization. Meanwhile, it is relevant to the stability and flexibility of legislation (Shouwen Zhang 2002).[9]

In the discussion above, VAT legislation in China has constantly been in the "experiment" state. In the early stages of reform and opening-up, the finance and taxation administrations considered introducing the French VAT system and conducting experiments in several industries across several cities. To solve the issue of legality of the reform with regard to industry and commerce, tax conducted by the State Council, the Standing Committee of the National People's Congress passed the Decision to Authorization on September 18, 1984, which approved the reformation scheme proposed by the State Council to reform the industry and commerce tax. Based on such a decision, the State Council published six "Regulations (draft)" including the "Regulation on VAT (draft)" which enabled VAT legislation to gain legality, at least, on the surface.

During the experimental period of the Regulation on VAT (draft), the State Council continuously expanded the sphere of VAT and the original 12 items were extended to 31. For such an "extension", the State Council did not amend the "Regulation (draft)" according to the authorization in 1984, nor did it promulgate any "Interim Regulation" according to the National People's Congress authorization in 1985. Therefore, the legality of such an extension is doubtful.

As the replacement, completion, and supplement to the Regulation on VAT (draft), the Interim Regulation on VAT came into effect in 1994, and the legal ground for this Interim Regulation is, as is commonly believed, the "Decision to Authorization" in 1985, the core of which is that the National People's Congress "authorizes the State Council to, when necessary, make interim regulations concerning issues relevant to the reformation of the economic system and opening-up in accordance with the Constitution without violating relevant laws and basic principles of decisions made by National People's Congress as well as its Standing Committee" (The Third Conference of Sixth National People's Congress 1985).[10] For this is the sole basis upon which the issue of legality can be solved.

Yet if the "Decision to Authorization" in 1985 is the legal ground for the Interim Regulation on VAT, it has to comply with the limitations made by the National People's Congress concerning the legislative sphere, necessity, and legality, without which the legal ground or legality is still problematic. The following questions need to be answered: is VAT legislation an issue of economic

54   Unification of distribution systems

system reformation and opening-up? Is it necessary for the State Council to make such a regulation? Does VAT legislation made by the State Council conflict with laws and basic principles of decisions made by the legislators?

If we apply a broader interpretation of the concept of "economic system reformation and opening-up" and consider reformation to taxation system and relevant taxation legislation in the domain which the State Council has been "authorized" to conduct legislation, then such problems could be solved. That is why there is no serious investigation against such events. However, strictly speaking, the "Decision to Authorization" of the National People's Congress should be clear, specific with a fixed term (instead of being ambiguous), broad, and indefinite (given that in such a state, the authorization could be essentially indefinite). In fact, in the "Decision to Authorization", terms such as "issues regarding the economic system reform and opening-up" and "when necessary" are broad and ambiguous (Shouwen Zhang 2011),[11] resulting in the State Council gaining tremendous space to legislate. This has given rise to a flood of "Interim Regulations" in various areas. Though the acceleration of the legal system construction has been achieved within a relatively short period of time, whether the "Decision to Authorization" is appropriate remains worthy of our profound consideration.

Besides, the "Decision to Authorization" requires that the legislation should be in accordance with the Constitution and not in conflict with laws. Yet in practice, little attention is paid to whether the taxation legislation conducted by the State Council is against the law as well as the basic principles of the law. According to Article 8 of the Law of Legislation and the principle of statutory taxation, regulations concerning basic principles of taxation or basic tax elements should be prescribed by the law and relevant taxation laws should be made. Of importance, especially under the current circumstances, the level of taxation regulations should be upgraded given that the VAT system has been experimented for many years and that there are abundant foreign experiences available to learn from.

Based on the abovementioned factors, in the field of VAT, the state legislative institution should pass legislation instead of constantly using the "Decision to Authorization" passed in 1985 which makes the administrative institution the main body to make taxation legislation. The "experiment to transformation" or "experiment to extension" should not become the reason to delay direct legislation by the National People's Congress. Only through this could the Law of Legislation and principle of statutory taxation be obeyed and the issue of the legality of VAT legislation be better solved.

In accordance with the requirements of statutory taxation, the taxation element should also be stipulated by the law. Therefore, the adjustment to relevant taxation elements with regard to each VAT legislation "experiment" should strictly be governed by laws. In fact, the "experiment to the initiation of the tax" at the beginning of the reform and opening-up or the "experiment" of Interim Regulation on VAT, or the "experiment to extension" of VAT involves the change of taxation items and rates. While the "experiment to transformation" of VAT involves the exercising of taxpayers' rights to deduction, it directly affects the adjustment to the basis of the tax. Such change or adjustment to the taxation elements should

Unification of distribution systems   55

strictly abide by the principle of statutory taxation, which is the only approach to guarantee the legality of the "experiment".

In general, during the transitional period from a product to goods economy and further to market economy, the VAT system in China has constantly undergone "experiments", a phenomenon far from the requirement of the rule of law and which seriously affects the stability of the system. Although the shift of economic institution and system has caused the emergence of new types of transactions which are increasingly complicated and which have become a vital foundation for VAT, the shift has also rendered the VAT system rigid and exceptionally "flexible".[12] Therefore to reinforce the balance and coordination between stability and flexibility within the taxation law system becomes important. Even if the level of "stability" of taxation law could never be achieved as with some traditional laws, at least relative stability should be pursued. Especially the institutional reformation of VAT, as the biggest tax, directly affects the freedom of operation of corporations and property rights of citizens as well as the distribution of interests of various agents. For such reasons, the stability and predictability of VAT laws should be maintained. Also, the "certainty" based on its stability is more important (Hayek 2002).[13]

Besides, the "Decision to Authorization" in 1985 by the National People's Congress once required that the published regulations, "after being examined by practice, when the time is mature, should be made into laws by the National People's Congress or its Standing Committee", which means the principle of legal reservation is still emphasized and insisted. However, according to past practices, the focus was on "authorization" while the attention to the ultimate legislative power and ultimate responsibility of the legislature was absent. Therefore, the partial understanding of the "Decision to Authorization" has to be corrected and from the perspective of ensuring legality, the National People's Congress and its Standing Committee have to bear the responsibility to legislate and to promote and upgrade the level of VAT legislation.

3.1.3 The issue of fairness in legislative "experimentation"

The legislative "experiments" of VAT involve not only the issue of legality but also the issue of fairness which has attracted more attention from the public. In fact, various legislative "experiments" are institutional reform mostly targeting some sort of issue of unfairness. For example, the "transitional experiment" of VAT aims to solve the issue of unfair deduction, the "extension experiment" aims to solve the issue of duplicate taxation or unfair tax burden,[14] while one significant goal of the experiment on real property tax reform intends to solve the unfairness of income distribution or the distribution of real estate resources.[15] Because various legislative "experiments" involve the value of fairness and aim at solving specific issues of unfairness, the legislative experiments have thus been justified to a certain extent.

One vital goal of the VAT system in different countries is to solve the issue of unfairness brought by duplicate taxation. As a typical "neutral" tax, VAT is not

56 *Unification of distribution systems*

supposed to bring extra costs or interests to taxpayers. However, because of complicated reasons, such benefit in practice is not abundantly achieved in the realistic system, thereby revealing the unfair nature of the system. Besides, the unfairness resulting from "experiments" and the limitations in solving the issue of fairness is generally neglected. Hence, focus on the legislative experiments of VAT requires attention to the following points.

First, the legislative "experiment" may create new unfairness. Each "experiment" is conducted in a specific "spot" in a specific area. This means it is in conflict with the principle of universality. The experiments are conducted in specific areas or industries which require the special application of the law. Sometimes, this causes the emergence of a so-called "low-lying land effect", directly affecting the distribution of interest and the realization of the value of fairness among different agents in different areas and industries. For example, from the perspective of substantial fairness, though the "transitional experiment" conducted in the northeast in 2004 was necessary and the industries and amount of wealth involved were not significant, it did cause a difference compared with other regions and industries and it made agents in other regions and industries feel indignant. That is one of the significant reasons why the state extended the application of relevant institutions to the central area as well as the whole nation. Besides, the more "universal" the VAT system is, the better the effect it has to solve the duplicate taxation, and the better the chances of protecting fairness. Meanwhile, "experiments" in isolated industries or regions would not contribute to solving the issue of duplicate taxation. In fact, they may even create new cases of unfairness. For instance, the "extension experiment" once negatively affected the fairness of the tax burden because of the inconsistency of the taxation chain among relevant industries.

Second, the legislative "experiment" cannot solve the issue of fairness among different types of taxpayers. VAT is widely applied and VAT payers are hugely diverse. Yet, as a tax that targets agents instead of individuals, it does not focus so much on the difference and fairness between different agents, therefore whether the legislative "experiment" will be applied or not cannot solve the issue of difference resulting from the diversity of internal agents as well as the unfairness in institution and implementation.[16] For example, in terms of the use of VAT Specific Receipt (*fapiao*), the standard of deduction and actual tax burden, ordinary taxpayers and small-scale taxpayers are treated differently. Though Pareto improvement in legislation could be achieved, the unification of treatment and status among taxpayers still could not be realized. Neither the "transitional experiment" nor "extension experiment" of VAT can solve the issue of unfairness in the tax burden resulting from the difference in identity and status of taxpayers. Although VAT emphasizes "neutrality" or "no difference", the differences among taxpayers and institutional design problems cause differences in the exercising of rights or tax burdens of various agents, bringing about vertical unfairness.

At last, it is difficult for the legislative "experiment" to solve the issue of the fair distribution of taxation revenue. On one hand, VAT, as a commodity tax, is closely linked to the place of sale of the relevant commodity (Fikentscher 2010)[17] and thus, should be administered by the corresponding jurisdiction which closely

Unification of distribution systems 57

connects to local taxation revenue. On the other hand, VAT is a typically shared tax which is relevant to the taxation revenue of the central government. The fairness in the distribution of VAT income is vitally important. In fact, the scheme for "business tax to VAT" had been brought long ago, yet it was not implemented only because of the fact that it would affect the core interests of the local government. For this reason, when "extension experiment" was implemented the state emphasized that this should not affect the taxation interest of the local government.[18] As long as the conflict of interests exists between central and local government, the interests represented by the two sets of taxation administrations will have "permanent differences" that are difficult to solve.

It could be concluded that the legislative "experiment" of VAT involves various issues of fairness but, sometimes, it brings about new issues of unfairness. The unfairness between regions and industries where the experiments are and are not conducted is in conflict with the "unification of law" and the "unification of the taxation system" required by the market economy; it affects fair competition and distribution and it should be solved.

3.1.4 Considering the efficiency of the legislative "experiment"

In addition to the abovementioned issues of legality and fairness that are involved in VAT legislative "experiments", the issue of efficiency is also relevant. The real property taxation legislative "experiment" in Shanghai and Chongqing aims at safeguarding comprehensive economic efficiency by promoting the healthy development of real property markets, preventing the overheating of the economy, and avoiding the economic bubble from bursting. From the perspective of efficiency, every type of legislative "experiment" needs to comply with the requirement of both economic and administrative efficiency.

Based on the principles of economic efficiency, the legislative "experiment" of VAT should contribute to the development of the economy. In fact, both the "extension experiment" aimed at preventing or reducing duplicate taxation and the "transitional experiment" aimed at extending the scope of deduction intend to excite the energy of enterprises, promote the efficiency of the economic operation, and to advance economic development. From this sense, these two types of "experiments" both comply with the principle of economic efficiency.

Besides, as the typical indirect tax, the "extension experiment" of VAT reduces the overall tax burden of some agents that were originally subject to business tax, and further affect the price as well as the final agent that bears such a tax. Therefore, such reform could contribute to relieving the pressure of enterprises and citizens and could promote the development of the economy, thereby complying with the principle of economic efficiency.

From the requirement of administrative efficiency, the legislative "experiment" should lower the cost of the tax administration or the cost of taxpayers for such costs are ultimately borne by taxpayers. The rising cost of taxation is not only the result of administrative inefficiency of taxation administrations, it equally affects the efficiency of the economy because of the increasing burden of

58 Unification of distribution systems

taxpayers. Besides, the cost of taxation of the whole taxation system should be examined, especially the cost of coordination among taxation administrative bodies (Streit and Kasper 2000).[19]

For example, the "extension experiment" directly involves coordination between the two sets of taxation administrations. The issue of the cost of coordination or institutional reform should be considered comprehensively based on the principle of efficiency and from the perspective of cost-benefit analysis. It is common knowledge that without the design of two sets of taxation administrations, the costs, including the cost of tax collection and the obedience of taxpayers, the cost of coordination, and the reform of institution, will be lowered. If two sets of institutions could be combined, and as long as the institutional arrangement is reasonable and the power, type, and benefits of taxation could be effectively defined, the interest distribution between central and local governments could be solved. Otherwise, even with the two sets of institutions and without a steady institutional arrangement to the distribution of taxation income, the issue of the relationship between central and local government will continue to exist. When the taxation revenue gained by the local government is not sufficient to support the performance of its functions, the financial pressure of the local government increases and the "land finance" or other types of "non-taxation financial revenue" become difficult to deal with.[20] Therefore, the key is the reasonable distribution of taxable income and the shift of government functions which are not solely resolved through the setting up of taxation administrations. The configuration of power to taxation and the arrangement of various "institutions" are required.

3.1.5 Further thinking on the "experiment method" for taxation legislation

The issues of legality, fairness, and efficiency with regard to the VAT legislation "experiment" are common in various types of taxation legislation and they further have a vital influence on the distribution of income of relevant agents. To solve such problems, the three fundamental principles of taxation law shall be maintained. Because of the fact that the "experiment" of VAT legislation is very typical, the corresponding issues are thus quite typical to undertake research on the "experiment method" of taxation legislation. Given that there is prior discussion during the process to implement the "experiment method" of taxation legislation, the following questions should be further considered and focused on.

3.1.5.1 Should the legislation "experiment" focus on legality at multiple levels?

Both regular taxation legislation and the legislation "experiment" as reformation exploration should emphasize the issue of legality. Prior discussion on the VAT legislation "experiment" has already reflected the common problem existing in taxation legislation as well as the whole economic legislation. For a long period of time, China has been in the process of reform and transformation. As long as the 1985 "Decision to Authorization" still forms the legal ground, only a "permission by the State Council" could lead to the "experiment" or "amendment" of the laws in most areas of taxation – an action which is relatively easy to undertake. The legality of such conduct has already received criticism. There are also doubts regarding putting the "Decision to Authorization" as the legal ground for "experimentation". The existence of the prior issues would have a profound influence on the seriousness and compliance of the taxation law as well as on the development of rule of law in taxation.

Considering that the Law on Legislation has substantially stipulated the power and level of taxation legislation, it is worth discussing whether the "Decision to Authorization" made at the beginning of the Reform and Opening-up should be abolished, and whether a transition period should be set for the purpose of ending such authorized legislation.[21] From the overall development trend, the "Decision to Authorization" should be abolished at the proper time, given that the authorization was vague and broad and that the principle of statutory taxation should be strengthened (Shouwen Zhang 1996).[22]

The main target of the legislation "experiment" concerning various types of taxation is to reform the current system, a practice which sometimes leads to emphasis on the regulation, control, and collection of tax while neglecting the protection of the freedom of operating and property rights. To effectively balance these two aspects has always been a significant task in terms of the rules of taxation in the construction of the law. In order to better achieve the goal of rule of law in taxation collection, the principle of statutory taxation must be fully respected when dealing with the common issue that, in practice, the principle of "tax elements by law" is not strictly respected.

To emphasize the legality of the taxation legislation "experiment", the focus should not only be on the compliance to statutory principles with regard to the grounds of legislation and institution adjustment but also the legislation "experiment" must abide by the requirement of constitutionalism and protect the fundamental interests of citizens. From the requirement of legality at a higher level, the taxation legislation "experiment" should never violate the comprehensive and long-term interests of citizens, otherwise it would lose its legitimacy or legality. Therefore, the experiment of real property tax reform should not only conform to the basic statutory principle, but also to the overall and long-term interests of citizens. It should protect the individual interests of taxpayers, which is fundamentally important to ensure the effectiveness of taxation law (Shouwen Zhang 2012).[23]

3.1.5.2 The legislation "experiment" should be both fair and efficient

The taxation legislation "experiment" may affect property rights and the right to business operation of citizens and may constitute an extra burden to taxpayers which may likely affect the fairness of tax burden. Meanwhile, an unfair taxation system may generate a twisting effect which would negatively affect efficiency. Therefore, good taxation legislation must focus on the close connection between fairness and efficiency, and must strictly conform to the principles of fairness and efficiency of taxation law in institutional design as a way of protecting the

60 Unification of distribution systems

relevant values of order and justice. During the process in which taxation law exercises its function to regulate and distribute, it is relevant to present the new unfairness that may possibly be brought by the legislation "experiment" while pursuing the "Pareto improvement" in efficiency.

3.1.5.3 The future for "experiment methods"

Based on the issues of legality, fairness, and efficiency existing in legislation "experimentation", the following questions should be further investigated: whether the taxation legislation "experiment" method should be maintained and how the negative effects produced by "experiments" should be viewed.

As is mentioned earlier on, the experiments implemented at the beginning of the reform and opening-up were indeed necessary and reasonable, yet while China has already accumulated legislation and gathered experience for many years, including from foreign countries, the question that remains to be answered is whether the frequent and widespread "experiment" is necessary.[24] In fact, if a relatively accurate prediction could be made for the real effect of legislation, then legislation "experiment" is not necessary; needless to say that if the choice of "experiment" scheme is improper, the whole situation of legislation would be affected.

With the establishment and development of the rule of law, when the principle and system are both relatively clear, the establishment of a stable institutional framework should be emphasized, instead of conducting "experiments" which are neither just nor necessary. From a practical perspective, maybe someone would believe that the "structural tax reduction" is a temporary measure to deal with the crisis and therefore an "experiment" would not be a problem. Yet from the perspective of the law, the reduction of tax is always a serious legal issue regardless of the reason because it involves the basic rights of citizens, including property rights, which should be treated with caution. Hence, although "business tax to VAT" is a significant element of the "structural tax reduction", experimenting with it should not be normalized.[25]

3.1.6 Summary

Taxation legislation involves a complicated distribution of interest and affects wide spheres. The circumstance for its implementation also varies considerably thereby making the "experiment before widespread application" method reasonable and worthy of extensive application accounting for the "experiment method" for taxation legislation. Although the purpose of "experiments" is usually to solve current institutional issues, it is worth noting that legitimacy may be absent during the process of "experimenting" and that it may negatively impact fairness and efficiency. Therefore, the flaws of an experiment scheme or the demerits of institutional designs, as well as the deficits of the "experiment method" should be noted and deeply researched.

Based on the importance and typicality of the VAT legislation "experiment", the previous part emphasized analyzing existing problems and brought out the

Unification of distribution systems   61

common issues involving various taxation legislation "experiments" including the issue of legality and justifiability reflected in fairness and efficiency. First, in terms of legality, the legal ground, adjustment to taxation collection elements, or specific institutional design, and the protection of the rights of taxpayers in the "experiment" of taxation legislation are particularly worthy of our attention. In the field of taxation legislation, the most outstanding issue is the issue of authorized legislation, and the "Decision to Authorization" by the National People's Congress must be cancelled at the proper time and real taxation legislation in accordance with the Law on Legislation should be conducted. Meanwhile, the adjustment or specific institutional design for collecting taxes should abide by the principle of statutory taxation upon which the interest of the public and the long-term interest of the citizens should be considered so that the basic rights of taxpayers can be protected. Second, in terms of justifiability, the taxation legislation "experiment" should be visible through the improvement of institutions via the accumulation of experience, and through the assimilation of values including fairness and efficiency. On the ground of meeting the requirement of legality, the taxation legislation "experiment" must solve the existing issue of unfairness and avoid triggering new cases of unfairness. Meanwhile, the efficiency of the economy and administration should be promoted and for such purpose, the institutional problems existing in fiscal and taxation institution should be further solved.

When focusing on the necessity and justifiability of the existence of an "experiment method", the deficits should especially be considered, in addition to the conditions and costs of "experiments". Since the economy and society have gained tremendous development and the experience of legislation and economic management has been increasingly abundant, and based on the spirit of rule of law, unless absolutely necessary, the "experiments" should be reduced so that different treatments that might exist could be eliminated allowing for the unification of basic legal institutions. Therefore, the level of the rule of law can be promoted and the modernization of the state governance system can be enhanced.

3.2 Unified regulation to differentiated distribution

To realize justice in distribution, the distribution system should be differentiated. This is otherwise known as differentiated distribution. The degree of difference is difficult to define, and this may lead to further increases in the distribution differences and may affect justice in distribution. Therefore, the power involving distribution must have legal grounds and should be exercised in a unified manner. For instance, "structural tax reduction" reflects the difference in the distribution system, namely through making tax reduction arrangements in specific tax systems to achieving tax reduction for certain, not all, agents. Although "structural tax reduction" is a type of differentiated arrangement, it requires the coordination of various relevant tax law systems, especially in terms of legal basis and exercising the power of tax reduction, which should be unified. For this reason, the following part discusses the power to reduce taxes involving "structural tax

62 *Unification of distribution systems*

reduction" as an example to discuss the "difference and unified regulation" in the distribution system.

3.2.1 The multiple definitions of the power of tax reduction

The implementation of "structural tax reduction" must be grounded on statutory power to tax reduction, which is the foundation for "unified regulation". Without the power to reduce taxes, any tax reduction, regardless of its nature, would lack legality. In accordance with the principle of statutory taxation and regulations of relevant laws including the *Law on Taxation Collection*, no agent is entitled to make decisions to reduce taxes autonomously and by so doing, violate the law.[26] Considering the fact that the approaches for "structural tax reduction" vary, the appropriate ground for such tax reduction should be the "power to reduce taxes in the broad sense".

This so-called "power to reduce taxes in the broad sense", namely the power to decrease the collection of tax, includes the power to reduce the types and items of taxation, to reduce the rate and foundation, to suspend one type of tax, and to reduce the amount of tax, all of which aim to decrease the burden of taxpayers. As a vital part of the power to impose taxes, the "power to reduce taxes in the broad sense" corresponds to the "power to increase the tax". The difference compared with the "power to reduce taxes in the narrow sense" is that the latter is the foundation for the "tax reduction measures", which belong to special taxation measures. Special taxation measures do not align with basic taxation elements including tax items and foundations – "tax reduction measures" being one of them. The "power to reduce taxes in the broad sense", which will be thoroughly investigated in this chapter, corresponds to the multiple approaches to tax reduction and involves not only various tax elements but also considerably exceeds tax elements and connects to the maintenance/abolition of taxation as well as the overall change of taxation law structure.

Based on such broad understanding of tax reduction power, this chapter discusses the power of legislation and administration to tax reduction, which is not equal to the "power of administrative review and approval to tax reduction" exercised by taxation administration as part of law enforcement. According to the principle of statutory taxation, the power of legislation to tax reduction is the foundation for the exercise of tax reduction and the power of administrative review and approval that is more specific. During the process of implementing "structural tax reduction", the target of exercising power to reduce taxes might be multiple, i.e. fair distribution, macro regulation and control, improvements in the lives of the people, social stability maintenance, etc. Such targets should be incorporated into relevant taxation law norms through exercising the power of legislation to tax reduction and be fulfilled through law enforcement activities of tax reduction.

From the overall theory of power to taxation, the state power to taxation includes both the power to increase tax and the power to reduce tax.[27] In the past, people tended to understand the power to impose tax solely as the power to increase tax while neglecting the power to reduce tax. In fact, both tax increase and deduction are normal for a state to exercise its power to taxation. To realize "the encouragement and promotion to positive elements" and "the restriction and prohibition to negative elements" through the adjustment of the tax burden are exactly a significant aspect of the functions of taxation law.

Besides, from the perspective of constitutional law or constitutionalism, the abovementioned power to reduce taxes is essentially the state's "power to make decisions concerning tax reduction", which is relevant to the citizens' "right to request for tax reduction". Based on such right of citizens, the state should consider whether to exercise the tax reduction. Of course, exercising the right to request a tax reduction should be connected with the state's power to make decisions concerning tax reduction through the legislative activities of the National People's Congress or parliaments. Though the nature and level of such power and rights are different, they are closely linked with each other under the framework of rule of law and are both vital elements that may influence the rule of law system.

On the constitutional law level, based on the "binary structure of objects" of the state and citizen, and also on the idea and regulation that "all power belongs to the people",[28] the right to request a tax reduction is more fundamental and the state must seriously consider the realities of the demand of citizens and the situation of the development of society and the economy, and pay attention to the legality of the collection of tax. In this way, the state's exercising of power to make decisions concerning tax reduction must be restricted. Besides, if the "contract hypothesis" between state and citizens is accepted, then the right of citizens to request a tax reduction also corresponds to the state's power to request tax collection, and the exercising of such two types of rights would be reflected by the public goods game on pricing. Nevertheless, whatever theory is chosen, the citizens' right to request a tax reduction should be emphasized and the state's power to implement a tax reduction, which means "statutory power to tax reduction, should be restricted".

3.2.2 Statutory power to reduce taxes and relevant issues

The foundation for "structural tax reduction" is the statutory power to reduce taxes. Based on the principle of statutory taxation, all powers and rights concerning taxation must be regulated by the law, including the tax reduction powers. Based on the protection of the property rights of citizens, normally the issue of "power to increase the taxes" is raised more frequently, while the "tax reduction power" is rarely mentioned. In fact, the exercising of both powers would affect the interests of the state and citizens, and merit strict regulation by the laws. The state exercising power to reduce taxes is not only relevant to the protection of the state's taxation interest or fiscal interest but also has the potential to directly affect the property interests of citizens and may result in an unfair tax burden to taxpayers. For that, the exercising of tax reduction power is directly linked to the adjustment of relevant types of taxation, items, rates, foundations, and preferential measures. In addition, the initiation, suspension, and change of taxation

64 Unification of distribution systems

elements should strictly abide by the principle of statutory taxation and the exercising of power to reduce taxes should also strictly comply with such a principle.

Article 56 of the Chinese Constitution stipulates that "it is the duty of citizens of the People's Republic of China to pay taxes in accordance with the law". Thus, the foundation and basis for citizens to perform their duty to pay tax are only through laws, just as the basis for the relief or exemption of the duty to pay tax is on the law. Besides, the law directly affects the determination of taxpayers' duty to pay tax by regulating the types of tax and taxation elements. It is important that the exercising of the power to reduce taxes through the change of tax types and taxation elements aimed to relieve the taxpayers' duty must comply with regulations of laws. In addition, the law should decide whether the duty to pay tax can be waived. This is the requirement and reflection of the principle of statutory tax and is a vital restriction to exercising the power to reduce taxes.

In China, the relevant taxation laws have more clearly stipulated the power to tax reduction.[29] For example, Article 3 Clause 1 on the Law on Tax Collection of China stipulates that:

> The initiation, suspension, reduction, exemption, return and making up should be in accordance with the stipulations of laws. When the law authorizes the State Council to make relevant regulations, then the administrative regulations made by the State Council shall be followed.

The abovementioned suspension, tax reduction, exemption and return relevant to these stipulations are directly linked to the exercise of the "power to reduce taxes in the broad sense". The legal requirement that such conducts should "be executed in accordance with the stipulations of laws" reflects the principle of statutory taxation. Also, this article emphasizes the strict principle of statutory taxation by stipulating that only when the law authorizes the State Council to make regulations can such measures be conducted "following the administrative regulations made by the State Council".

These stipulations are also the practice and reflection of the content of Article 56 of the Constitution. According to the principles of the Constitution,[30] the principle of statutory taxation must be strictly implemented. Therefore, Article 3 of the Law on Tax Collection focuses on the "power to reduce taxes in the broad sense" on the laws as well as on the administrative regulations when there are legal authorizations. This is because departmental rules and regulations made by departments of the State Council (i.e. the Department of Finance, State Taxation Administration, and General Administration of Customs) and local regulations are not mentioned in this article. Hence, if this article strictly abides by departmental rules and regulations, then local regulations cannot serve as the basis or legal grounds for the exercise of power to tax reduction. Correspondingly, departments and committees cannot serve as agents exercising the power to tax reduction.

Furthermore, among the Law on Tax Collection and relevant implementation regulations, there are stipulations concerning "the right to request for tax reduction" and correspondingly, the taxation administration that disposes of the

Unification of distribution systems 65

"power to approve the tax reduction". Tax elements cannot be changed during such request or approval processes and without statutory procedures, the tax elements cannot be adjusted. This means the order could be maintained during the process of tax reduction, thereby protecting the overall order of distribution.

The abovementioned "tax reduction elements" mean there are various important elements directly connected with the tax reduction, i.e. the suspension of one type of tax, the adjustment of tax items and rates, the adjustment of the method to determine the tax foundation, and the adjustment of the scope of tax reduction or exemption. All these measures may bring about the effect of tax reduction. They are factors that affect the tax burden, and they are specific approaches through which tax is reduced. Such adjustment to "tax reduction elements" profoundly affects the state's power and citizens' rights to taxation behaviour and relevant taxation interest (Shouwen Zhang 2003)[31] as well as to the fairness of taxation and the distribution of income. As a consequence, caution is needed in dealing with them.

Because of the importance of such "tax reduction elements", some states even make restrictive stipulations on the initiation of certain types of taxes in their constitutional laws. For example, the US Constitution once stipulated that "no State shall, without the Consent of Congress, lay any Duty of Tonnage".[32] The duty of tonnage in China corresponds with regulations made in the 1950s for a long period of time until 2012 when the new regulation was published.[33] Yet till today, legal stipulations are absent and this is contrary to the requirement of the principle of statutory taxation.

China has not made explicit stipulations on what types of taxes can and cannot be imposed, because of the fact that it is still not clear which types of taxation a benign taxation system should include, and the taxation system and taxation law system are still changing and developing. Yet, with the development of the market economy and the gradual maturing of the taxation law system, the taxation law system in China should also become relatively stable. The main types of taxation that the taxation law system should include as well as the basic taxation elements of each taxation system should be clear. This is especially important for making effective legal definitions to the adjustment of various "tax reduction elements".

To emphasize the principle of statutory power to reduce taxes and adjust "tax reduction elements" according to the law does not provide significant value to the development of taxation law theory and even to public law theory.It also contributes tremendously to the practice of relevant distribution systems. Analyzing the institution of tax reduction may reveal existing issues concerning the statutory power of tax reduction and illustrate why the tax reduction power must be exercised in accordance with laws.

3.2.3 The proper exercising of the tax reduction power in accordance with the laws

It is not difficult to realize, through reflecting on the institutional practice of "structural tax reduction" in China, that numerous legal issues exist in terms of the agent, the scope, and procedure in the process of exercising power to reduce

66 *Unification of distribution systems*

tax. It is only through ensuring the legality and justice of the assertion of control to reduce taxes that such issues could be better solved and effective regulation to distribution achieved.

From the perspective of legislation, the taxation law structure of one state would directly affect "structural tax reduction". Within a certain taxation law system, the types of taxes that should be abolished, suspended, or merged would directly affect the distribution of interests among relevant agents and therefore tax reduction should not be conducted at will. On the contrary, various factors should be considered, and the power to reduce taxes should be exercised with legality and justice in mind. For such a purpose, the agent, scope, procedure, and principle to exercise the tax reduction power should especially be considered.

First, in terms of the agent to exercise the power, stipulations of the Constitution and relevant laws must be complied with, and the source of the tax reduction power, as well as the legitimate agent to exercise such power, must be clearly identified. China had emphasized multiple times that the power to introduce taxation legislation (including tax reduction legislation) should comprehensively be recollected by the central government while the local governments could exercise the power to reduce taxes only within the scope where the laws have authorized them to do so. Meanwhile, even at the level of the central government, the power to reduce taxes by various agents should also be clearly identified and the ultra vires of relevant agents should be prevented. These are vitally important for the maintenance of a unified regulation. Based on the stipulation of the Law on Legislation in China,[34] taxation legislation that involves basic taxation systems must be regulated by the law. Therefore, the National People's Congress and its Standing Committee should be the main agent exercising the legislative power to impose tax reductions, and the State Council should not be allowed to exercise such power because it is beyond its legal authority. For example, the Regulation on Agricultural Tax was passed by the Standing Committee of the National People's Congress and, therefore, the decision to abolish agricultural tax should be made by the Standing Committee of the National People's Congress. For its part, the State Council should not act beyond its statutory functions to abolish this type of tax. Even if the elimination of such tax is necessary, the legislative procedure must be followed, and it should not be left to the local government to stop the implementation of the law which is still in effect. Identifying the agent to exercise such power is significant in preventing the ultra vires concerning the legislative power to impose tax reduction and to protect the just exercise of power to reduce taxes in accordance with the law.

An important characteristic could be seen through the process of "structural tax reduction" in China where in most cases, the legislative power to impose taxes is actually exercised by the State Council and, correspondingly, the State Council has become an important agent to exercise the legislative power to reduce taxes. The formation of such characteristics is directly connected with the Decision to Authorization of 1984 and 1985. After deciding to employ the market economy system, and as the process to improve the modern taxation system continues, it is indeed problematic to continue with the abovementioned decisions. The Standing

Committee of the National People's Congress is clearly aware of such issues so it specifically abolished the Decision to Authorization of 1984 in 2009.[35] However, the Decision of 1985 is still valid and the authorization has almost no limitation in terms and scope. This has led to a significant number of problems, so the timely abolition of such a Decision is required (Shouwen Zhang 1996 & 2012).[36] Tax reduction is connected with basic property rights and many other relevant rights of various agents. To exercise such power by the National People's Congress and its Standing Committee could meet the requirement of the principle of statutory taxation and it complies with the regulations of current laws. Hence, the agent to exercise the legislative power to impose tax reduction should gradually transfer from the State Council to the National People's Congress and its Standing Committee.

Second, the scope of exercising power to impose tax reduction, which corresponds to the specific approach of "structural tax reduction", involves both the continuance, abolition, merging, and transfer of types of taxation, and the adjustment to various important "tax reduction elements", especially the adjustment of items, rates, foundations, and preferential measures. Currently, in terms of the scope of exercising power, the first and immediate task is "to fulfil the principle of statutory taxation comprehensively".[37] For such a purpose, legal authorizations should be given to relevant agents in order to exercise tax reduction powers which would contribute to solving the issue of the lack of a legal basis and to further protect the legality and justice in the process of exercising of power to reduce taxes. For instance, in 2007, China amended Article 12 of the Law on Personal Income Tax, stipulating that "the initiation, reduction, suspension and implementation of taxation on deposit interests should be stipulated by the State Council". Based on such authorization, the exercising of power to impose tax reduction on deposit interests now has legal grounds.

Considering the complexity of the taxation law and the social relationships it adjusts, the scope of the exercise of the power to reduce taxes should reflect the combined compliance to both policies and laws, as well as the unification of stability and flexibility in order to achieve the spirit of "differentiated treatment" or "discriminated distribution", and to realize the institutional function of taxation law. Normally in areas concerning the protection of individual property rights, the requirement for legality toward tax reduction is higher, and the exercise of the power to reduce taxes or the change of approach to tax reduction would attract more public attention. Therefore, the legal and proper exercising of power to impose tax reduction should be emphasized.

In addition, in terms of the procedure regarding the exercise of power, irrespective of whether it is legislative power or executive power that imposes tax reduction, the emphasis should be on the issue of proper procedure. It should be noted, however, that in the practice of "structural tax reduction", some procedures are still not sufficiently transparent. For example, adjustments to the amount deducted from a salary for the personal income tax or the adjustment to the rate of stamp duty for security transactions (aka the "Midnight Cockcrow" incident) (Ming Sheng Yuan 2008)[38] which both reflect a lack of transparency in the procedure. The public normally would not reveal their doubts from the perspective of ultra vires or abuse of

68   *Unification of distribution systems*

power, yet they would at least believe that this is the improper use of power and would further question the fairness and justifiability of the relevant distribution. Therefore, the power to reduce taxes must be exercised strictly in accordance with relevant procedures, and the institutional construction for the taxation procedural law should be further strengthened so that the rule of law in taxation can be promoted and the relevant distribution problems can be effectively solved.

At last, in terms of the principles regarding the exercising of power, it is not only the aforementioned principle of statutory taxation that must be abided by, but there is also a need to put into practice the principles of fairness and efficiency. The principle of fairness would be presented as the principle of moderation or proportion (Schliesky 2006)[39] which requires that the exercise of power be moderate in terms of the scope and degree of tax reduction. Meanwhile, the relationship between compliance to policies and laws needs to be handled in order to better achieve the functions and goals of "structural tax reduction". Based on the principle of moderation which reflects the spirit of fairness, the exercise of the power of tax collection needs to be modest or controlled, especially the power to impose tax reduction, through which the legal rights and interests of various agents will be protected and the stable development of society as well as the stability of the state realized. For that, the "structural tax reduction" may grant specific agents in specific areas of taxation interests, if the exercise of the legislative or executive power to reduce taxes is improper, the value of fairness embodied in the principle of fairness would be violated and therefore, "structural tax reduction" should especially value the substantial fairness and to effectively solve the issue of distribution. Otherwise, the necessity for the State's implementation of "structural tax reduction" would be difficult to explain from the perspective of formal fairness alone.

Other than the requirement of the aforementioned principle of fairness, the exercise of the power to reduce taxes also needs to benefit economic development and fulfil the requirement of efficiency by substantially reducing the burden on taxpayers. For example, the unification of the corporate income tax system in China reduced the burden of corporations and promoted fair competition and economic development. Therefore, such a "structural tax reduction" is one that meets the principle of efficiency. If the "structural tax reduction" is promoted in name and new types of taxation are added in substance, then the overall burden of taxpayers rises, the economic development would be hindered, and the requirement of efficiency would not be met.

To fulfil the abovementioned principles of taxation law, the exercise of the power to collect taxes needs to be moderate. In other words, the collection of tax by the state is intended to satisfy the needs of the public for public goods, without producing an oppressive government. Instead, the burden of taxpayers should be reduced so that they can survive (Jun Wang 2009).[40] To emphasize on the "moderation" of the power to collect taxes contributes to the protection of the rights of citizens, to the better promotion of the development of a market economy, to the efficiency of resource configuration, and to facilitate the operation of the economy. Also, it would guarantee the fiscal revenue of the state and lead to

Unification of distribution systems 69

a "win-win" situation for national finance and citizens' benefits. In addition, a benign relationship of "give–receive" would be established.

During the process through which the state exercises its power to collect taxes, "expansion" and "moderation" usually happen simultaneously. The "expansion" of tax collection powers corresponds to the power to increase taxes while moderating the power to reduce taxes. The exercise of both powers is normal for the state to exercise its tax collection power and it reflects the regulating nature of the taxation law. This means combining the characteristics of "encouraging and promoting the positive factors" and "restricting or prohibiting the negative factors". Therefore, it is necessary to restrict its "expansion" from the perspective of principles of statutory tax, fairness, and efficiency.

In recent years, China has conducted "structural tax reduction" but the burden of market agents remains high. This phenomenon reflects that fact that the power to reduce taxes is not exercised properly in accordance with laws, that the fulfillment of the principles of the taxation law is not adequate, and that the systematic thinking and comprehensive design for tax reduction are lacking. The "structural tax reduction" in China is implemented inadvertently during the process of the continuous resolution of multiple issues in various fields. Therefore, the top design needs to be strengthened and the tax law structure needs to be optimized so that a scientific and justifiable taxation law system can be established that will act as a solid institutional foundation for "structural tax reduction". It is solely through this that problems, like in VAT system reform, that are susceptible to be exposed during continuous experiments, can be avoided.

3.2.4 The issue of tax reduction power in VAT system reform

The most important "structural tax reduction" currently underway is "business tax to VAT". Because of the fact that the VAT system in China has constantly been in the process of reform or "experiment" and the overall intention has been to continuously reduce the burden of taxpayers through a better reflection of the principles of VAT, it is necessary to explore this specifically by combining the past VAT system reforms as well as the issue of the power to reduce taxes regarding the practice of "business tax to VAT".

The VAT system reform in China includes both the adjustment to internal taxation elements brought by "VAT transformation", and comprehensive adjustment among different types of taxes brought by "business tax to VAT". Hence, the aforementioned two "structural tax reduction" approaches are both reflected in the field of VAT, and such two closely linked approaches both involve the issue of the power to reduce taxes. The following part will briefly discuss this.

3.2.4.1 The issue of tax reduction power in previous VAT system reforms

As the type of tax with the largest scope, VAT not only covers a wide sphere but also once constituted around half of the overall tax revenue. Although in recent years, tax reduction has been conducted through adjustments to the tax

70 *Unification of distribution systems*

foundation and rate, VAT revenue has always constituted over 40% of the total tax revenue. However, given that is it such an important tax, the system reform has never stopped. The relevant issue of tax reduction power is especially typical and common.

As is mentioned before, from 2004, China has initiated the "structural tax reduction" and the reform of the VAT system is one element. At that time, the "VAT transformation" experiment in the northeast that aimed at "expanding the area of deduction"[41] has been a vital step toward "structural tax reduction",[42] and it contributed to adjusting the industry structure of the northeast region and also led to the optimization of the structure of taxation law. Though the new system applied to limited industries and regions, due to its tax reduction effect, the central region also applied such policies[43] and finally in 2009, it became an important system that was applicable to the whole nation.

The direct motivation for the extension of the "VAT transformation" across the nation was the urgent need for "structural tax reduction" after the occurrence of the financial crisis. Because of the further expansion of the sphere of deduction due to system transformation, the base of VAT was directly decreased. Meanwhile, the reduction of the taxation rate for small-scale taxpayers also reduced the overall tax burden of VAT. Through the internal adjustment of tax elements within the VAT system, the obvious "tax reduction effect" could then be generated.

The aforementioned "VAT transformation" belongs to the second approach of "structural tax reduction" and scholars have not yet paid sufficient attention to the tax reduction power involved. The direct basis for the expansion of "VAT transformation" from limited experimentation to the whole nation is basically the "regulations" or "interim methods" made by the Department of Finance and the State Administration of Taxation. Though these documents reflect the intentions of the State Council, the level of effectiveness is still too low for such an expansion of the scope of deduction. Adjustment to the rate corresponds to substantial stipulations of taxation elements whereas such affairs should be stipulations under the law.[44] Such a basis for "VAT transformation" obviously does not fit the requirement of the principle of statutory taxation.

Besides, in the process of spreading the "VAT transformation" experiment, though the regulations concerning expanding the scope of deduction have a tax reduction effect, it should be noted that such measures were experimented only in certain industries or areas rather than applied to the nation. It is against the principle that the collection of VAT should be unified within the nation[45] and the chain of VAT should remain integral. This violates the principles of taxation and taxation law and also fails to reflect the spirit of the rule of law. In addition, the principles of statutory taxation, fairness, and efficiency are not exercised either.

Thus, it could be concluded that though the reform of "VAT transformation" is important and it could generate the effect of "structural tax reduction", predominant issues exist in the relevant basis and ways of the exercise of power to tax reduction. These issues also existed in the previous "VAT transformation" and "business tax to VAT".

3.2.4.2 The issue of power to reduce taxes in the practice of "business tax to VAT"

"Business tax to VAT" has attracted special attention from the central and local governments given that it is the most important step in the "structural tax reduction" and it is also the main direction toward which China improves its overall taxation law system. In addition, it involves the relationship with and significant interests of central and local governments, the adjustments to industry structure, the protection of the rights of taxpayers, and the future of China's taxation law.

From the perspective of overall design, the targets of taxation for VAT and business tax are binary objects (goods and service), and the "business tax to VAT" reform involves very broad areas. With the completion of the reform, the original "co-existing of two types of tax" will become "one type of tax covering all areas". The replacement by VAT could, when the chain of deduction is complete, avoid the duplicate collection of taxes in the area of business tax, and could reduce the actual burden on taxpayers. Therefore, the effect of "structural tax reduction" would be obvious, would contribute to the development of many industries which were subject to business tax before, and would contribute to the fulfilment of the goals of adjustments to the economic structure.

"Business tax to VAT" tries to realize "structural tax reduction" through the overall adjustment to types of tax and it belongs to the first approach to "structural tax reduction". Business tax, with its long history, was absorbed by VAT, which vastly changed the VAT system with regard to the scope of taxation, the specific foundations, the confirmation of the rate and the structure, etc. In addition, the substantial interests of many taxpayers were affected. The property rights, freedom of business operation, and choice of occupation of market agents are directly influenced; therefore the legality of such changes must be seriously considered.

During the practice of "business tax to VAT", the direct basis for the exercise of tax reduction power is the "Experiment Schemes", "notices" published by the Department of Finance and State Administration of Taxation that are "agreed" upon or "approved" by the State Council.[46] The level of effectiveness of these documents is the same as the documents concerning "VAT transformation" and therefore the issue of legality also exists here. From the initiation of the VAT system reform and the practice of other taxation law systems, the issue of the lack of legality to exercise the power to reduce taxes has become a "chronic illness" that has remained unhealed for a long period of time and a predominant problem that requires a solution during the process intended to improve the rule of law in China.

Although in substance, the following areas are led by the State Council: to promote "structural tax reduction" through "business tax to VAT", to strengthen the competitiveness of corporations, and to facilitate structural adjustment and industry update. And, the basis for the State Council to exercise the power to impose tax reduction seems to be the "Decision to Authorization" by the National People's Congress in 1985. As we have discussed, the "Decision" has already been questioned widely for it does not only violate the principle of statutory taxation but is also against specific legal stipulations of the Law on Legislation and

72 *Unification of distribution systems*

the Law on Taxation Collection Management. Therefore, its legality is obviously flawed and should no longer constitute a basis.

The aforementioned "VAT transformation" only involves the internal adjustment of one single type of tax, while "business tax to VAT" involves the change of systems of two significantly important types of tax and it has a greater influence on the basic rights of taxpayers. Since "business tax to VAT" involves the vital adjustment to taxpayers, items, rates, and foundations, and experiments on relevant tax items have been applied to the whole nation, the State Council had to amend the Interim Regulation on VAT and abolish the Interim Regulation on Business Tax. For such adjustment to the fundamental taxation affairs that involve the basic rights of taxpayers, the National People's Congress should make relevant legislation, in accordance with the stipulations of the Law on Legislation and the principle of statutory taxation, to complete upgrading the effectiveness of VAT laws. It is through this method that the long-existing issue of legality in the VAT system reform can be thoroughly solved.

In recent years, the issue of the lack of a legal basis exposed by the VAT system reform has been increasingly intensified and advocates for an increase in the level of VAT have also appeared. In fact, during the process to promote the rule of law in taxation, the form and the procedure are both important. If the conditions to pass legislation by the National People's Congress are temporarily insufficient, at least the Standing Committee could adopt a practical approach by first announcing relevant "Decisions" and proceeding, when the time is ripe, to passing the unified Law on VAT.

In conclusion, all types of taxation system reforms, including "business tax to VAT", must pay attention to the concept of legal basis when exercising the power to reduce taxes, and the "Decision to Authorization" made by the National People's Congress should no longer act as the basis for the unlimited implementation of "experiments".[47] For the implementation of economic reform, economic growth is not the only point that needs to be pursued. The legal basis for such reform should also be considered. The theories and practice in many states prove that changing the taxation law system has always been closely linked to the "economic constitution". In China, to "strengthen economic legislation and to improve macro-regulation and control" in view of maintaining a steady growth of the national economy constitute both the basic requirement of the Constitution[48] and the reflection of the state ration and function. Therefore, to fulfil the requirements of the Constitution, the economic legislation in taxation areas must be strengthened to facilitate targets that facilitate the adjustment of economic structure and to ensure that the steady growth of the economy through "business tax to VAT" can be realized, based on which the principles of fairness and efficiency of taxation can be better executed and the basic rights of citizens can be better protected.

3.2.5 Summary

"Structural tax reduction" is an important institutional practice in China and it fundamentally affects the development of the economy, politics, law, and society.

Unification of distribution systems 73

For a better solution to relevant distribution issues, China has, at least since 2004, initiated structural adjustments to taxation law institutions.

To discuss the "structural tax reduction" in the broad sense would contribute to finding embodied legal issues within a broader time-space background, especially the crucial issue of the tax reduction area. Under the context where "structural tax reduction" is commonly treated as an issue of policy or economy relevant to the adjustment of economic structural adjustment, instead of a legal issue,[49] the issue of power to reduce taxes is not valued and the issue of the legality of "structural tax reduction" is usually neglected, thereby triggering problems from various aspects.

Therefore, it should be emphasized that the statutory power to impose tax reduction is the foundation for "structural tax reduction", without which "structural tax reduction" would have no legality. Either the legislative power or the executive power to impose tax reduction must be stipulated in the law, which is important to the legal adjustment of various "tax reduction elements". Besides, the statutory power to impose tax reduction must be fairly exercised in accordance with the law, and the requirement of compliance to the law and justifiability must be met in terms of various aspects including the agent, scope, procedure, and principles of the exercise of such power. Such "structural tax reduction" would better reflect the requirement of basic principles of taxation laws, including the principle of statutory taxation, the principle of fairness, and the principle of efficiency.

Besides, the VAT system reform which in recent years has been the focus of the "structural tax reduction", "transformation of VAT" and "business tax to VAT" reflect the two main approaches for "structural tax reduction". For this reason, this chapter specifically analyzes the relevant issues of the power to impose tax reduction and further reveals the long-existing issue of lack of legality when exercising the power to reduce taxes and to highlight the fact that the principle of statutory taxation should be strictly abided by and also the fact that the level of VAT legislation needs to be upgraded. The abovementioned issues and the solutions are also applicable to the improvement of other taxation law systems other than the VAT system.

Through the above discussion, it is also not difficult to find out that "structural tax reduction" is directly relevant to the adjustment and improvement of the taxation law structure and to the coordination of specific taxation law systems. The direct foundation for the coordination of various systems is the tax reduction power in taxation law, not a "policy" to put in place tax reduction. Policies cannot replace the stipulations of taxation law and this is an important issue that requires special emphasis. From the perspective of law, "structural tax reduction" always directly connects with adjustments to the structure of taxation law. It is a "legal" instead of a "policy" issue and is far beyond merely an "economic" issue.

"Structural tax reduction" as an important institutional practice, will continue for a long period of time. The above discussion has indicated that the issues of violation against the law during tax reduction must be reviewed and effectively solved. The legal stipulations and limitations to tax reduction power must

74 *Unification of distribution systems*

be emphasized. The above issues concerning the power to reduce taxes are also worth noting for taxation law, economic law, as well as the whole public law area. The comprehensive development of rule of law in taxation will be achieved and the overall theory about the power to reduce taxes, the theory of taxation power, and taxation law will be improved, as long as the power to reduce taxes is truly and effectively defined and exercised in accordance with the law under the structure of rule of law and constitutionalism, and the distribution of rights and interests of relevant agents is protected.

3.3 The internal differences in a distribution system

There are differences in many aspects of a distribution system, including the agents and objects within the distribution system which appear to be unified on the surface but have many differences. The existence of some differences is justifiable, but others need to be eliminated to improve the distribution system. For that, the unreasonable difference is a vital cause leading to the emergence of significant distribution problems and distribution crises. The internal differences within a system require our attention and action to undertake research on its justifiability.

The Law on Corporate Income Tax is important for the income distribution of corporations and relevant agents. However, different income tax systems are applied to different types of corporations, thereby generating huge negative effects on fair competition and distribution. Therefore, since 2008, China has applied a unified Law on Corporate Income Tax, although many institutional differences still exist today. For this purpose, the following part will, taking the unified, integrated Law on Corporate Income Tax as an example, analyze the existing issues of difference and highlight the issues that bring about the differences within the distribution system.

3.3.1 Introduction

The unification of the Law of Corporate Income Tax is the long-term ideal and a milestone for the fiscal and taxation legislation and even the economic legislation in China. As significant legislation that attracts the attention of the whole nation, the unified Law on Corporate Income Tax undoubtedly has a strong symbolic meaning because it indicates the dedication of the state to establish a legal system that fits the requirement of the market economy system with the spirit of rule of law. Hence, research on this law could expand beyond the technique of taxation law and radiate to broader areas including economy, society, and law.

The unification of the Law on Corporate Income Tax will not happen without the increasing acceptance of the ideas of "unified market, unified law, equal agents, fair competition". The expansion of these ideas lays the conceptive foundation for much important economic legislation and contributes to a series of important laws that are dispensable to a market economy, and further lays a solid foundation for the overall unification of legal system.

Among the many cornerstones, the fiscal and taxation legislation which directly affect the power, rights, and interests of the state and citizens are undoubtedly vital, especially the direct taxations like income tax which directly affects the production and operation of market agents as well as the fair competition and interests of various agents. The unification of income tax law and the unified application of specific norms are significant to the interests of all the parties. Therefore, eliminating the diversified or binary legislation in the area of corporate income tax[50] becomes the most basic consent of all groups.

The unification of the Law on Corporate Income Tax is a requirement of the development of economy, society, and law whose conceptive foundation is also relatively solid. For this reason, the publishing of the unified Law on Corporate Income Tax was praised for unification, especially for the unification regarding its application to different agents, the unification on the pre-taxation deduction system, and the unification on rate and preferential measures which has already been amply discussed.[51] Meanwhile, the fact that there are limitations for the unification of the Law on Corporate Income Tax should not be neglected given that it would be beneficial for the improvement of legislation and execution, and in providing a better solution to distribution problems.

Therefore, the following part intends to analyze the internal limitation of such unification and the reflection of such limitation on the system and explores the cause and relevant principles of such limitation. It will be based on the foundation for emphasizing the "principle of difference" of the economic law, objectively perceive the "outward unification and inward difference", and the "harmony with difference" of the unification of laws, thus achieving a better understanding of the internal difference of the distribution system.

3.3.2 The internal limitation of the unification and its reflection on the system level

Similar to the multiple limitations of the universality of taxation law,[52] the unification of Law on Corporate Income Tax would also comprise of multiple limitations, including the realistic level of development of the economy and society, the state economic and political institutions, the condition of the rule of law, the level of perception of the people, etc. Such limitations are vital factors affecting the unification of the Law on Corporate Income Tax and as elements that constitute the outside environment of legislation, they decide the basic appearance of the unified and integrated Law on Corporate Income Tax as well as the overall level of legislation. Such limitations could be described as outside limitations affecting the unification of taxation elements of corporate income tax. At the same time, internal limitations should also be considered. The particularities and differences of the taxation elements of corporate income tax would result in constrained elements that affect the unification of the system. In fact, whether such outside limitations exist or not, internal limitations may play a role. Therefore, the unification of the Law on Corporate Income Tax would be profoundly influenced by internal limitations.

76 *Unification of distribution systems*

Some would believe that the unification of the Law on Corporate Income Tax should realize the unified application of the Law on Corporate Income Tax to all agents. Yet, in fact, because of the effect of the constrained elements including subjects, objects, standard for the quantification of duties, etc., the degree of unification of the Law on Corporate Income Tax is very limited and far from the degree of comprehensive unification and integration imagined or expected by people. For such purpose, the following part intends to discuss the specific reflection on the institutional level of various internal limitations.

3.3.2.1 The intrinsic limitation of the difference among agents

The intrinsic limitation of the difference of agents results from the realistic differences of taxpaying agents. The taxpaying agent is a vital standard for the classification of income tax because it is directly linked to the taxation interests of relevant agents and is a typical direct tax. The corporate income tax system in the history of China was classified based on differences of ownership or whether the agent was involved in foreign elements. This indicates that such a system considered the difference of agents. Though the legislation aims at achieving the universal application of a unified taxation law to different types of corporations, especially domestic corporations and foreign-invested corporations, as long as different agents exist, specific measures need to be taken in some areas in accordance with the specific circumstances and different rules required to be applied based on the differences among agents, instead of the universal application of the same rule – an action which is impossible.

From the performance of the current system, the Law on Corporate Income Tax is not actually equally applied to different agents. First, the implementation of the Law on Corporate Income Tax is limited, which means it is not applied to all types of corporations. For example, it is not applicable to partnerships and sole proprietorships, thereby making the scope of the application of this Law smaller than what its name indicates. Second, the application of the Law on Corporate Income Tax, in some areas, exceeds what its name indicates. It is not only limited to corporations, but also "other forms of organizations that obtain incomes" including governmental bodies, official functional institutions, and social groups. This means the reality of the application of this law exceeds the sphere of "corporations". Third, differences still exist among corporations that are under the jurisdiction of the Law on Corporate Income Tax. Sometimes, the same taxation law norms cannot be applied by the same standard. For instance, the differences between residence corporations and non-residence corporations still objectively exist and the legal application to such two types of agents are not always unified. Also, the existence of taxation preferential measures is based on the differences among agents. In reality, the taxpaying agents are diversified and the state would inevitably discriminate against these agents due to economic, social, or political considerations leading to the emergence of a complicated taxation preferential measures system. The existence of taxation preferential measures implies that not

Unification of distribution systems   77

all agents enjoy such preferential measures in the same manner, and therefore the distribution of income would inevitably be affected.

Therefore, differences with regard to taxpaying agents are vital intrinsic limitations affecting the unified application of the Law on Corporate Income Tax. These differences make it difficult for the total integration of the Law on Corporate Income Tax, hence it is impossible to apply unified, identical norms to different types of corporations. And, as long as the differences among agents still exist, differences in taxation law norms will continue to exist for a long period of time.

3.3.2.2 The intrinsic limitation of subjective quantification

According to the theory of taxability, the nature of income and profitability is vital for determining whether an object is taxable or not (Shouwen Zhang 2000).[53] In each area of taxation, "no taxation without income" exemplifies the principle of fairness in taxation. In the area of income tax, the "income" should be specifically emphasized. Without taxable income, income tax cannot be collected. This is a basic requirement of the principle of taxation by capability. Therefore, when designing the system of corporate income tax, the fundamental questions that need to be considered are how to determine whether relevant agents have gained taxable income, how to determine the taxable income, and how to quantify the objects of taxation.

In the area of the Law on Corporate Income Tax, because of the obvious differences existing among agents, both in theory and in practice, the object of taxation collection is the taxable income, yet huge differences exist in the specific quantification to the objects. The reason is that income tax, being different from other types of tax, is quite complicated in terms of factors that affect the determination of taxable income, and such determination is closely linked to the identity of the agents. Different types of taxpayers are actually subject to different rules of taxation law and they enjoy different statuses under taxation law. Because it is difficult to unify these rules and statuses, the quantification of objects becomes an intrinsic limitation that affects the unification of the Law on Corporate Income Tax.

For example, during the process of the unification of the Law on Corporate Income Tax, the legislators strived to include various "organizations that obtain income" into the net of taxation and law,[54] resulting in a situation where governmental bodies, official functional institutions, social groups, and the military were all subjected to corporate income tax as long as they received income. Although the nature of these organizations is different and the differences between corporations and non-profit organizations are huge, the norms applied to quantify taxpaying objects are diversified. Organizations that do not frequently undertake business activities, or whose goal is not to make profit, should first deduct the amount of income that is not subject to taxation, including fiscal appropriation, administrative functional charges obtained in accordance with the law, governmental funds, etc., which are closely connected to the performance of duties or presume governmental functions representing the government (providing public

78 *Unification of distribution systems*

or semi-public goods to the general public).[55] Therefore, it could be concluded that the quantification of non-corporate taxpaying objects could not be totally unified with the quantification to the taxable income of pure enterprises.

Besides, even compared with different types of corporations, huge differences exist among corporations in different areas and industries which have different legal natures. Therefore, the quantification of their taxable income would be different. For example, compared with resident corporations, the whole amount of non-resident corporation interest of stock, interests, dividends, a fee of concession is subject to taxation without any deduction. Or in different tax collection modes, the ways to collection applicable to corporations with different scales are different, and the applicable rules to the quantification of their taxable income are different. These are limiting factors affecting the integration of laws in terms of the aspect of quantification of taxation objects.

The difference in the quantification of the objects results largely from the difference in the agents. Therefore, the research on the quantification of objects should combine with the specific taxpaying agents solely through whom the system of object quantification can be improved and the grounds for taxation effectively determined. This has the potential of laying the foundation to correctly weigh the taxpaying duty of taxpaying agents and the protection of the legal rights and interests of both parties – the collector and the payer.

3.3.2.3 *The internal limitations to the quantification of duty*

The difference in taxpaying agents is closely linked to the quantification of objects and duty. In fact, the precondition for the quantification of duty is the quantification of objects, without which the quantification of duty is impossible, for the realization of quantification to duty is ultimately through the application of relevant rates or preferential measures or a heavier burden to quantified objects. Therefore, the quantification of the objects is the foundation for the quantification of the duty. It may even be categorized as the quantification to the duty. From the general principles, the formation of abstract taxpaying duty normally relies on the application of rate to specific tax foundations. Where there are preferential measures, it also relies on the application of preferential measures or heavier duties.

Though the Law on Corporate Income Tax is considered to unify the rate and preferential measures, the unification of the tax rate system and tax preferential measures system is still incomplete.[56] For instance, there are multiple levels of rates even though the rate of corporate income tax is officially 25%. The rate for withholding income tax to non-resident corporations is 20% (most of the taxation treaties between China and other countries stipulate that the rate should be 10%), and the preferential rate is 20% or 15%,[57] etc. These rate differences indicate that there are "general principles" and "particular situations" in the area of state taxation law adjustment. Also, the state would consider which areas need to be regulated, controlled, and guided, and in which areas the distribution of interests should focus on. In different circumstances, different rates should be applied to different agents, which implies that it is impossible to completely unify the tax rate.

Unification of distribution systems 79

Besides, the system of tax preferential measures has more influence with regard to the quantification of the duty. Tax preferential measures enjoyed by different agents are more diversified, and the difference in the actual taxpaying duties of agents is more pronounced. The state would directly stipulate preferential measures including reduction, exemption, preferential rates, additional deduction, reductive calculation of income, etc., to decrease or even eliminate income tax by corporations including grand-agriculture, high and new technology industry, public infrastructure construction, environmental protection and energy-saving projects, etc. These measures are directly correlated to the long-term economic and social policies made by the state in accordance with the current conditions. As for numerous corporations that are not included in the above sphere, they are excluded from such preferential measures regardless of the nature of ownership. For a better exercise of the function of tax preferential measures, the law would not apply the same preferential measures to different types of agents. The unified preferential measures are against the original purpose of the system of preferential measures.

In conclusion, the difference in the agents as well as the behaviour of agents directly affect the quantification of agents and duty and this affects the unified application of legal norms, thereby highlighting an internal limitation of the Law on Corporate Income Tax – its inability to integrate.

3.3.3 *The cause for the internal limitation and relevant principles*

In general, the existence of various internal limitations is due to the particularity of the objects of the Law on Corporate Income Tax, especially the visible complicity and differences among the taxpaying agents. As a direct tax, income tax directly involves the agents and their interest distribution. Such complicity and difference would inevitably result in the complicity and difference of the income tax legal norms that adjust to the interests of agents, hence making it difficult for the income tax norms to be unified among various types of agents.

The unification of the legal system or law is "relative". The unification of the Law on Corporate Income Tax is only achieved in general and concerning certain important aspects. The original binary income tax system that discriminates against domestic and foreign corporations has been relatively unified, yet in terms of many fractions and many specific institutions or norms, divisions still exist. The external unification and internal division are caused by the internal contradiction of the Law on Corporate Income Tax. As long as the differences in the nature and specific behaviour of taxpaying agents exist, the situation of "external unification and internal division" is inevitable.

In fact, in the Law on Corporate Income Tax, there are many cases where "principles and exceptions simultaneously exist", a reflection of the "divisions among unification" and "unification among divisions". For example, in terms of the agents, many people believe that the current Law on Corporate Income Tax adopts a legal person in the taxation system, thereby highlighting the independence of taxpaying agents. The reason is that the legal person shall be responsible

80 *Unification of distribution systems*

for himself/herself, and shall bear his/her own taxpaying duties as its independent status indicates. In that sense, the "independent taxpaying principle" could be confirmed in the field of taxation law. However, there are exceptions to such a principle. In some circumstances, there exists consolidated taxpaying or collective taxpaying. Though they are exceptions to the principle of independent taxpaying their existence is justifiable (Shouwen Zhang 2007).[58] Besides, in reality, the dependence (or affiliation) might be in conflict with the independence required by the law. This means targeting the objective situation of the affiliated corporations and by emphasizing its independence, the Law on Corporate Income Tax makes specific stipulations which enable affiliated corporations' systems or anti-tax avoidance systems to emerge.

Directly relevant to the anti-tax avoidance system, it should be noted that the purpose of the agents' behaviour is also important when focusing on the independence of agents. The purpose of corporate behaviour is mainly commercial otherwise tax evasion would directly affect the legality of such behaviour, and the principle of "substance precedes the form" may become applicable.[59] Therefore, the taxation law should also distinguish between corporations with different purposes and it should equip relevant norms to react to such behaviours so that different corporations may enjoy different taxation law statuses, thus achieving the justice of distribution, which means, each entity gets what it deserves.

In summary, the "external unification and internal division" of the Law on Corporate Income Tax" is manifested by the taxation law norms and systems that stipulate different treatment to different types of agents. The main reason is the existence of differences among taxpaying agents, their behaviour, as well as the relevant internal limitation elements such as the quantification of the objects and duties. Only through discrimination based on existing differences can taxation based on capability and taxation according to the law be better applied to achieve justice, and to further the principle of taxation efficiency in order to realize the fundamental principles of statutory taxation and fair taxation. Meanwhile, it is by maintaining the division of relevant norms to various types of agents that macro regulation and control can be better conducted, which may contribute to the better realization of functions of taxation and taxation law, and to the fulfilment of the multi-purposes or goals of the Law on Corporate Income Tax.

Besides, the difference in the system generated from the difference in the agents reflects an important principle of economic law – the principle of difference. Unlike traditional civil and commercial law, the adjustment by economic law is based on the difference and non-balance of the agents as well as many other aspects, and the goal of such adjustments is to solve the issues of difference that have to be settled to realize substantial justice and to guarantee overall efficiency. Therefore, economic law needs to incorporate huge amounts of norms that reflect the economic and social policy to discriminately adjust different agents and different behaviours, forming various specific institutions that "are in harmony yet not the same". The internal limitations for the unification of the Law on Corporate Income Tax is an important reflection on the principle of difference, which makes the Law a vital system that is in "harmony yet not the same". In other words, though there are differences within various systems, they collectively form a harmonious entity and could better correspond to the reality of society and realize its system performance.

3.3.4 Summary

The release of the Law on Corporate Income Tax in China was unified with the corporate income taxation law on the surface (Krause & Walt 2005),[60] yet due to the restriction by internal and external limitations, such unification is not complete and the unified law has only be applied to a limited degree. Because of the existence of multiple and mutual limitations, such as the difference in agents and quantification to objects and duties, the specific taxation law norms applied to different types of taxpayers are not identical. Corporations in different regions, industries, and areas are all taxpaying agents stipulated under the Law on Corporate Income Tax. However, the applicable specific norms may be vastly different from one another. Meanwhile, there are many specific issues that are worthy of our attention, in terms of the unification and division of system, the independence and affiliation of agents, and the commercial purpose and taxation-related purpose of behaviours. Such issues reflect the principle of difference in economic law. It would be immensely beneficial for the effective implementation and future improvement of the law, and for the coordination of relevant systems in the taxation law area, if these issues could be comprehensively understood and the relevant distribution issues effectively solved.

3.4 The national factors in the difference of distribution systems

In relevant distribution systems, based on considerations to national interest or in the name of national interest, there exist different institutional arrangements. For example, corporations which are all taxpaying agents of the abovementioned Law on Corporate Income Tax may be affected by discrimination in taxation laws because of the so-called national factors. Among these systems, the collective taxpaying system for enterprise groups reflects such discrimination and would directly affect the distribution of taxation interests of relevant corporations. For such purposes, the following part will use it as an example to reveal the national factors that constitute the difference in distribution systems.

3.4.1 The issue and its definition

Among the complicated taxation law systems, enterprise groups' collective taxpaying system is a type of new-emerging system. Research into such an important system is currently focused on the aspect of taxation management.[61] Yet, this system not only involves taxation collection and management but it is also connected to economic issues such as accounting and industry policy, as well as various other aspects like politics and law.[62] The influence it has is far-reaching

82 *Unification of distribution systems*

and therefore legal research, from the perspective of department laws including taxation law, needs to be conducted.

Due to the complexity of taxation law, especially the complexity of the process through which the taxation law system forms, many concepts in taxation law need to be defined to avoid confusion. "Collective taxpaying" is one such concept. In fact, in the past, to, the term "collective taxpaying" was also used in the income tax and VAT systems and the application of such concept was more common in the area of income tax.[63] Within the field of income tax, the term "collective taxpaying" is mainly applied to two areas with as many meanings. The first is collective taxpaying that directly corresponds to the determination of the foundation for income tax. The other is collective taxpaying relevant to the deduction of the taxation amount in the taxation offset and deduction. The latter could be illustrated through the concept of taxation offset and deduction in international or domestic taxation law. The former meaning, therefore, is more common when people use the concept of collective taxpaying.

Such definition also originates from realistic institutional stipulations. Article 14 of the Interim Regulation on Corporate Income Tax which came into effect in 1994 in China stipulates that "unless otherwise stipulated by the State, the taxpayers of corporate income tax shall pay corporate income tax to the local taxation administrations". As for the part that requires the State to make specific stipulations, Article 43 of *Implementation Regulation on the Interim Regulation on Corporate Income Tax* further stipulates that:

"As for railway operation, civil aviation transportation, post, and telecommunication enterprises, [the corporate income tax] shall be paid by the organizations that are responsible for the operation and management and are in control of such enterprises."

Therefore, since 1994, the State Administration of Taxation has released a series of regulatory documents including both comprehensive regulations to collective taxpaying by corporate groups and specific regulations to specific types of corporate groups in relevant industries. Such industries include finance (especially the four biggest state-owned commercial banks, policy banks, insurance companies, securities companies, etc.), telecommunication (including large-scale enterprises such as China Mobile, China Unicom and China Telecom), transportation (including railway, civil aviation, etc.), and the collective taxpaying system of Chinese corporate groups have thus emerged.

From the perspective of the institutional construction, the core of the collective taxpaying system for corporate groups is to emphasize that the corporate groups and affiliated enterprises that fit the legal conditions be seen as one entity in terms of collectively calculating and paying corporate income tax. To be specific, collective taxpaying means the method that relevant corporations "calculate the amount of taxable income (or loss) according to relevant regulations and the headquarter or the taxpayer designated by the law pays the income tax collectively".[64] For that, the collective taxpaying system allows agents to add up the income and expenditure of relevant agents. In general, this would affect the confirmation of the foundation of the tax for relevant corporations and therefore would affect the final amount of income tax. This is far from the basic requirement of normal principles of independent taxpaying and jurisdiction. Therefore, it is an exceptional and special system.

Although the collective taxpaying system is special, since the agents subjected to it (large-scale corporate groups in special industries) are of crucial importance to the schemes of the state and the life of the people, and their operation network covers the whole nation that profoundly and widely affects life, the scope of its application is not narrow. The relevant existing problems are not only about taxation law but also connected to company or corporation law, accounting law, competition law, industry law, as well as constitutional law and administrative law. Therefore, deeper research needs to be conducted from various angles.

As for the particularity and the difference compared to other systems of corporate groups' collective taxpaying systems, and for the basic issues including the institutional goals and configuration of taxation power, despite their importance, relevant research is still lacking among scholars. Besides, the following issues require further investigation: the conflict between the corporate group collective taxpaying system and the independent taxpaying system, the reflection to basic requirement by taxation law, and the connection with the transfer pricing system and loss transfer system. Such an effort may contribute to revealing the particularity of a collective taxpaying system and its value while enhancing and improving current systems.

3.4.2 The particularity of the collective taxpaying system

The particularity of corporate groups' collective taxpaying system means this system is "special" and "different" compared with other types of taxpaying systems. As mentioned earlier, as a special system in the field of corporate income tax, it is an exception to the common "independency-jurisdiction" taxpaying system. Originally, according to the requirement of the principle of taxpaying by "independency-jurisdiction", the branches of companies' head offices, especially for subsidiary companies controlled by parent companies, could act as independent taxpaying agents and pay tax directly to the local taxation administrations, instead of together with other branches or subsidiaries that collectively pay taxes with the head offices or parent companies. For that, if there are losses incurred by the branches or subsidiaries when paying tax collectively, the overall taxable amount would be decreased and the whole amount of tax payable by the corporate group and the taxation revenue of the state would be decreased.

As a special type of taxation law system, a collective taxpaying system is not universally applicable as ordinary taxation law systems due to the limitation to the agents. This could be considered a limitation of the applicability of taxation law.[65] Such limitation is connected with the whole "principle of difference" in economic law. In the area of taxation law, because of the difference in the status, strength, or taxpaying capability of taxpaying agents, the State makes many

84 *Unification of distribution systems*

special considerations in terms of economic policy and social policy and applies differentiated treatment to different agents concerning taxation law, thus constituting many exceptional systems in taxation law. The collective taxpaying system emphasizes the difference in defining the taxation foundation with regard to different agents, or in other words, the particularity of certain agents in terms of taxation law treatment.

The particularity of the collective taxpaying system is directly related to the particularity of the agents to which such a system is applied. According to current stipulations, the agents entitled to the right to apply for collective taxpaying must be corporate groups that meet the requirement of the regulations (which are all "large-scale enterprises"). This is different from the emphasis on preferential measures on "medium and small-scale enterprises" by past taxation laws. Currently, agents that have been approved for collective taxpaying are mainly large-scale groups in finance, telecommunication, and transportation, i.e. banks, security and insurance companies, and telecommunication enterprises[66] which are all directly related to the foundation of the existence of the State and the life of the people. With regard to their nature, these huge corporate groups cover ample areas and have complicated branches, and normally have extensive monopoly attributes (economic monopoly, administrative monopoly, natural monopoly, or a combination of these). Some agents (i.e. policy banks) theoretically have a public interest nature. Such particularities are vital to the formation and development of a collective taxpaying system.

The nature of trans-territory and complex branches is the common attribute shared by these enterprises. Yet, there are other corporate groups in other industries that share this attribute.[67] Why is the collective taxpaying system not applied to these corporate groups? Why is the taxation law treatment different with regard to different types of corporate groups? The perception of these issues is diverse. For example, some believe that to treat different corporate groups differently with regard to taxation is obviously unfair and to apply a collective taxpaying system to all corporate groups is exactly the direction for the future amendment to taxation law (Lei Liu 2006).[68] This opinion is justifiable. Based on past practices and relevant principles, the influence of one certain industry or corporate group to national schemes and the life of the people, and the relevant nature of monopoly and public interest would affect the policy nature of the system. Meanwhile, the policy nature of a system is the particularity of system differences. In fact, the aforementioned corporate groups like finance, telecommunication, and transportation are with a significant nature of monopoly or public interest and are fundamentally important to the national schemes and life of the people, and to the stability of the economy and society, and they constitute the vital foundations for the application of such a special collective taxpaying system. The state, based on the economic, political, and societal considerations takes special care of state-owned or state-holding enterprises, which constitutes an important motivation for the confirmation of such a special collective taxpaying system. Therefore, the formation of a special distribution system actually incorporates the interests and factors of the State.[69]

3.4.3 Aims of the collective taxpaying system

The previous discussion about the collective taxpaying system included the aims of such a system. For what purpose should the special collective taxpaying system be established beside the basic systems (independent taxpaying system and system of taxpaying) according to jurisdiction? What are the aims or values of such a system? Under the collective taxpaying system, the offset of profits by losses would decrease the whole taxable amount of the corporate group and further lower the overall amount of taxation, thus it would be beneficial to the corporate groups. In this sense, the main aim of the collective taxpaying system is to encourage and promote the development of corporate groups in relevant industries, enhancing its competitiveness and increasing economies of scale. Since most of the corporate groups subjected to a collective taxpaying system are typically state-owned or are state-holding enterprises and are protruding monopolies with a huge impact on the public interest of society and the foundation of the national economy, the implementation of collective taxpaying system is, in essence, the promotion by the state of relevant industries and enterprises through transferring the interest of taxation, which in many aspects reflects the "factors of the state". In conclusion, the main purpose of the collective taxpaying system is to directly affect the industry policy through the taxation system, especially to optimize the industry structure and promote the ability of risk resistance and market competitiveness of enterprises by influencing the industry organizing policies and industry structure policies. Therefore, the ability of the state to develop the macroeconomy could be facilitated, and the national economy and public interest of society could be protected.

Judging from the aims of the system, collective taxpaying is not only a technical issue, it also contains various considerations to policies. Meanwhile, collective taxpaying is not a normal operation in taxation but reflects considerations to taxation preferential measures. Thus, the collective taxpaying system is a predominant facet of the natural economy and regulation.[70] From the perspective of the economy, for relevant taxpaying agents, collective taxpaying is more economical in general and would reduce their cost for taxation or reduce the taxation burden. From the perspective of regulation, a collective taxpaying system may combine positive encouragement and positive prohibition, reflecting the state's will to support and promote the development of a series of important corporate groups, a phenomenon which is significant for the promotion of competitiveness of enterprises in relevant fields and the safety of the state economy.

Similar to the situation in China, in many countries, the aims of corporate groups' collective taxpaying system could be summarized as follows: to impact industry policy, to optimize the allocation of resource, to raise the efficiency of the economy, to promote the development of the economy, and to protect the public interest. Historically, the development of corporate groups in many countries is directly linked with the impact of taxation laws, and such a connection is so close to a degree that some believe "the trace of legal policies concerning corporate groups in Western countries almost always appear first in taxation law"

86 Unification of distribution systems

(Changbin Wang 2004).[71] Each country tries to promote the development of corporate groups through the adjustment of taxation law and therefore, in terms of collective taxpaying, no matter what specific mode, the US and Germany mode, or Australia and Netherland mode,[72] the aims of the system are similar. However, in these countries, the ownership of enterprises is not emphasized. The focus is more on fair competition among market agents. Therefore, in general, these systems do not differentiate corporate groups and the core of such collective taxpaying systems is to regulate the "collective taxpaying" behaviours of relevant agents within one corporate group.

What needs to be further clarified here is that, at present, some scholars hold that the terms "collective taxpaying" and "combined taxpaying" should be distinguished.[73] In China, regulatory documents concerning collective taxpaying use the term "collective taxpaying" more frequently, yet some documents adopt the term "combined taxpaying" or "collective (combined) taxpaying" or "combined (collective) taxpaying", all of which demonstrate the chaos in the use of basic concepts in taxation law, as well as the lack of coordination among regulatory documents in the use of terms. From the development of the system, normally when regulating issues concerning collective taxpaying, the content of combined taxpaying is contained while combined taxpaying has already become an object that the collective taxpaying system specifically regulates. Therefore, when talking about the concept of collective taxpaying, the extension of such a term already includes combined taxpaying.

Besides, the aim of a collective taxpaying system is also directly relevant to the basis of such a system and it should be reflected in relevant legislation. Article 52 of the Law on Corporate Income Tax in China stipulates that "unless otherwise stipulated by the State Council, corporations shall not pay corporate income tax collectively". This article emphasizes the principle of independent taxpaying (namely, non-collective taxpaying is the principle), meanwhile reserving space for the existence of a special and exceptional collective taxpaying system (namely, the combined taxpaying system targeting special agents). However, relevant laws do not make specific regulations on topics including the aims of the collective taxpaying system. From the perspective of effective implementation of a system, there should be a systematical stipulation of the collective taxpaying system including the clear stipulation of the aims of such a system. It could also contribute to preventing the abuse of collective taxpaying systems by relevant agents.

3.4.4 The allocation of taxation power in the collective taxpaying system

The allocation of taxation power is the core of any taxation law system. In terms of the corporate groups' collective taxpaying system, the allocation of taxation power also appears as the significant "binary structure of levying and paying". From the perspective of the levying agent, the collective taxpaying system targets national, transregional corporate groups, and therefore the legislative power concerning collective taxpaying system should be kept by the centre, in other

Unification of distribution systems 87

words, it should be stipulated mainly by the National People's Congress and State Council. In terms of the power to levy and regulate, because the collective taxpaying system is a type of special and vital system with strong nature of policy and it involves the "tax expense" of the state, it should be treated with caution. To that end, the state explicitly applies the approval system which means it is the State Administration of Taxation that owns the power to approve collective taxpaying and specifically determines which corporate groups in which industries could enjoy collective taxpaying. Such power seems to be merely procedural, yet it is essentially important to taxpaying agents.

To emphasize the exclusiveness of this power, from 2000 the State Administration of Taxation has released many documents repeating that collective taxpaying has to be approved by the State Administration of Taxation, so the local tax administration is not entitled to make such decisions. Therefore, if local tax administrations have approved collective taxpaying or expanded the scope of collective taxpaying, that situation must be corrected. It could be concluded that collective taxpaying approval is closely connected to the taxation interest of the state, the taxation interest of the local government, the corporate groups, and various relevant corporations, and should be decided by the central administration based on the overall situation. In this sense, the centralization of power is justifiable. However, if there is no limitation to the types of corporate groups to which collective taxpaying is applicable, then the high centralization of the power to approve collective taxpaying is unnecessary.

Corresponding to the power to impose taxes by the agents that levy tax is the taxpaying obligation of agents that pay tax. Originally, if the behaviour or facts of a corporation meet the statutory taxation requirements, it should be subject to taxation according to the principle of independent taxpaying. Yet, considering various factors including the economy, society, and politics, the state specifically sets up the collective taxpaying system to enhance the development of corporate groups in relevant fields. Due to that, the amount of taxation of such corporate groups could be decreased in general, and therefore collective taxpaying is, in essence, a type of preferential tax policy. Enterprises are motivated to apply for collective taxpaying which makes the right to apply for collective taxpaying by relevant corporate groups an important procedural right.

The collective taxpaying system is constantly changing. According to the original arrangement, the agents entitled to apply for collective taxpaying have to be corporate groups meeting relevant requirements. At that time, corporate groups with such a right were mainly: 1) 120 large-scale corporate groups that could conduct such "experiment" as determined by the State Council; 2) corporate groups that were experimenting corporate group policies and collective taxpaying policies approved by the State Council; 3) railway operation, civil aviation transportation, post, telecommunication, and finance corporations (including non-banking financial institutions as securities and insurance companies) stipulated by the taxation law; 4) corporations under the culture system reform experiment; and 5) corporations with the nature of corporate group which were decedents of corporations subject to collective taxpaying after restructuring. Collective taxpaying may

88 *Unification of distribution systems*

apply to the aforementioned corporate groups after approval, and once approved, the members of such groups, including the branches and wholly owned subsidiaries, could pay tax according to collective taxpaying guidelines. If the situation about member corporations changes, and the list of member corporations needs to be amended, the corporate group should submit applications within limited time and wait for approval by the State Administration of Taxation. During the process of re-grouping, adjusting, or asset restructuring, if one wholly-owned subsidiary becomes a non-wholly-owned subsidiary,[74] then from the current year that subsidiary should cease to be subject to collective taxpaying and principles of independent taxation, and taxation according to jurisdiction should apply. Such a subsidiary should pay its corporate income tax to the local tax administration instead of enjoying the right to collective taxpaying.[75]

Thus, it could be concluded that in terms of the taxpaying agent, the issue that corporate groups could pay tax collectively is, in essence, an issue of the eligibility to the right of collective taxpaying. Inside a corporate group, the types of enterprises that should be eligible for collective taxpaying is relevant to the independence or degree of independence of such enterprises. Such issues should be the focus when allocating the power to impose taxation.

3.4.5 *Several issues that need further investigation*

The above part briefly discussed several basic topics including the particularity, goals, and allocation of power to impose taxes with regard to the collective taxpaying system. A series of important issues need further investigation. For instance, the relationship between collective taxpaying and the principle of independent taxation, whether collective taxpaying aligns with the measures, whether the fairness of taxation is affected, as well as the difference in the allocation of power to taxation with other systems. To that end, the following part intends to discuss such issues.

3.4.5.1 *Collective taxpaying: exception to the principle of independent taxation*

As mentioned earlier, the collective taxpaying system is just a particular exception to the common rule. From the perspective of the theory of taxpaying agent and the management of tax levying and regulation, independent taxation and taxation according to jurisdiction are basic principles. Based on the principle of independent taxation, all the independent taxpaying agents, according to taxation law, should pay tax independently instead of collectively with other agents. This practice is relevant to the allocation of the taxpaying obligation and the independent performance of taxation duties. However, from the perspective of the collective taxpaying system, many subsidiaries fully constitute independent taxpaying agents according to taxation law. However, for its particular affiliation with their parent companies, in order to meet relevant regulations that encourage and facilitate the development of corporate groups, they could pay their tax according to collective taxpaying methods. Still, such exception is not the total denial of the basic principle of independent taxpaying, for on the one hand, when relevant agents fail to meet the equity requirements, etc., they should again be subject to independent taxation. On the other hand, even under collective taxpaying, the relevant information concerning taxation should be submitted to local taxation administrations for supervision, which is in conformity to the principle of independent taxpaying. Therefore, the conflict between the collective taxpaying system and the principle of independent taxation is relative and the principle of independent taxation remains fundamental.

In principle, the dependence of enterprises or companies on taxpayer qualification may result in dependency in taxpaying, which means that when relevant enterprises are dependent and the state has set up a collective taxpaying system, the application of the principle of independent taxation can be avoided. However, the key precondition is that there must be a collective taxpaying system established by the state, otherwise, even when there is dependency, a collective taxpaying system could hardly be applied.

The difference between two modes of corporate income tax, namely the classical system and the integrated system, could inspire us to comprehend the connection between the principle of independent taxation and the collective taxpaying system. To solve the issue of repeated economic tax levying, the classical system, represented by the US and based on the realistic theory of the legal person, emphasizes that the company and its shareholders are independent agents, so they should independently bear their duties to taxation in accordance with the principle of independent taxation. The integrated system, represented by some states in the EU, is based on the fiction theory. It emphasizes that a company and its shareholders may be deemed as one agent and therefore the taxation duties of companies and individuals could be combined and solved together.[76] Such integration is similar to the spirit of the collective taxpaying system. Therefore, if the integrated mode could be spread based on the internal arrangements between companies and their shareholders (here specifically indicating the parent company or the head office), the taxpaying of these agents could be combined in an integrated approach for collective taxpaying.

Comparatively, though it is not appropriate to simply equate a collective taxpaying system with the abovementioned modes (sometimes the collective taxpaying system is similar to a mixture of both), generally speaking, the collective taxpaying system emphasizes the maximization of the overall interest, and therefore is more similar to the integrated model, reflecting the idea of holism. It is internally related to the overall strategy of corporate groups, with the comprehensive considerations of the state, and with the whole effect pursued by the taxation law adjustment.

Besides, from the principle of taxation according to jurisdiction, which is directly connected to the principle of independent taxation and to which administration the taxpayer pay taxes directly, relates to the issue of the jurisdiction of the taxation and the power to gain taxation interests. Collective taxpaying changes the common principle of jurisdiction and the situation of the taxation interest of the

90   Unification of distribution systems

local government, thereby affecting the distribution of taxation between the central and local government. It is, therefore, likely to affect the relationship between the central and local government.

3.4.5.2 Viewing collective taxation from the perspective of the requirement of basic principles of taxation law

As discussed above, the principle of collective taxpaying is the opposite of the principle of independent taxation. Is it a type of preferential measure? After all, the original motivation for the state to levy tax is to gain taxation interests, both in the short term and in the long term. Yet under collective taxpaying, the state has to give up part of its taxation interest. From the perspective of the state's "giving up" and decreasing the burden of enterprises, collective taxpaying fits the general definition of taxation preferential measures, and some economic scholars therefore treat it as a type of preferential measure. Of course, such preferential measures are based on foundations and the effect is similar to the transfer of loss.

If collective taxpaying is treated as a preferential measure, then the issue of fairness should be involved, and problems such as whether collective taxpaying comply with basic principles of system goals of the taxation law would emerge. For according to principles of taxation law, taxation preferential measures are taxation special measures which should comply with and reflect the three basic principles of taxation law, namely, the principles of statutory taxation, fairness, and efficiency. Therefore, issues relating to collective taxpaying could be researched from the perspective of requirement by basic principles of taxation law.

According to the principle of statutory taxation, the collective taxpaying system should also be statutory, including the applicable agents, scopes, conditions, and approaches, which all require explicit stipulations by the law. Judging from current regulations in China, though there are bases and reflections in the collective taxpaying system in state legislation, the core content has been established by a series of regulatory documents released by taxation administrations. As far as the documents are concerned, it suffices to say that their level is too low and the conditions for application are unclear, resulting in the expansion of administrative discretion. This is still considerably far from the requirement of the principle of statutory taxation.

In terms of realization of the fairness of taxation, the current collective taxpaying system is also very problematic. For instance, from the perspective of horizontal fairness, why are certain corporate groups eligible to enjoy collective taxpaying? Why are only a few types of corporate groups approved while there are many other corporate groups that meet the criteria? Though explanations based on policy considerations exist, sometimes the justifiability of policy is questionable. Therefore, satisfactory answers are required for normative fairness and substantial fairness. Besides, from the perspective of vertical fairness, compared with a relatively disadvantaged medium and small-scale enterprises, corporate groups have strong economic capabilities and enjoy more public goods, therefore they should contribute more to the state in terms of taxation. Is it appropriate to instead give corporate groups taxation preferential measures? Especially for corporate groups that are obviously with monopoly status, will such measures further increase their monopoly status and influence economic efficiency and consumer interest?

Closely related to the two abovementioned principles is the issue of, from a taxation efficiency perspective, whether collective taxpaying will twist the resource allocation by the market and further decrease the efficiency of the economy. Are the costs of taxation levying of the administrations and the cost of taxation by relevant enterprises really lowered? Further calculation is needed instead of simple speculation from stipulations on the paper.

Various questions related to basic principles of taxation law may have already been highlighted, yet deeper questions exist that need to be explained in theory. For example, does the development of corporate groups or the encouragement of corporate groups by the state represent the public interest? How should we define public interest? How should fairness and efficiency be defined and how should the relationship between them be arranged properly? Besides, how could the scale benefit of groups be increased and how could the competitiveness of corporate groups be increased? Which entity should bear the cost of corporate groups? Is it appropriate that the taxpayers collectively pay for the results of collective taxpaying? There is bound to be increasing consent with regard to these questions given the increasing enterprise independence and market competition as well as a deepened understanding of the public interest.

3.4.5.3 Interrelations between collective taxpaying and the system of transfer pricing and loss transfer

Apart from the collective taxpaying system, taxation law systems that are closely related to corporate groups also include the system of price transfer and loss transfer. These systems share similarities though they have distinctions. Therefore, the merit further investigation and discussion in order to increase the understanding of issues including the allocation of taxation power and the protection of interests.

As is widely known, in the field of corporate income tax, that there exists a specific type of system, namely transfer pricing, which is specifically applicable to affiliated enterprises within corporate groups. The core of such a system is to solve the issue of transfer pricing among affiliated enterprises. In fact, the branches and subsidiaries of corporate groups are typically affiliated enterprises and, in accordance with stipulations of taxation law, when transactions occur among them, the principle of independent transaction has to be followed in terms of charges or paying of funds. Otherwise, if pricing (therefore profit) is transferred through internal transactions among affiliated enterprises, the result of such transactions would not be admitted by taxation law. That explains why the taxation administration is entitled to adjust the amount of taxation.[77] It could thus be concluded that the system of transfer pricing emphasizes the fairness of transactions among affiliated enterprises indicating that such transactions should be conducted in a way that is similar to market agents without affiliations. In other words, it emphasizes the independence of affiliated enterprises.

92   *Unification of distribution systems*

Yet, the system of collective taxpaying is different. It focuses not on the affiliated transactions among affiliated enterprises within corporate groups, but on the issue of collective taxpaying based on profits or losses after examining the financial operation of affiliated enterprises. At this juncture, it does not emphasize the independence of affiliated enterprises, but instead the connection among them and the integration of the losses and profits of all these agents.

Such two systems are applicable to two phases. The system of transfer pricing is applicable to the phase of the formation of benefit/loss before taxation, which emphasizes the principle of independent transaction (aka principle of independent competition, principle of fair transaction), and it directly affects the formation of the foundation for taxation of individuals. Meanwhile, the system of collective taxpaying is applicable to the phase when the result of the operation of enterprises is clear and the benefit/loss has been subjectively realized. Collection would change the overall foundation for taxation. The aims and phases are different between such two systems. Besides, from the perspective of economics, transfer pricing is reasonable because it contributes to the decreasing cost of transactions and to the realization of the goals of multiple parties. Yet, from the perspective of the law, transfer pricing may generate numerous negative effects and therefore should be regulated through the taxation law, thereby reflecting the requirement of the independent competition of agents in the external market. It focuses on the individual. The system of collective taxpaying, however, emphasizes the dependent competitiveness of enterprises which reflect the requirement to decrease the cost of taxation through the integration of benefits and losses within the internal market.

In addition, the connection between the system of collective taxpaying and loss transfer is also worth researching. From the design of the system, loss transfer aims at adjusting the foundation for taxation through the offset of profit and loss in different years, enabling the enterprise to enjoy deferred tax and lowered rate by determining the taxable amount in a longer term.[78] Collective taxpaying tries to realize the offset of benefits and losses among affiliated enterprises, decreasing the burden on relevant agents by the integration of profits and losses. Besides, loss transfer also emphasizes the importance of individuals, in other words, enterprises as independent individuals may conduct loss offsetting. Collective taxpaying emphasizes the meaning of the entirety, maximizing the profits of the whole group. The difference of both, in this aspect, is similar to the difference between the system of collective taxpaying and the system of transfer pricing.

3.4.6 Summary

The issue of collective taxpaying for corporate groups is a complicated issue that demands deeper research by academia. The terms and scope of application and the relationship with relevant systems need to be cleared so that the relevant legal issues can be investigated more profoundly. Based on the basic definition of collective taxpaying, the previous sections discussed the particularity and goals of the system of collective taxpaying as well as issues such as the allocation of taxation

Unification of distribution systems 93

power within such system, emphasizing that the particularity of the system lies in its exception to normal systems of independent taxpaying and taxation according to jurisdiction, etc., and that such particularity is directly related to its system goals. In fact, without the attempt to achieve specific system goals, the doubtful system of collective taxpaying would not exist. It is to realize specific system goals that special allocation of power to taxation is needed in such a system, that emphasis on the exclusive power of State Administration of Taxation to approve of collective taxpaying is necessary, and that the overriding nature of policy or difference is apparent in terms of collective taxpaying.

Earlier sections also focus on the relationship between the system of collective taxpaying and relevant systems or legal principles, from which we could further analyze the particularity of the system of collective taxpaying and therefore better understand the aims of this system. In fact, many analyses of the relative conflict between collective taxpaying with regard to the system of independent taxation and taxation according to jurisdiction intend to further illustrate the particularity or difference of the system of collective taxpaying and to emphasize that it is only an exception to the norm, and its implementation should meet specific conditions. Analyses concerning the relationship between collective taxpaying and basic principles of the law of taxation attempt to illustrate that the realization of the goals of the system of collective taxpaying may conflict with the basic principles of taxation law and that, in practice, it may generate many problems or doubts. The discussion on the correlation between the system of collective taxpaying and transfer pricing and loss transfer implicitly contains the focus on the shift from an individualism standard to a holism standard concerning the allocation of taxation power or interest on taxation, as well as the shift from individualistic thought emphasized by traditional systems to holistic thought emphasized by modern systems.

Notes

1 The initiation of reform and opening-up and the economic law legislation were passed almost at the same time, and benign interaction happened between them. Taxation legislation, as the earliest economic legislation since the reform and opening-up, has tremendous influence. The deepening of reform or the expansion of macro-regulation and control involve taxation legislation.
2 Since the reform and opening-up, the first laws made in economic legislation are the *Law on Individual Income Tax* (1980) and the *Law on Foreign Corporate Income Tax* (1981). As laws passed by the national legislative body, their precedency is higher than the later taxation interim regulations.
3 Though in 2011 China announced that the socialist legal system with Chinese characteristics had been established, many important pieces of legislation in the taxation field had not yet been published, and the overall taxation law structure was still in the process of improvement.
4 On September 18, 1984, the State Council, in accordance with the decision to authorized legislation by the Standing Committee of National People's Congress, published relevant taxation regulations (draft), including the *Regulation on Commodity Taxation (draft)* and the *Regulation on VAT (draft)*.
5 Based on the *Decision to Authorized Legislation* in 1985 of the National People's Congress, the State Council made and implemented a series of interim taxation regula-

94 *Unification of distribution systems*

tions, ending the history of taxation "Regulation (Draft)". Currently, most taxation laws are "interim regulations" made by the State Council.

6 The Standing Committee of National People's Congress (1984). *The Decision to Authorize the State Council to Reform the Industry and Commerce Taxation System and to Publish and Experiment Relevant Taxation Regulations and Drafts.*

7 Shouwen Zhang. (2001). *The Universal Applicability of Taxation law and its limitations.* Peking University Law Review, 4(05), pp. 554–566.

8 In recent years, the employment of "experiment mode" in taxation legislation has been increasingly frequent. Apart from the expansion of experiments on VAT, real estate tax and resource tax are also under experiment.

9 Given that taxation law has the function to distribute income and conduct macro-regulation and control, its changeable nature makes it worthy of our attention. For relevant discussion, see Shouwen Zhang. (2002). *The Periodical Change of Macro-regulation and Control Law.* Peking University Law Journal, 5(06), pp. 695–705.

10 The Third Conference of the Sixth National People's Congress (1985). *Decision on Authorizing the State Council to Formulate Interim Regulations Concerning Economic Institution Reform and Opening-up.*

11 Similarly, Article 1 Clause 8 of the US Constitution grants the Congress the power concerning taxation levying, expenses, adjusting international trade and inter-state trade, and authorizing the Congress "to make all laws which shall be necessary and proper for the foregoing powers, and all other powers vested by this Constitution in the government of the United States, or in any department or officer thereof". However, the terms "necessary" and "proper" have been controversial for their ambiguity. Through the constant constitutional interpretations made by Associate Justice Marshall, etc., the power of the federation has been expanding. See Qianfan Zhang. (2011). The US Federal Constitution. Beijing: China Law Press, pp. 95–103. Therefore, both constitutional authorization and legislative authorization may result in the problem of ambiguity, yet the agents being authorized are obviously different in China and the US.

12 For example, though there are already many specific stipulations in the *Interim Regulation on VAT* as well as its implementation regulations, the fiscal and taxation department still needs to publish an expanse of documents. This is directly related to the complexity of economic activities, and reflects the changeable nature of the VAT system.

13 "Though to increase the certainty is the aim of the laws, however the laws are only capable in terminating part of the source of uncertainty". See Friedrich Hayek. (2002). *Law, Legislation and Liberty.* Vols. II, III. Beijing: China Encyclopedia Press, p. 213.

14 See the *Experiment Scheme to Change Business Tax to VAT*, which emphasized "to regulate the taxation system and make the burdens reasonable", and "basically terminate the duplicate taxation".

15 The real estate tax reform experiment started on January 28, 2011 in Shanghai and Chongqing. Both stipulated that the aim of such experiment is to "adjust income distribution, guide the real estate consumption and effectively allocate the real estate resource".

16 During the process of "the experiment of business tax to VAT", a common problem is that the burden of taxpayers with lower capital may rise. The increase of tax burden of logistic companies is an illustration.

17 Fikentscher believes that the jointing point decides whether a taxation fact is taxable. See Wolfgang Fikentscher. (2010). *Wirtschaftsrecht.* Translated by Shiming Zhang. Beijing: China Democracy Legislative Publishing House, p. 32.

18 Based on *Experiment Scheme to Change Business Tax to VAT*, during the experiment period, the basic fiscal institution should remain stable, and the income generated from business tax should belong to the original region. The corresponding reduction of fiscal revenue should be shared between the central and local government. Thus, the local taxation interest would not be affected.

Unification of distribution systems   95

19 In terms of the cost to obey and coordinate, see Manfred Streit and Wolfgang Kasper. (2000). *Institutional Economics: Social Order and Public Policy*. Translated by Chaohua Han. Beijing: Business Press, pp. 152–156.

20 When taxation income is insufficient, even though the local government does not rely on the income of the land, it will seek other fees or non-taxation income, and the whole income distribution system would become chaotic. Therefore, it is vital for the future development of China to shift the function of the government, relieving the government from "operational activities".

21 Under the efforts of various groups, the Standing Committee of the National People's Congress has already paid attention to this issue. Especially under the circumstance that the advocacy for "fulfilling the principle of statutory taxation" has been rising, the date when the *Decision to Authorization* will be abolished will not be far.

22 In terms of the problem of authorized legislation and the violation against principle of statutory taxation, see Shouwen Zhang. (1996). *On Statutory Taxation*. Chinese Journal of Law, 18(06), pp. 59–67.

23 Shouwen Zhang. (2012). *Three Basic Problems of Real Estate Tax Legislation*. Taxation Research, (11), pp. 50–55.

24 For various problems that may result from legislation "experimentation", the public has accumulated abundant understanding, and therefore the state emphasizes the grand design, instead of experimenting under all circumstance.

25 *Law on VAT* has been listed into the legislation scheme of the National People's Congress, and should be published as early as possible. This is vital to avoid the demerits of "experimenting".

26 Article 3 of the *Law on Taxation Collection* stipulates that no government bodies, units, or individuals could make decisions to initiate, suspend, reduce, or exempt rebate tax that is against current taxation laws and regulations. This article reflects the power to reduce taxes in the broad sense.

27 Taxation scholars divide the power to taxation into power to taxation legislation, taxation administration, and taxation income. From the perspective of increasing or reducing tax burdens, it could also be divided into the power to increase tax and the power to reduce tax. It is mainly relevant to the abovementioned power to taxation legislation, and would have a direct impact on the power to taxation administration and taxation income.

28 Article 2 of the Constitution of the People's Republic of China stipulates that "all power in the People's Republic of China belongs to the people". Similar stipulations exist in the constitutional laws of many other states. Therefore, the power to make decisions concerning tax reduction should be exercised mainly by the National People's Congress or parliament.

29 At present, China has not made *Tax Codex* or *General Rules on Tax*, and the basic stipulations of taxation institution laws concerning the distribution of power to taxation, and the specific stipulations on the power to reduce taxes are mainly in the *Law on Tax Collection*.

30 Some states have already included the principle of statutory taxation into their constitutional law. For example, Article 317 of the Constitution of the Bolivarian Republic of Venezuela specifically stipulates the principle of statutory taxation.

31 Power to taxation, taxation behaviour, and taxation interest are the three basic categories of the field of taxation and they reflect the core issues of taxation law. For relevant discussion, see Shouwen Zhang. (2003). *The Abstract and Value of the Category of Taxation Behavior*. Taxation Research, (7), pp. 43–49.

32 Article 1, Clause 10 of the US Constitution stipulates that "no state shall, without the consent of Congress, lay any duty of tonnage". This is crucially important to reducing the burden of enterprises and encouraging domestic free trade and fair competition.

33 China implemented the *Interim Regulation on Custom Duty of Tonnage*, published in September 1952. The new *Interim Regulation on Duty of Tonnage* came into effect on January 1, 2012.

96 *Unification of distribution systems*

34 According to Article 8, Clause 8 of the *Law on Legislation*, affairs concerning basic institutions of taxation could be regulated only by the law.

35 This decision was abolished by the Standing Committee of the National People's Congress on June 27, 2009.

36 Shouwen Zhang. (1996). On Statutory Taxation. *Chinese Journal of Law*, 18(06), pp. 59–67; Shouwen Zhang. (2012). Three Fundamental Issues Concerning Real Estate Tax Legislation. *Taxation Research*, (11), pp. 50–55.

37 Though in the *Decision to Reform* in 2013, the National People's Congress is required to fulfil the "principle of statutory taxation" with regard to legislation, the implementation of this principle in execution is equally important and it is the direction for the improvement of taxation legislation.

38 In late May 2007, officials of the Department of Finance insisted that the rate of security exchange stamp duty will not be increased, while four working days later, in the early morning of May 30, the Department of Finance announced that the rate would be increased. This resulted in a sharp drop in the stock market. The public doubted such behaviour. See Mingsheng Yuan. (2008). The Crazy Stock Market, Stamp Duty and Rule of Law of the Government: Thinking on the Adjustment to the Rate of Security Exchange Stamp Duty from the Perspective of Jurisprudence. *Law Science*, (8), p. 25.

39 The principle of proportion contributes to avoiding the violation of the state power against the legal interests of citizens. It is comparatively more important to emphasize this principle regarding the reduction of tax. If the measures of tax reduction violate the principle of proportion, then such measures are against the law. If the law is against the principle of proportion, then such law is against the constitution. See Utz Schliesky. (2006). *Öffentliches Wettbewerbsrecht.* Translated by Wenguang Yu. Beijing: China Law Press, p. 103.

40 Sima Guang ni Song Dynasty believed that through reducing the burden of the people, the source of taxation would be maintained, achieving the sustainability in tax levying. See Jun Wang. (2009). *The Institutional Change and Thinking Evolution of Fiscal Institution in China* (Vol 1, Part 2). Beijing: China Fiscal Economy Press, pp. 822–823. The thinking of Sima Guang is consistent to Laffer, yet it is much earlier than Laffer.

41 Approved by the State Council, the Department of Finance and State Administration of Taxation enacted the *Regulations on Several Issues concerning the Expansion of VAT Deduction in Northeast Regions*. It is the direct basis for the exercise of power to reduce taxes in the field of VAT in the northeast region.

42 The VAT transformation experiment initiated in the northeast region and the experiment for exemption of agriculture tax in Heilongjiang and Jilin are both important measures of "structural tax reduction". However, at that time, people did not view these events from such a perspective given that they failed to identify the vital position and meaning in restarting the taxation institution reform.

43 The *Interim Method for Expanding the Scope of VAT Deduction in Central Regions* is the direct basis for the exercise of power to reduce taxes in VAT area in central regions.

44 Some states even make strict restriction to the exercise of power to reduce taxes in constitutional laws. For example, Article 219 of the Constitution of Republic of Haiti stipulates that "no tax exemption, increase, decrease or elimination may be established except by law". Thus, the exercise of power to reduce taxes shall comply with strict principle of statutory taxation.

45 VAT is a typical neutral tax and should be applied with unified standard. More than that, various indirect taxes, including VAT, should be applied. Therefore, Article 1 Clause 8 of the US Constitution stipulates that "the Congress shall have Power To lay and collect Taxes, Duties, Imposts and Excises, to pay the Debts and provide for the common Defence and general Welfare of the United States; but all Duties, Imposts and Excises shall be uniform throughout the United States".

46 For instance, the *Experiment Scheme to Change Business Tax to VAT* published by the Department of Finance and State Administration of Taxation.

Unification of distribution systems 97

47 For specific discussion on relevant legal problems concerning VAT experiments, see Shouwen Zhang. (2013). The "Experiment Mode" of Taxation Legislation in China: Taking VAT Legislation Experiment as Example. *Law Science*, (4), pp. 61–68.

48 "The State strengthens economic legislation, improves macro-regulation and control" is explicitly stipulated by Article 15 in Constitution of China, which is crucial for the maintenance of the steady growth of national economy. For such purpose, Article 109 of the Basic Law for the Federal Republic of Germany stipulates the "overall economic balance", which is deemed as a core aim of the state. See Rolf Stober. (2008). *Allgemeines Wirtschaftsverwaltungsrecht: Grundlagen des Wirtschaftsverfassungs- und Wirtschaftsverwaltungsrechts, des Weltwirtschafts- und Binnenmarktrechts.* Translated by Libin Xie. Beijing: Commercial Press, p. 333.

49 Many problems in the process of economic structure adjustment in China are legal problems, which are vital for analyzing the issue of "structural tax reduction". For relevant analysis, see Shouwen Zhang. (2011). Economic Law Thinking on "Dual Adjustment". *Law Science*, (1), pp. 30–34.

50 The period of multi-legislation indicates the period when the standard of legislation is the ownership of enterprises. While the dual-legislation period indicates the period when the income tax system for domestic enterprises and for foreign enterprises coexisted.

51 After over ten years of preparation, the *Law on Corporate Income Tax* was finally passed in March 2007 and the approval vote was as high as 97.8%. At that time, it was studied or reported in many essays and in the news.

52 For the brief discussion on the universal application and limitations of taxation law, see Shouwen Zhang. (2001). The Universal Applicability of Taxation Law and its Limitations. *Peking University Law Journal*, 4(05), p. 554.

53 Shouwen Zhang. (2000). On the Taxability in Taxation Law. *Jurists Review*, (5), p. 12.

54 According to Article 1, Clause 2 of the *Law on Corporate Income Tax*, individual sole-invested corporations and partnership corporations are not subject to this law.

55 Such institutional arrangement is also an important reflection on the taxable principle. See Zhengwen Shi. (2007). Discussion on the Issue of "Income not Subject to Taxation" in Law on Corporate Income Tax. *Taxation Research*, (9), p. 44.

56 The different treatments do not exist in terms of rate and preferential measures. However, the difference still exists, and the unified application of the same norms or institutions to all types of corporations is impossible.

57 Article 28 of the *Law on Corporate Income Tax* stipulates that micro-scale enterprises fitting the requirements are levied at 20%, and the high-tech enterprises supported by the State are levied at 15%.

58 Shouwen Zhang. (2007). Legal Analysis to the Collective Taxpaying by Corporate Groups. *Law Science*, (5), pp. 41–49.

59 Taxation law theory and practice in both the common law and continental law system value this principle. In fact, in the whole economic law field, to fulfil the substantial justice, this principle must be established.

60 It is a vital problem, whether substantial unity is achieved, and whether certainty, predictability, and stability have been established. See Jody Krause and Steven Walt. (2005). *The Jurisprudential Foundations of Corporate and Commercial Law.* Translated by Haijun Jin. Beijing: Peking University Press, p. 193.

61 For instance, some scholars believed that collective taxpaying was one of the reasons for the "deviation", when discussing the issue of deviation between regional taxation and tax resource. See Wanjun Jin. (2007). Primary Thinking on the Issue of Deviation between Regional Taxation and Tax Resource. *Taxation Research*, (1), pp. 28–34.

62 Collective taxpaying, as a type of special system, changes the original principle of local tax and impacts the interest and competition of enterprises as well as the taxation interest of local government. It will further affect the relationship between central and local government and correspondingly will bring forward political and legal problems. Research from the perspective of the department of law is required.

98   *Unification of distribution systems*

63 In other fields, the term "collective paying" similar to "collective taxpaying" is used. For instance, in terms of stamp duty, as early as in 1989, the State Administration of Taxation and the Department of Railway stipulated that the stamp duty of the carrier should be collectively paid by the railway administrations in order to simplify the taxpaying procedure and to enhance the taxation administration. Yet the exact meaning of "collective paying" is not the same as "collective taxpaying".

64 See the State Administration of Taxation. (1995). *The Interim Regulation on Enhancing the Levying of Corporate Income Tax for Collective Taxpaying Enterprises.*

65 For relevant discussion, see Shouwen Zhang. (2001). The Universal Applicability of Taxation law and its limitations. *Peking University Law Journal*, 4(05), p. 554.

66 For instance, The Ministry of Finance and Taxation. (1996). *The Reply Concerning the Calculation and Paying of Income Tax of State-owned Commercial Banks;* (2001). *Notice Concerning the Income Tax of Entities subject to CAAC*, State Taxation Letter No. 502.

67 As for other enterprises, the State Administration of Taxation stipulated the *Regulation on the Administration of Tax Levying of Income Tax for Enterprises Conducting Interregion Business*, which came into effect on January 1, 2013. However, the scope according to this Regulation, is limited to the branch without the legal person status. Therefore, the meaning is different.

68 Lei Liu. (2006). On the Formation of Modern Enterprises and Income Tax. *China Economic Studies*, (2), p. 56.

69 A vital reason is that such tax income belongs to the revenue of central government, and should be paid to the central treasury in full amount. Therefore, the applicable system is naturally different.

70 The nature of the economy and regulation is a basic characteristic of economic law including taxation law. See Shouwen Zhang. (2004). *The Reconstruction of Economic Law Theory*. Beijing: People's Press, pp. 221–226.

71 Changbin Wang. (2004). *Comparative Studies on Corporate Group Laws*. Beijing: Peking University Press, p. 155.

72 Some believe that the US and Germany apply a collective-sharing system, which means that the entities subject to one corporate group calculate their taxable income respectively, and the total amount of such taxable income constitutes the taxable income of the entities of the higher level. While in states such as Australia, a total-combination system is applied, where the corporate groups are treated as independent taxpaying agents. See Wenchuan Xia. (2007). Thinkings on Collective Taxpaying of Corporate Income Tax. *Taxation Research*, (1), p. 44.

73 The collective taxpaying by headquarter and branches would be called collective taxpaying, and the collective taxpaying by parent company and subsidiaries would be called combined taxpaying, which is reasonable.

74 In many developed countries, the companies subject to combined taxpaying are not limited to wholly-owned subsidiaries. For example, the US once stipulated that owning over 80% of shares with the power to vote is one of the conditions for applying combined taxpaying.

75 The State Administration of Taxation. (2006). *Notice on Regulating the Scope of Collective Taxpaying of Corporate Income Tax,* State Tax Letter No. 48. Currently, this Notice is abolished, which reflects the process of change of the collective taxpaying system.

76 Some scholars call these two modes the American independent taxation system, and European unified taxation system. See Kaneko Hiroshi. (2004). *Tax Law*. Translated by Xianbin Zhan. Beijing: China Law Press, p. 198.

77 Article 41 of the Law on Corporate Income Tax stipulates that "where a transaction between an enterprise and its related party is not conducted pursuant to the arm's length principle and this results in the reduction of Taxable Gross Income or Taxable Income of the Enterprise or its related party, the tax authorities shall have the authority to make adjustment using appropriate methods".

78 For example, article 18 of the Law on Corporate Income Tax stipulates that "the loss incurred during a tax year by an Enterprise is allowed to be carried forward to the following years and set off against the profits of the following years, but the carrying forward period shall not exceed a maximum of 5 years".

4 The legal protection of distribution rights and interests

The emergence and expansion of distribution risks and crises are directly related to inadequacies in the protection of relevant rights and interests by distribution systems. For example, the right to economic development involves the survival and development of various agents and as an important economic right, it contains the right to participation in distribution. If the right to economic development cannot be effectively protected, the distribution risk may increase and the possibility of the occurrence of distribution crises would arise. Therefore, the focus needs to be on the resolution of distribution issues in development while the right to the economic development of various agents needs to be valued.

Directly related to the right to economic development is the decreasing of the tax burden of market agents which helps to protect and promote the development of relevant agents, and to better solve the relevant distribution issues. For this reason, China has implemented many "structural tax reduction" measures, among which is the "transition" and "expansion of the scope of application" of VAT. These measures have attracted significant attention given the fact that they are all important institutional adjustments aimed at dealing with the distribution crisis. For this reason, this chapter mainly reveals the distribution issues involved by illustrating the issues related to the protection of the deduction right concerning the transition of VAT. In addition, the chapter demonstrates the influence of the distribution right or power of relevant taxpayers or the state.

Besides, real estate, as a type of property with extreme importance, would hugely affect the realization of the basic human rights of individuals. Meanwhile, real estate ownership would directly affect the distribution of income of residents. Issues such as whether and how to levy tax on property owned by individuals and how to improve the current property tax legislation not only influence the development of the real estate market or the adjustment of relevant economic structures but also involve the prevention of relevant distribution risks. The relevant issues of the protection of different rights are also worth researching. Therefore, this chapter also discusses the issue of improving property tax legislation and reveals the important influence of distribution interests among relevant agents using different approaches to such improvement.

In the grand scenario of distribution, apart from focusing on the distribution rights and interests of enterprises and individuals, the distribution of interest of the government also needs attention, especially the distribution of interest of local governments, which, has currently gathered significant steam and may trigger distribution risks and distribution crises including local government debt risk. For these reasons, this chapter investigates the issues of the distribution of interests of local governments and the relevant legal protection, combining the notable problems caused by the development of a binary system of taxation in China and the important characteristics of the binary system.

4.1 The issue of distribution and the protection of the right to economic development

That fact that the issue of distribution has become crucial is directly related to the lack of protection of the right to economic development. The right to distribution forms part of the right to economic development and when the right to distribution cannot be effectively protected the issue of distribution would naturally become obvious. To analyze the issue from the perspective of rights to economic development would contribute to the further understanding of the reasons for the protection of rights and interest of distribution of relevant agents, and the reasons why the enhancement of economic law regulation is needed in order to resolve distribution issues.

4.1.1 The right to economic development that directly relates to distribution

Development is the current theme for all countries, so it is especially important for developing countries to understand how to develop or what approach should be taken to achieve development. Development economics, development sociology, and development politics have already researched such issues,[1] while development law, as a newly emerging discipline, has not yet conducted sufficient research in this area.[2] Since economic law is the law to promote development, it is particularly necessary to strengthen the research of economic law on legal issues related to development.

Throughout history and till today, countries face extremely complicated "development problems" in their endeavour to achieve multiple goals including industrialization, modernization, urbanization, and informatization. This requires the clarification, in the law, of power or rights of states and citizens in terms of development, thereby giving way to a complicated "right to development" system.

The right to development is usually comprehended as the right of individuals (i.e. a natural person) or a community (i.e. a state or nation) to participate and promote the comprehensive development of the economy, society, culture, and politics and to enjoy the fruits of such development.[3] In the past, research and discussion on the right to development have occurred mainly in the field of international law, especially in the field of human rights. In notable historical documents, such as the *Charter of the United Nations*, the idea of the right to development already existed.[4] Since Kéba M'Baye brought the concept "right to development",

102   *Legal protection of distribution rights*

in documents such as *The Declaration on the Right to Development*, the right to development has been repeated over and over again[5] and has become a vital object in international law research. However, many scholars have realized that the achievement of the right to development of different agents would be impossible without the protection of domestic laws including, most importantly, the protection of economic development.

Based on existing theories on the right to development, all the countries (traditionally mainly developing countries) may choose their approach to economic development according to the conditions of the world and of each country. This constitutes the "right to economic development" within the right to development of one country, which is essential. The exercise of the right to economic development is vital to protect the economic development of relevant states and nations, and to establish a new international economic order. To realize the right to economic development, different countries are entitled to employ various measures to promote and protect economic development including legal measures, among which economic law measures are central.

In previous economic law research, some scholars integrated "development" into the discussion on the ideas, values, and principles of economic law in fields including value theory, and have achieved considerable results.[6] However, the overall research to the right to development (especially the right to economic development) is quite insufficient. Since the occurrence of the financial crisis in 2008, based on the profound influence to the crisis by distribution, "how to develop" and how to solve the crisis resulting from distribution issues has become a major topic for all countries. China, based on the complicated international environment and domestic conditions, has made a major strategic decision to change its way of economic development, which is related to both international and domestic laws. For example, at the level of international law and based on the right to development, China is completely autonomous in terms of deciding how to develop and how to change its way to develop. Meanwhile at the level of domestic law, to realize the goals of changing its ways to develop, the right to the development of various agents needs to be further clarified and defined, with the support of domestic laws including economic laws. Considering that the changing of ways to develop is a long-term strategy of the state, the right to economic development of various agents needs the protection of economic law. Therefore, it is quite necessary to focus on and study the issue of the right to economic development.

In fact, the approach to economic development of one state is directly related to the right to economic development. The realization of the right to economic development, especially the right to distribution, especially calls for protection by economic law. Economic law is "the law to promote development" and relates to the increasing relevance of the nature of regulation,[7] the adjustment of which would directly affect the right to economic development and the interest of development of relevant agents. To consider the issue of the right to economic development through the perspective of economic law may contribute to solving the issue of the protection of domestic laws aimed at enhancing the

Legal protection of distribution rights   103

right to development that has long been brought up in the area of international law and yet has never been effectively solved, thereby transforming the issue of the right to development into an issue of domestic law. It may contribute to the establishment of a new international economic order and a new domestic economic structure in this new historical era. It may also facilitate the development and improvement of the theories of economic law and even the entire development law.

Therefore, the following part hails from the perspective of economic law. It locates the right to economic development within economic law, thereby revealing the right pedigree of economic law agents and their complicated hierarchical structure, and explores the relationship between basic power and the right of economic law agents with various types of rights to economic development. Based on that, the following section discusses the issue of economic law protection of the right to economic development and highlights relevant issues that affect the right to economic development and that require immediate solutions. The expectation is that this may promote the development of economic law theory, the improvement of relevant institutions, and it may facilitate "development law" and international law.

4.1.2 *The position of the right to economic development in economic law*

It is generally agreed that the right to development includes the right to economic development, the right to social development and the right to political development, etc. The right to economic development is widely admitted as the core to the right to development and it is the foundation for the effective realization of other types of rights to development. Some scholars believe that the right to economic development is the most active element in the law and social development motivation system, and it is the right for a state or nation to demand the establishment of a fair and justifiable economic order, deciding and adjusting its economic structure and its development policy (Xigen Wang 2008).[8] Since the right to economic development directly relates to the domestic adjustment of economic structure and economic development of a state, it is necessary to define such right in domestic laws, including economic law, in terms of its types and specific precedency.

From the perspective of economic law, the right to economic development is a type of important comprehensive right owned by economic law agents whose realization is based on the power and the rights of economic law agents. Therefore, there is higher precedence. Because of such a status, the right to economic development is both closely related to various specific types of power or the rights of economic law agents being studied by academia, and also, obviously different from such other powers or rights.

It is necessary, with regard to the position of the right to economic development, to further clarify, through investigation, the content and category of the right to economic development. In fact, the content of the right to economic development is abundant and is embodied in various types of rights. In economic law research at least, the following types need our attention.

104   *Legal protection of distribution rights*

First, based on the binary structure of state-citizen, the right to economic development could be divided into the state's right to development and the citizens' right to development. The citizens' right to development could include the rights of both enterprises and individuals to development as well as the third sector's right to development, etc. At the international level, if the broad definition of the right to development is considered, both developed countries and developing countries may enjoy the vital right to economic development.[9] While at the domestic level, the right to economic development of enterprises and other individuals is neglected and especially requires protection by economic law.

The state right to development involves national interest and social and public interest, while citizens' rights to development involve personal interests. The exercising of state right to economic development directly affects the results of the approach to economic development, while different approaches to economic development would significantly influence citizens' right to economic development. Generally speaking, it should be an important goal to adjust economic law that could effectively guarantee the right to the economic development of various agents and to ensure the fair distribution of various kinds of interests.

Second, based on the binary structure of the community and individual, the right to economic development could be divided into the right to the development of the community (or the collective right to development) and the right to the development of individuals.[10] The right to the development of the community concerns the interest of the whole group or the community, while the right to the development of individuals concerns individual interests. To achieve the benign development of the economy, the rights and interests of economic development of various agents have to be effectively coordinated and protected. Based on the experience and lessons of development since the initiation of reform and opening-up in China, while protecting the right and interest to the economic development of individuals there has been a focus on the right to development of the community. The contradictions between the profitability of individuals and social public interest require constant effort to solve. Efficiency and fairness need to be balanced, and the fairness of distribution needs to be guaranteed so that balanced, sustainable development can be achieved, and the benign operation and coordinated development of the economy and society can be promoted comprehensively. These are the highest goals of the adjustment of economic law.

Third, based on the binary structure of government and market, the right to economic development could further be divided into the right to promote development and the right to self-development. The right to promote development is the right for the government to achieve the comprehensive development of a country by promoting the development of other agents. For example, the state may implement measures such as macro-regulation and control, market regulation, etc., to facilitate the economic development of the macro-economy. While the right to self-development enables market agents to realize their self-improvement and self-development through their own conducts. Taking medium and small-scale enterprises as an example, the state may facilitate the development of such enterprises through the implementation of *The Law on Facilitating Medium and*

Small-scale Enterprises. A reflection of the right to self-development is when such enterprises strive to achieve self-development through exercising relevant rights stipulated by this law. Besides, the state facilitates the development of enterprises through quantitative fiscal and taxation systems and financial systems, while enterprises are fulfilling their self-development through such systems, which are both a reflection to the abovementioned two types of rights to economic development. It is not difficult to conclude that such categorization lays bare the increasing importance of economic law.

In the field of economic law, the abovementioned types of rights to economic development are all comprehensive power or rights with high precedency owned by economic law agents while the effective protection of such rights directly relates to the achievement of the goals of economic law adjustment. To clarify the position of the right to economic development in the field of economic law would contribute to conducting the study on the typology of different rights to economic development, especially to the development of economic law theories and improvement of systems.

For example, in the past, based on the binary structure of economic law agents, the difference between the power to economic regulation of the regulator and the decision-making right of market agents, constituting the binary structure of the duty and right of economic law agents. From the perspective of the right to economic development, such regulation and control reflect the state's power to promote development, while the decision-making right corresponds to the right to self-development of citizens, which both belong to a higher ranking in the right to economic development. Therefore, a common upper concept between the power to regulate and right to decision making is found. This constitutes a significant category which could be applicable to different economic law agents, containing power and right, namely the right to economic development. This could, at least from one specific aspect, solve the problem that the powers and rights of different agents lack the same upper concept in the power-right structure theory in economic law. This situation could further facilitate research on the economic law norms theories.

Another example is that after the financial crisis in 2008, most countries began to realize the importance to adjust their economic structure. The famous economist Joseph Stiglitz believes that the crisis in 2008 "is not only a financial crisis" because adjustments to the economic structure are necessary. It should, however, be understood that such adjustments to the economic structure cannot occur spontaneously. The government must play a core role in the process of the transition of economic structure (Stiglitz 2011).[11] The Chinese government has been positively promoting a change of approach to development in recent years and the adjustment to the economic structure is central to such a process. Meanwhile, legal support is provided for such adjustment. The adjustment of the economic structure involves the optimization of the industry structure, the distribution structure, the consumption structure, etc., and for the effective realization of the goal to structural optimization, the power to adjust the industry structure, the distribution structure, and the consumption structure need to be established within the law.[12]

106 *Legal protection of distribution rights*

Although the abovementioned structural adjustment power exists, it is still subordinate to the higher right to economic development and it is directly relevant to various types of basic power or rights to economic law agents.

The basic power or right closely related to the abovementioned right to economic development and power to undertake structural adjustment mainly reflects the power to economic regulation and the decision-making right of economic law agents, which contains different layers of powers or rights and which constitutes the hierarchical structure of the right of economic law agents. The fundamental power of regulation and the right to decision making owned by economic law agents are important protections for the fulfilment of the comprehensive right to economic development.

The aim of the exercise of fundamental power or the rights of economic law agents, irrespective of whether it is the power to regulate that lies with the regulatory administration or the right to decision making owned by the objects of such regulation, is to protect the right to economic development which represents the idea of development. During the implementation of economic law, different agents try to promote the overall development of the market economy through the exercise of the power to macro-regulation and control and the power to market regulation. Such protection is compatible with the development of market agents and it fits the development orientation of the state. It is therefore consistent with the power to promote the development of the state. Meanwhile, market agents also try to achieve self-improvement and self-development through the exercise of the right to decision-making and the maximization of its self-interest – and endeavour for consistency with the right to self-development of market agents. Therefore, the right to economic development is more related to the goals and fundamental interests of agents to some extent. Compared to the upper and more comprehensive right to economic development, the economic regulation powers and decision-making rights are more instrumental and the issue of the connection between the purpose and instrument of right or power is worth deeper investigation.

4.1.3 Legal protection of the right to economic development

In accordance with the state's right to economic development, a state is entitled to choose its approach to development, to decide whether to change the approach to development and to adjust the structures. It is also entitled to conduct macro-regulation and control and market regulation to promote economic development. As the fundamental power of the regulatory agent, the power to macro-regulation and control and the power to market regulation stipulated by the economic law of one state especially requires the limitation of law and should be exercised by the law. Besides, in accordance with citizens' rights to economic development, enterprises, residents, and other types of agents are also eligible to participate in development in accordance with the law and to share the fruits of the development of the state and society. Also, they are entitled to eliminate the factors hindering their development.

Theoretically, the right to economic development of different agents should all be protected by the law. Even the state's right to economic development requires the protection of economic law given that protection from international public law or international economic law is insufficient. The infringement to the state's right to economic development is from some domestic market agents. Of course, in reality, people tend to believe that compared with the state, citizens are in a disadvantaged position and it is easier to infringe upon their right to economic development, therefore, the citizens' rights to economic development attract more attention and it is protected more by the economic law.

Based on the diversity and hierarchy of the right to economic development, relevant legal protection is reflected at multiple levels. For example, in the field of macro-regulation and control, the power to issue currency and levy taxes that are relevant to finance and taxation regulation and control directly affects the right to economic development of both the state and citizens, as well as the distribution of income of relevant agents. Whether a state is able to issue currency independently and to exercise the power of taxation independently involves the core interest and long-term development of the state, and directly affects the right to economic development of the state. Therefore, it is necessary to make relevant stipulations in constitutional law or other important laws. If legal protection is insufficient in a state, the power to issue currency and levy taxes would be interfered or violated by other states or individuals, and economic development would inevitably be negatively affected.

Meanwhile, the exercise of the power to issue currency may generate an important influence on the economic development of other states (for example, considering the special status of US dollar, the US power to issue currency would affect other relevant states). At a domestic level, this may directly affect the right to economic development of citizens because the power to issue currency is directly connected to the amount of currency supply, the inflation affecting the value of currency, or the stability of prices. This implicates the economic stability of the whole economy and therefore influences the distribution of interests of enterprises and individuals.[13] The economic development of enterprises and individuals requires a stable currency environment and a relatively stable property situation, while the abuse of power to issue currency constitutes a significant cause for inflation. In addition, it helps to worsen the property status of citizens. To effectively protect the right to economic development of enterprises and individuals, the state has to exercise the power to issue currency in accordance with the law and to impose strict regulations on those who abuse the power to issue currency.

Besides, the power to levy taxes should also be limited in order to protect the rights of citizens to economic development. Though there are still many debates concerning whether the tax burden in China is high or low, a comparatively reasonable consensus is that China is definitely not a low-tax burden country. To make the tax burden fair and reasonable, the state is considering how to reduce duplicate taxation, especially commodity tax which is at the centre of the reform. For example, to extend the scope of the application of VAT to solve the issue of duplicate taxation of business tax, the state has specifically implemented the experiment

108 *Legal protection of distribution rights*

for "business tax to VAT" (Department of Finance and State Administration of Taxation of PRC 2011).[14] In addition to that, the *Planning Outline for the Twelfth Five-years* of the state stipulates specifically in one chapter that "the distribution relations need to be reasonably adjusted". This goes a long way to emphasize that a justifiable and orderly income distribution system needs to be speedily established, that the percentage of residence income in the national income needs to be increased, and that the percentage of labour compensation in the initial distribution needs to be raised as a way of reversing the ever-increasing gap between the rich and the poor (The Twelfth Five-Year Plan of PRC 2011).[15] For this purpose, "structural tax reduction" must be conducted so that the tax burden of relevant agents can be reduced. It is solely through this method that the re-distribution adjustment institution can be improved and the adjustment of the distribution structure promoted. Taxation is a vital limiting factor for the development of modern enterprises, and to promote the development of enterprises through taxation leverage is an issue that every state needs to solve and which especially relies on the continuous improvement and effective regulation by taxation law.

The abovementioned power to issue currency and levy taxes involves the financial interest and taxation interest of the state. Meanwhile, as a monopoly power of the state, they would directly affect the distribution of relevant interests and influence the competitive environment of enterprises and the living conditions of individuals. To promote the economic development of enterprises, the right to free operation and to fair competition of enterprises needs to be protected and there is the necessity to establish an external environment of fair competition. After all, the condition to issue currency and levy taxes corresponds to the power to issue currency and levy taxes. This has the tendency of affecting fair and effective competition among enterprises which cannot be resolved by relying solely on competitive laws and regulations. Therefore, a joint force from the overall economic law adjustment to the protection of the right to economic development is necessary.

4.1.4 Significant issues affecting the right to economic development that need to be solved

According to the *Declaration on the Right to Development* passed by the UN Congress in December 1986,

> States have the right and the duty to formulate appropriate national development policies that aim at the constant improvement of the well-being of the entire population and of all individuals, on the basis of their active, free, and meaningful participation in development and in the fair distribution of the benefits resulting therefrom.
>
> (UN Congress 1986)[16]

Therefore, various agents within a state are entitled to participate in development and to enjoy the fair distribution of development interests because the continuous

Legal protection of distribution rights 109

improvement of the group and individual welfare is intrinsic to the right to economic development. Correspondingly, the right of market agents to participate in development and fair distribution is extremely important. With regard to such aspects, the reality is that there are many outstanding issues directly affecting the realization of the overall right to economic development meaning that adjustments by economic law are required.

In fact, as early as March 1979, the Human Rights Committee of the UN reiterated, in the form of a resolution, that the right to development is one item of human rights and it emphasized that "the equal opportunity to development is the right of a nation and of individuals within a nation". In order to protect the equal opportunity to development of various types of market agents including individuals, it is necessary for such agents to be able to fairly participate in the competition. Therefore, it is crucially important to protect the right to participate in the competition of individuals of one nation. Without the chance to fairly participate in the competition, the realization of the right to economic development of market agents is improbable.

From a fair competition perspective, all the market agents should be entitled to participate in fair and just competition devoid of illegal monopoly or unfair competition. If this does not happen, those responsible should be punished based on the stipulations of anti-monopoly and anti-unfair competition laws. In this sense, the market regulation based on competition law is an important protection of participation in fair competition.

However, the situation in China is not that satisfactory. The regulation of competition law is flawed with limitations in many aspects. From the perspective of market entrance, sometimes the right for different types of enterprises to participate in fair competition cannot be equally guaranteed. Private-owned enterprises have long been treated unfairly compared with state-owned enterprises with regard to entry into the market. In order to promote the development of the private economy, the State Council released *Several Instructions concerning Encouraging and Guiding the Healthy Development of Private Investment* (Guo Fa [2010] No.13, also known as "the New 36 Articles") in 2010, having followed the publishing of *Several Instructions concerning Encouraging, Supporting and Guiding the Development of Non-public Economy Including Self-employed Business and Private Business* (Guo Fa [2005] No.3, also known as "the Original 36 Articles") in 2005. Despite the fact that the general spirit and contents of these documents are beneficial because they try to protect the rights of private enterprises to participate in market competition in some fields through effective measures, it not easy to achieve comprehensive fair competition between private enterprises and state-owned enterprises due to multiple reasons. There is still a long way to go prior to the actual implementation of such documents. The issues of usurious loans and the difficulty in financing for private enterprises indicate that it is necessary to enhance the protection of the right of private enterprises to participate in fair competition, only through which the right to economic development can be better realized.

In reality, the state usually stipulates different regulations to enterprises with different ownership, in different regions, with different scales and nature with

110 *Legal protection of distribution rights*

regard to a specific financial system, taxation system, fiscal system, industry system, investment system, and foreign-trade system. Different market agents may enjoy quite a different treatment. It reflects the principle of differentiation of the economic law, while economic law also needs to exercise its adjustment function against such situation. In terms of the participation in fair competition of market agents, competition policy or system alone is insufficient. The assistance from competition law and other types of legal systems, and coordination from economic law and economic policy are necessary, for that fiscal and taxation system, financial system, etc., are all significant limitations to the fair competition and effective self-development of market agents.

In terms of comprehensively realizing the right to economic development, to fairly participate in competition and development only means to fairly participate in distribution and to increase the welfare of the group and individual. For this reason, the *Declaration on the Right to Development* once emphasized that "States should undertake, at the national level, all necessary measures for the realization of the right to development and shall ensure, inter alia, equality of opportunity for all in their access to basic resources, education, health services, food, housing, employment and the fair distribution of income" (the UN Congress 1986).[17] Therefore, the state is obliged to ensure equal opportunity in basic resource, fair distribution, etc. Hence, when studying their participation in fair competition, special focus should also be paid to the participation in fair distribution.

Currently, there exists the major "problem of distribution" with regard to participating in fair distribution. Since the reform and opening-up, China has always focused on "two types of distribution", namely the distribution of citizens' individual interest, and the financial distribution of the state. In addition, "two types of distribution" is an important motivation that promotes the reform and opening-up (Shouwen Zhang 2009).[18] However, due to multiple reasons, the problem of distribution has become increasingly urgent given that the distribution structure is not balanced, that the distribution gap is too large, and that distribution is unfair. These factors have already affected many aspects including economic growth, social development and political stability. Economic law as the typical "law of distribution" must exercise its function effectively, conducting effective allocation to the right to income distribution of relevant agents, and promoting the resolution of various distribution issues (Shouwen Zhang 2011).[19]

For example, the imbalance of the distribution structure and the imbalance of income distribution of the state, enterprises, and residents are significant. Among these, the percentage of income of residents in the national income and the percentage of labour compensation in the initial distribution are both relatively low. These would seriously affect the right to economic development of residents and require the adjustment of the law including economic law through the adjustment of the right to income distribution. Since the reform and opening-up, the percentage of fiscal revenue in GDP has shown an apparent U-curve. In recent years, the rise of the fiscal revenue has been notably faster than the rise of the GDP, while the percentage of resident income in GDP has been obviously descending. This situation tends to generate a negative influence on the right to the economic development of market agents. Therefore, comprehensive adjustment involving fiscal laws, taxation laws, and financial laws within economic law must be conducted to solve the issue of the relative decrease of resident income.

Besides, in terms of the distribution gap and distribution unfairness, the Gini coefficient of China has been near 0.5 for many years. The gap in income distribution between urban and rural areas, or among different regions, and the gap in income distribution among different groups is significant and it affects the right to the economic development of relevant agents. Under the circumstance that the gap in distribution is significant distribution is unfair, the issues of distribution fairness and distribution justice have already attracted considerable attention from the public, influencing the right to the economic development, social development, and political development of relevant agents. It requires comprehensive adjustment using economic law as well as other types of legal systems and policies.

In general, both fair competitions relating to the economic development of private enterprises and fair distribution relating to the difference among regions as well as the gain in distribution involve the issue of the right to economic development and are vital factors affecting the economic imbalance or developmental imbalance. Therefore, the degree of economic law adjustment needs to be increased to obtain an ongoing solution to the problems that hinder economic development.

4.1.5 Summary

The research for the right to economic development is relatively weak, yet issues in this field worth investigating are abundant given that this is an interesting perspective for research that addresses issues of distribution. Generally speaking, the right to development, or the right to economic development, is not only a research object for international law or international human rights law, but should also be an important field for the economic law research.

The right to economic development as a vital upper concept contains comprehensive powers and rights, including the power to structure adjustment, and meanwhile relies on fundamental power and right, including the power to regulate and to control and the right to countermeasures of economic law agents. It provides a new approach for examining the right spectrum of economic law agents. Research through this new approach would contribute to enrich the theory on the right-obligation structure of economic law and promote the corresponding construction of institutions.

Correspondingly, the right to development may also become an important factor in "development law". Despite the fact that scholars may have different understandings of the concept of right to development, the fundamental connotation has been gaining increasingly wider acceptance. If the research relating to it is limited to international law without introducing it into the domestic law area, then the research and protection of the right to development would be seriously hindered. The right to development should not become a tool for developing

112 *Legal protection of distribution rights*

countries to struggle with regarding their legal rights and interests, but instead, it should become a right that could be fulfilled in domestic law. How to protect the right to development is a significant task in the research of "development law", while how to protect the right to economic development is specifically the task of researchers of economic law.

In economic law study, the focus should be on the types of rights to economic development. The national right to economic development is an important basis for China to change its economic development approach. During the process to change the economic development approach, the protection of the right to economic development of various types of citizens especially needs to be strengthened. The right to development of the group and of individuals should both be protected by integrating the "right to development-promotion" and "right to self-development". For such purpose, legal confinement to the power to structure adjustment and to the more fundamental power to macro-regulation and control and market regulation is necessary, especially to the power to issue currency and levy taxes that directly affect the right to the economic development of various subjects. The exercise of such power must be confined to the railway of rule of law, only through which the right to economic development and development interest of various types of agents can be protected.

Predominant issues affecting the right to economic development including the hindrance to fair participation in development (or fair participation in competition), and to fair participation in distribution still exist. These may affect economic efficiency and fairness, social effect, and justice, and may endanger the future development of the state and the nation. Given that fair competition and fair distribution are both significant issues in the field of economic law, it is necessary to comprehensively employ various institutions of economic law as well as of laws in other fields to gradually solve these problems. Also, it is necessary to further enhance the institutional protection of the right to economic development, to promote the realization of the right to distribution of relevant agents, and to better achieve the goals of development.

4.2 The protection of the right to distribution through the "transformation" of VAT

The direct motivation for China to introduce VAT is to deal with the negative effects of financial crises to enterprises since it is directly linked to the issue of distribution. Before the transformation of the VAT system, the right to the deduction for taxpayers as a significant right to distribution had never been comprehensively protected. In fact, the extent of the right to deduction directly influences the final tax burden and the distribution of the economic income of taxpayers. Adequately protecting the right to the deduction for taxpayers through the "transformation" of VAT would contribute to raising the capability of the distribution of taxpayers and further to solve the issue of distribution.

In practice, the transformation of VAT was first brought by academia and stakeholders and was then experimented in limited areas. Yet, until the financial

Legal protection of distribution rights 113

crisis in 2008 when the tax burden of enterprises became heavier and the distribution pressure grew, the comparatively more comprehensive "transformation" was finally realized through the amendment to the *Interim Regulation on VAT*.[20] The transformation of VAT from "productive" to "consumptive" is meaningful not only in the economic sense but also is, in essence, a "significant reformation" and an improvement in legislation. The "transformation" of VAT and the relevant improvement in legislation directly affect the distribution of interest of relevant agents and this warrants a deeper discussion.

VAT has become one of the most important taxes in China and the institutional reform of VAT would generate a huge impact on the right and interest of taxpayers and the state, and also on microeconomic activities and operation of the macro-economy. The amended *Interim Regulation on VAT* has realized the "transformation" of VAT and could solve some of the problems exposed in the past practice, while there are still many flaws. First, some of the significant issues are left unsolved including the precedency of the legislation. Second, there are some issues that fail to attract enough attention, including the issue of ideal legislation. In fact, the legislative transformation of VAT only solves part of the important issues. VAT legislation is a continuous process and requires further improvement after the "transformation".

Therefore, it is necessary to further discuss the legislative improvement of VAT and the corresponding issue of protection of the right of distribution, combining the "transformation" of VAT and the distribution of the right/obligation and interest adjustment. The following part will emphasize the idea, value, legislation precedency, and legislation technique, etc., of VAT legislation based on the importance and correlation of issues. Also, the right to deduction and the power of the agents to levy taxes will also be discussed because they are important issues of power allocation in legislation. The aim is to contribute to the better protection of the right to distribution of relevant agents.

4.2.1 The legislation idea and value orientation of VAT

4.2.1.1 The issue of legislation idea

The so-called legislation idea normally contains many aspects including the conception, ideal, and belief in legislation represented in the spirit and principle of legislation (Qicai Gao 2006).[21] Though the legislation idea can be described in a variety of ways, generally speaking, the idea of the rule of law is emphasized most frequently.

As a significantly important element to the whole construction of the taxation legal system, the VAT legislation must meet and reflect the idea of the rule of law, which is vital to the protection of the right to distribution of relevant agents. Based on the general idea of the rule of law, it is important to stress that "good" laws are indispensable to realize the governance of the state according to the law, and to reach the level of "good governance". It is only by enhancing legislation, continuously improving legislation, and increasing the quality of legislation that "good governance" can be made possible; the universality, stability, and justifiability of laws be guaranteed; and the continuity, consistency, and predictability

114   *Legal protection of distribution rights*

of the application of law be realized. The abovementioned idea of rule of law also applies to the legislation of VAT.

It can be concluded, from improving the legislation of VAT and combining the transformation of VAT that to implement the idea of rule of law, the universality, stability, and predictability of VAT legislation should especially be increased. Therefore, VAT legislation must present the basic principles of VAT and comply with relevant economic regulations and normal regulations of legislation. The characteristic of "neutrality" of VAT should be emphasized with regard to its principles. The comparative surpassing status, i.e. the fact that taxation legislation must reflect taxation principles and taxation regulations, of the VAT legal system should also be emphasized. Such a system should not be altered at will for solving temporal economic or social issues. Only such a VAT system with independence could be applied continuously and widely, and only such a system could be more stable because it reflects the basic principles and relevant regulations. And it may also contribute to the better realization of distribution justice, protecting the taxation right and interest of various taxation agents.

Principles are central. Since the initiation of the overall reform of taxation law in China from the 1980s, the power to legislate for VAT actually belongs to the State Council and its functional departments. Though the efficiency of legislation is higher, which is an advantage, shortages do exist, such as the dispersion of power to legislation and the chaos in legislation.[22] Based on economic, social, and legal reasons, from 1994 when the State Council released the *Interim Regulation on VAT*, the Department of Finance and the State Administration of Taxation had to publish numerous regulations or regulatory documents to explain and implement the stipulations of the Regulation, which increased the cost for legislation and execution and also the cost of compliance to laws for taxpayers. This is partly due to the fact that VAT is comparatively complicated and the local practical experience is insufficient, yet the lack of systematic comprehension to the principles of VAT and the absence of the idea of the rule of law are also factors partially responsible for the current situation.

In fact, the absence of the idea of the rule of law would directly affect legislation, resulting in the lack of unification, rationality, and scientific accuracy. Problems would frequently emerge and relevant agents would be tired of handling urgent issues. From long-term practice, with the occurrence of changes brought by the transformation of the economy and society, many specific VAT systems remain unchanged seriously affecting the stability of the VAT system and also the universal applicability of the system in terms of many aspects including time, space, and agent. The inconsistency in the application of the system, in turn, directly affects the fairness and the participation to the system and the protection of the distribution rights of taxpaying agents.

The legislator did not choose the consumptive VAT system in 1994 not because it did not understand the basic principles of VAT. On the contrary, it was because the government department that actually exercised the power to legislate at that time intended to solve the issue of the "overheating" of the economy. Yet after 15 years in 2009, the direct motive for the comprehensive implementation of VAT

Legal protection of distribution rights 115

transformation was not to solve the issue of the overheating of the economy, rather it was to solve the issue of economy "over-cooling" due to the global economic crisis. As the legislative body, the central government still deemed VAT transformation as an important tool to conduct macro-regulation and control and to increase domestic demand. The reflection of the basic principle of avoiding duplicate taxation of VAT is just a coincidence. The idea of the rule of law requires that VAT legislation should not change frequently with the fluctuation of economic circles. VAT should not just be an important tool to deal with the economic condition, instead, the basic principles of VAT should be reflected as the most basic and fundamental content in VAT legislation based on its reasonableness, scientific nature, and ability to better protect taxpayers' rights to distribution. Of course, to emphasize the idea of the rule of law does not indicate that the function of taxation legislation to regulate and control is not important. To regulate and control is the intrinsic function of taxation and the shift of VAT from productive to consumptive would, no doubt, encourage enterprises and increase domestic demand. However, because of the fact that the neutrality of VAT is relatively important and in its capacity as an indirect tax, it is more convenient for VAT to transfer the taxation burden. This means it is not appropriate to overestimate the function of VAT itself to regulate and control.[23]

Based on the above analysis, in terms of the legislation of VAT, the basic principles of VAT should be sufficiently manifested and the VAT legislation should be more scientific and reasonable to better exercise its intrinsic function of resource allocation. Because of the fact that the goals and principles of the legislation for each taxation are different, the legislation of one single type of tax should not bear multiple goals.[24]

Therefore, based on the idea of the rule of law in various forms of taxation legislation, the basic principles in this area should be emphasized, and such principles should constitute the foundation for the exercise of the functions of taxation in resource allocation or macro-regulation and control. Meanwhile, considering the possibility of economic fluctuation in certain areas, the space for adjustment could be reserved through "legislative authorization" (instead of "authorization to legislation") to deal with the change in the situation. This is largely beneficial to keep the seriousness and fairness of taxation law and for the steady growth of the economy.

4.2.1.2 The issue of legislative value-orientation

Directly relevant to the abovementioned idea of legislation is the value-orientation of VAT legislation, especially external values including fairness, efficiency, order, and security, which are equally important for the protection of the right to distribution of relevant agents. From the perspective of the economy, VAT as an indirect tax emphasizes more efficiency compared with direct taxes such as income tax. From the perspective of law, the VAT system, as a type of "legal system", needs to balance various values. Therefore, in VAT legislation, both the value of efficiency and the values of fairness, order, etc., need to be considered.

116 *Legal protection of distribution rights*

In fact, the value-orientation for specific systems of VAT is not entirely the same. Sometimes, one single system may contain various values which also exist in other types of taxation law systems.

For instance, from the perspective of taxation law agents, in accordance with stipulations of the VAT system, various agents in the economic chain, especially sellers and buyers, are taxpaying agents for VAT as long as they engage in "sales" or "activities equalling sales" that reflect the equal treatment to all market agents. Therefore, the value of fairness is emphasized thereby reflecting the "justice in distribution". Furthermore, VAT taxpayers are divided into normal taxpayers and small-scale taxpayers, both of which have a bearing on the efficiency of levying taxes. Meanwhile, to some extent, an equal tax burden is taken into consideration. While regarding the management of special receipts (*Fapiao*) for VAT and export tax rebate, the focus needs to be on the order. Thus, it could be concluded that value-orientations including fairness, efficiency, and order are all reflected in specific systems of VAT.

Since 2004, VAT transformation experimented first in the northeast regions and then spread to the central regions. It was actually a "semi-taxation preferential measure" to the abovementioned areas through experimenting, before the implementation of such reforms to the whole nation. Because of the fact that it has a "preferential" nature (Tifu An 2008),[25] limitations with regard to regions and industries were set, instead of following a universal application. This is mainly based on the consideration of substantial equality to coordinate the balanced development among different regions. Promoting the transformation of VAT to the whole nation represents the focus on formal fairness and, at the same time, contributes to increasing the efficiency of management.

4.2.2 The legislative precedency and technique of VAT

4.2.2.1 The issue of legislative precedency

Academia and market agents have advocated for years for the issue of legislative precedency of VAT. Since VAT is the most important tax which is largely influential on the distribution of tax interest for the state and citizens, the state should actively promote the legislation and comply with the requirement of the *Law on Legislation* and in accordance with the strict principle of statutory taxation, and therefore increase the legislative precedency of the VAT system. This has become an increasingly common consensus.

Though higher precedency does not necessarily produce a better effect, VAT is a crucially important type of tax with complicated contents and with a wide influence, with significant effect on the property rights of citizens and the taxation interest of the state. "A benign law is the precondition for good governance". To increase legislative precedence is not only important for improving the legal system construction of taxation law but it is also beneficial to solve the issue of legal compliance in the field of VAT and to better protect the right to distribution of relevant agents. Emphasizing the idea of increasing the legislative precedence for VAT is not based on narrow or dogmatic preference for certain theories and

Legal protection of distribution rights 117

systems, but instead, constitutes a judgement that considers multiple factors from the perspective of the systematization of legal system construction or the taxation rule of law system. Both functional departments of the State Council and the specific legislative bodies should continue to increase the legislative precedency of VAT and try to release a high-level *Law on VAT*.[26] In a broader sense, VAT legislation should be multi-level. In addition to the *Law on VAT* with high precedence, specific regulations and rules should be included. It is due to the fact that VAT is too complicated that the legislation with high precedency should stipulate comparatively stable and abstract rules that reflect basic principles and regulations, including basic issues such as the institution and operation system of VAT system, while regulations and rules with lower precedence should specify the relevant stipulations of the *Law on VAT* by focusing on specific rules that are close to the reality. Thus, the overall stability of the VAT system could be maintained, and at the same time, flexibility according to various situations could be realized.

4.2.2.2 The issue of legislative technique

The issues discussed above including legislative idea, legislative value-orientation, and legislative precedency all involve the right and interest to distribution by relevant agents. Besides, from the broader legislative technique, to better protect the right to distribution of relevant agents, specific institutional design issues including coordination, justifiability, compliance, and universal applicability of the legislation should be considered, combining the legislative idea and value-orientation.

First, just like with all the modern legislations, VAT legislation has to coordinate economic, social, and legal goals in specific institutional design and this should be reflected in specific articles. For instance, from the perspective of the economy, it is the efficiency and outcome of VAT legislation that need to be focused on. The influence of VAT legislation on the operation of the economy, especially the state fiscal revenue and to the citizens' individual income is important. From the perspective of the society, it is the influence of VAT legislation on social development, including social justice and social welfare, and also on social psychology and on the protection of disadvantaged groups that need to be focused on. From the perspective of law, it is the allocation of power, rights, and obligations of various agents, and the legal responsibility for violation against obligations that need to be focused on as a way of effectively protecting the taxation law rights and interests of relevant agents. All these values and goals in different aspects call for reflection on specific systems in VAT through certain legislation techniques. For these reasons, it is relevant that coordination in the legislation is considered.

In addition to the coordination or systematization of legislation, the reasonableness of legislation is equally important because it indicates, first, the reasonableness from an economic and social aspect. For instance, it indicates how to protect the right to deduction of VAT payers; whether the particularity of VAT specific receipt (*Fapiao*) should be strengthened, how to keep the continuity of the VAT

118   *Legal protection of distribution rights*

chain, how to protect the neutrality of taxation, how to balance the efficiency and fairness of taxation, etc. Second, the reasonableness on the legal aspect, i.e. how to realize an appropriate, effective, and coordinated legislation. Because of the complexity of VAT, during the 15 years after the implementation of the *Interim Regulation on Taxation* in 1994, China successively passed numerous amendments which made many of the stipulations in the *Regulation* invalid in substance. Such a circumstance is an important motivation for legislative improvement and also indicates the insufficiency of the legislative technique. Though the actual effect of quantitative departmental regulations and regulatory documents is significant, the issue of inconsistency is predominant. Therefore, it is necessary to coordinate different systems and stipulations.

To effectively protect the right to distribution of relevant agents, compliance with VAT laws and legislation needs to be emphasized. The legislation should comply with the regulations and spirit of constitutional law and the requirement of other laws such as the *Law on Legislation*, and should be in line with economic regulations and relevant principles. Therefore, VAT law should be a benign law that reflects economic regulations and scientific principles, balancing the interest of both state and citizens. Only such a law could gain universal compliance by the taxation law agents.

To this end, effective systematic arrangement is required to solve the issues of difference in agent status as well as the taxation treatment between normal taxpayers and small-scale taxpayers.[27] Also, there are other special issues that need to be resolved including the significant differences between the nominal tax rate and actual tax rate, duplicate taxation, too many preferential measures, export tax rebate, special receipt (*Fapiao*) and so on.

The above part mainly discusses, in the broad sense, the issue of legislative technique at the macro-level, while from the micro-level perspective, in the narrow sense, it discusses the legislative technique, the scientific degree of relevant concepts and terms that need to be focused on. For example, "taxable behaviour" is an important term in VAT law and, in the legislations of different states, the taxable behaviour includes behaviour associated with selling, supplying, transactions, payments, provisions, etc.[28] Closely related to these are behaviours that are deemed as sales and mixed sales. To scientifically identify and accurately state the complicated taxable behaviour contribute to the protection of the right to distribution of relevant agents.

4.2.3 The issue of the allocation of taxpayers' rights to deduction

In the field of VAT, the allocation of various substantial rights is of crucial importance because it directly affects the distribution of income of relevant agents. The taxpaying agents' rights to deduction receives the most attention because it directly involves the distribution of substantial rights and interests of both parties: the taxpayer and the tax administration. From a broad view of taxation law, clauses concerning the right to deduction by taxpayers constitute a high proportion. Unfortunately, legal scholars have not yet conducted profound research on such issue. In fact, from an economic point of view, the so-called VAT

Legal protection of distribution rights 119

transformation is a shift from "productive" to "consumptive". However, from the point of view of law, it represents the expansion of the right to deduction by taxpayers. Theoretically speaking, after the implementation of consumptive VAT, taxpayers are empowered to deduct the payable VAT with regard to fixed assets.[29]

In fact, the right to deduction directly affects the scale of the taxpaying obligation of taxpaying agents. If the VAT system fails to reflect the "neutral" nature of VAT and the requirement of no-duplicate taxation, then the taxpayer right to deduction would be affected, and further, the realization of transactions and the development of the economy would be hindered. Therefore, it is important to grant taxpayers the right to deduction with regard to the representing of taxation principles. In other words, the right to deduction should be expanded through improvements in legislation.

The expansion of the right to deduction may result in the relative decrease of the taxpaying obligation of some taxpayers contributing to the lowering of the overall tax burden of market agents, and thus affecting the relevant distribution of interests. Though VAT is an indirect tax and it is easy to transfer, the diminishing of taxpaying obligation would generate a better effect on increasing efficiency in the use of funds, thus further facilitating the transactions and the development of the economy.

As an important right of taxpayers, the allocation of the right to deduction is directly linked with the abovementioned legislative ideas and value-orientations, and the improvement of the VAT legislation should focus on such matters. Through the transformative legislation of VAT, the right of taxpayers to deductions has expanded, while it is still an important goal to further legislation and to realize sufficient protection of the right to deduction of taxpayers, according to the basic principles of VAT.

It is worth noting that the right to the deduction of VAT by taxpayers as well as exercising such a right are complicated. First, the inequality of taxpaying agents would bring the difference in the right to deduction. Normal taxpayers enjoy the "right to direct deduction", while small-scale taxpayers only enjoy the "right to indirect deduction" under certain circumstances.[30] Second, the discontinuity of the VAT chain would result in inconsistency, thereby making the right to deduction incomplete, and to some extent, affecting the taxpaying obligation of relevant agents.[31] Third, the validity of VAT specific receipts (*Fapiao*) would affect the legality of the exercise of the right to deduction, especially when the VAT specific receipt (*Fapiao*) is fake or is obtained by a trustee, or when relevant agents receive invalid receipts in good faith. These circumstances would have different impacts at different levels with regard to the right to deduction by relevant agents. At last, as a special form of right to deduction, the right to export tax rebate is a right to the deduction by taxpaying agents at a certain stage, and the form would be affected by the adjustment to the system of export tax rebate. Each aspect makes the exercise of the right to deduction of taxpaying agents extremely complicated. Therefore, in the VAT legislation, stipulations need to be made concerning the type, agents, scope, and application of the right to deduction.

In terms of allocation to the right to deduction, the determination of the amount of output tax and input tax, and the items eligible to deduction are comparatively

120 *Legal protection of distribution rights*

stable, while stipulations concerning the right to export tax rebate are dynamic, constantly changing, and fluctuating with the rate of export tax rebate. Besides, there exists disagreement concerning the reasonableness and legality of the change to the right to deduction, based on different preferences for efficiency or fairness, as well as consideration regarding the stable order of taxation law and the security of the whole economy. In realistic taxation law practice, there are differences in the exercising of rights to deduction for taxpaying agents in different stages and different fields. All these factors mean that legislation should make comprehensive considerations for the better reflection of relevant principles, thus making more prudent and reasonable configuration to the complicated right to deduction, for the better protection of the right and interests of relevant agents, and exercising the comprehensive function of VAT legal system.

4.2.4 The issue of the configuration of the power to administration of taxation levying bodies

Closely related to the configuration to the right to deduction, the configuration to the power to taxation administration of the levying bodies is equally important. The right to deduction directly relates to the taxation law right and interest of taxpayers affecting the distribution of income, while the power to administer directly relates to the distribution of national taxation interest, involving the realization of the right to taxation income of governments at different levels, and further affecting the relationship between central and local governments.

Normally, systems relevant to the power to the administration of taxation levying agents (power to administer agents that levy taxes) in the field of VAT mainly include the system of jurisdiction, the system of power of determination, and the system of the power to tax rebate. From previous VAT legislations, the stipulations and emphasis on the power to administer are relatively abundant while its limitations are relatively insignificant. Though from the perspective of public law, to stipulate more articles concerning the power to administration of levying agents is reasonable, yet without proper configuration and if it fails to establish an organic combination with the taxpaying agents, or if the internal structure of the power system of the levying agents is inappropriate, such factors would affect the performance of the VAT system.

In terms of improvements to VAT legislation, the power to jurisdiction, determination, and tax rebate particularly needs to be further specified and normalized in order to better solve the economic substance and legal judgement issues. The following part will briefly discuss the configuration issues of the power to jurisdiction and determination.

4.2.4.1 Configuration to the power of jurisdiction

Jurisdiction does not only involve the place where the taxpaying agents pay the tax, but it also has an effect on the exercise of power by the taxation levying agents, which further relates to the distribution of interests among governments at different levels and different local governments. The main point of the current configuration of power to jurisdiction is to emphasize the principle of jurisdiction in general while considering the difference in the agents. To this end, in terms of institutional design, taxpayers are divided into two categories, namely domestic transaction taxpayers and export trade taxpayers. The latter should pay tax to the local custom, meaning local custom owns the direct power to jurisdiction. Besides, the domestic transaction taxpayers are further divided into fixed unit and unfixed unit. The former is administered by its local taxation administration, while the latter by the taxation administration where the economic activities (the place of sales or labour) happen. Thus, it could be concluded that the location of the institution and where economic activities take place are significant with regard to the determination of the power of jurisdiction of levying agents. Also, since the location of the institution is more important in the legal sense and it is comparatively more stable, it is most important for the determination of the power of jurisdiction and is the basis for the final verdict.

With the improvement of VAT legislation, sufficient considerations should be made concerning the issues of how to unify the power of jurisdiction of VAT and consumption tax. For the principle of jurisdiction, especially for the emphasis on the location of institutions, it is worth considering whether the focus on levying and regulation efficiency is excessive, and whether it sacrifices relevant regions to gain fairness in taxation interests. Since VAT is shared by different levels of government, the fair distribution of VAT income involves multiple horizontal and vertical relationship, including the central and local government, developed regions, and developing regions, and relates to issues including economic development and political stability. Therefore, it is not only the efficiency of levying and regulation that should be considered in legislation; deeper issues including fairness also require consideration.

Concerning future legislation, the configuration of the power of jurisdiction regarding special transactions, i.e. how to levy VAT on e-commerce, will be tricky in terms of the power of jurisdiction. There have already been many discussions and future legislative improvement needs to gradually solve such issues.

4.2.4.2 The configuration of the power of determination

The power of determination is an important power of the levying administration in the process of tax levying and regulation. Relevant laws and regulations have made multiple stipulations concerning this.[32] For instance, in accordance with the current *Interim Regulation on VAT* and its *Implementation Rules*, if the taxpayer sells commodities or provides services at an unnatural price without a reasonable cause, or if the taxpayer engages in business operations that are not subject to VAT at the same time, but mixes both in accounting, or the taxpayer engages in mixed sales without separate accounting, the taxation administration should determine the amount of sales based on how the power of determination of taxation administrations is established.

122 *Legal protection of distribution rights*

Though the power of determination is vital for the prevention of the loss of taxation income and for the protection of the taxation interests of the state, necessary limitations should be applied to avoid the abuse of such power and the violation of the interest of taxpayers. More specific stipulations are required in legislation.

Based on current stipulations, the space for the taxation administration to exercise its discretion with regard to the power of determination will lead to many problems. Because such power directly affects the burden of taxpayers in terms of how to "determine" and how to exercise this power, more specific and operational stipulations regarding the standard, procedure, etc., should be made.

4.2.5 Summary

To effectively protect the right of distribution of relevant agents with regard to the improvement of VAT legislation, more attention should be paid to the legislative idea and value-orientation, especially the idea of the rule of law and the balance among values including fairness, efficiency, and order. Meanwhile, a legislative precedency and technique need to be raised to constitute a multi-level institutional system of VAT. The legislative technique, both in the broad and the narrow sense, should be constantly improved, on the macro and micro aspects, and the quality of legislation also needs to be improved. Coordination, reasonableness, legality, and applicability should also be enhanced while specific stipulations should be more specific. Besides, the configuration of the basic taxation right of both parties, the levying and the paying, needs to be considered in order to improve the stipulations regarding the right to deduction of the taxpayers and the power of the taxation administration to levy and regulate taxes. The configuration of the basic right or power of taxation should thoroughly reflect the abovementioned legislative ideas, value-orientation, and technique, which is substantial for solving the distribution issues inherent in VAT.

In-depth research on the above issues contributes not only to the improvement of VAT as well as other types of tax legislation but also to the protection of the right to distribution of relevant agents, thus better solving relevant distribution issues.

4.3 The consideration to distribution in the real estate tax legislation

The improvement of real estate tax legislation is an important issue that has attracted the attention of the general public. It is because the real estate tax involves not only the fluctuation of real estate price and the development of the real estate market but also to the fair distribution in the real estate tax legislation. Since real estate and the real estate tax have become significant factors affecting social distribution, it is vital to strengthen the improvement to real estate tax to prevent the distribution risk and crisis.

Though real estate is an important type of property, and property tax is an important type of tax, in the whole taxation system, the real estate tax is not a major type and relevant legislation is not considered as important for a long period of time. In recent years, with the rise of economic and social problems relevant to real estate, the real estate tax has been assigned special missions and expectations from different groups of society. Therefore, the discussion on the levying of real estate tax has become intense.

Such fierce discussion is directly relevant to real estate tax legislation. Though the contribution of real estate tax is insignificant in terms of tax revenue,[33] it covers a wide range of affairs, and the relevant legislation directly relating to the interest distribution of relevant agents is complicated. Because of this, opinions are diversified. By going back to basic issues and tracing back to the source, the direction and structure of such legislation can be clarified, reasonable distribution arrangements can be made, and improvements to real estate tax can be promoted.

Therefore, the following part intends to discuss three most basic issues that are fundamental and need to be clarified in terms of real estate tax legislation, combining the discussion on theories, institutional practice, and the experiment experience of real estate tax. In other words, we will discuss the purpose, basis, and mode of real estate tax legislation, which are directly related to the protection of the right to distribution and the balance to the distribution of interest.

4.3.1 The purpose of real estate tax legislation

The purpose or aim of legislation should first be clarified in order to enact real estate tax legislation. Influenced by the legislative technique of "Interim Regulations on Taxation" in China, the current *Interim Regulation on Real Estate Tax* does not stipulate the purpose of such legislation, yet it defines the direction and goals for the legislation in terms of the establishment, amendment, abolition, and interpretation to the real estate tax system, which is essential for systematically strengthening the construction of the real estate tax system.

Based on the multi-functions of taxation and taxation law, the purpose of real estate tax legislation especially needs to be clarified. Is the purpose of the formulation and implementation of the real estate tax system by the state to acquire tax revenue, or to strengthen macro-regulation and control? Is it to adjust social distribution, or to maintain economic stability?[34] Whatever the aim or the combination of aims is, specific analysis is needed, combined with the actual function of taxation law.

First, if the purpose of the real estate tax is to acquire fiscal revenue, then is it for the central government's revenue or local governments' revenue? And if it is the latter, will real estate tax be a major tax of local governments? Could it be a major tax that could solve the current problem of "land finance", filling the deficit of local government revenue? Consensus in terms of these issues is required.

Based on the theory of taxation power and the current binary-taxation system, the income of real estate tax, as property tax, belongs to local governments. Yet under the structure of "separation between the construction and the land", the real estate tax revenue is far less than the income generated from selling the land. If the current system and institutional restrictions are not changed, real estate tax could hardly become a major tax.[35] Meanwhile, the real estate tax system, excluding the

124 *Legal protection of distribution rights*

factor of the land, can hardly fill the deficits of the local fiscal revenue and therefore cannot solve the problem of "land finance". The experiment on real estate tax reform has already proved this.[36]

Second, if the purpose of real estate tax legislation is to strengthen macro-regulation and control, then could real estate tax become an important tool to regulate and control the operation of the economy and exercise the function to regulate and control? Originally, "property is immovable wealth". So, the regulatory function of the property tax through which to affect the economic operation is relatively indirect. Because of the limitations of property tax in regulating and controlling, China has not used real estate tax as an important tool to regulate and control. With the rapid development of the real estate industry and related industries, and with the over-heating of the real estate market, real estate tax, business tax, and land VAT have begun to act as tools to regulate and control,[37] becoming instruments regulating the real estate market.

However, macro-regulation and control is not one-dimensional. It is not only necessary when the market is over-heated and real estate prices need to be lowered, but also necessary when the market is over-cooling and needs to be activated. This reflects the "regulatory nature" that combines the active encouragement and negative limitation or prohibition thereby meeting the definition of macro-regulation and control. Besides, regulation and control using real estate tax can only function indirectly to a limited extent. Therefore, the result should not be overestimated. After all, it is not the same as administrative measures with more direct results including "limitations on purchase". Therefore, the influence of real estate tax to real estate price, or the function of regulating and controlling the real estate market, should not be overestimated or relied on.[38]

Third, if the purpose of the real estate tax is to regulate social distribution or maintain economic stability, then we must admit that the achievement of these economic or social goals is based on the fulfillment of the income goals or regulation and control goals. If real estate tax cannot effectively adjust to the income distribution of different agents and cannot reduce the gap between different types of real estate owners, then the fulfilment of the aim to adjust social distribution is difficult. If the aim of regulation and control cannot be effectively realized, then the aim to stabilize the economy is difficult to achieve. After all, among the four aims of the macro-economy, to stabilize prices (especially the real estate price) is an important factor directly impacting the stability of the macro-economy.

In conclusion, though the aim of the real estate tax is possibly (and could be) varied, the function of levying real estate tax in realizing these aims is limited and cannot be relied upon. Real estate tax is only a type of property tax and the most direct way to strengthen real estate tax is to facilitate the improvement of the taxation law system. Real estate tax legislation is only a part of the local tax legislation. To comprehensively solve the local tax problems to realize the economic and social goals, i.e. distribution, regulation, and control, etc., the real estate tax system alone is insufficient and requires close cooperation among different taxation law systems, between the taxation law system and other types of legal systems. This is the only way to facilitate the effective realization of such multiple goals.

4.3.2 The basis for real estate tax legislation

The basis for real estate tax legislation directly relates to the foundation of the legislation and the legitimacy of the system, the legislative agent, the power of legislation, the authorized legislation, and the principle of statutory taxation. The same goes for the abovementioned purpose of legislation, such issues should also be clarified before legislation.

The basis for legislation conducted by different legislative agents is different. The basis for the legislation of real estate tax is directly related to the legislative agent and the distribution of the power to legislate (i.e. the power to initiate the tax and the power to legislative amendment). Article 1 of the current *Interim Regulation on Real Estate Tax* does not specify the purpose or basis of such legislation. Though it is common for various "Interim Regulations" on taxation, it was mostly related to the legislative authorizations from the National People's Congress and its Standing Committee in the 1980s.

On September 7, 1984, the State Council presented the *Proposal for Authorizing the State Council to Reform the Industry and Commerce Taxation System and to Publish and Experiment Relevant Taxation Regulations (Draft)*[(84) State Council Letter No.126]. On September 18 of the same year, the Standing Committee of the National People's Congress passed *The Decision to Authorize the State Council to Reform the Industry and Commerce Taxation System and to Publish and Experiment Relevant Taxation Regulations and Drafts*, which mainly stipulated that

> [the National People's Congress] decides to authorize the State Council to, during the process of reforming the industry and commerce taxation system and the 'profit to taxation' for state-owned enterprises, formulate relevant taxation regulations, publish such regulations in the form of draft, and amend such regulations according to the experiences from the experiments, and propose to the Standing Committee of NATIONAL PEOPLE'S CONGRESS for approval.

This is the famous "*Decision to Authorization*" in 1984. It was made specifically for taxation legislation and it aimed to solve the "profit to taxation" reform of state-owned enterprises, industry and the commerce taxation system at the first stage of economic institution reform.[39]

At that time, the State Council, in its proposal, had already mentioned that the real estate tax would be a type of local tax,[40] therefore the Decision to Authorization in 1984 is usually deemed as the basis for the *Interim Regulation on Real Estate Tax* in 1986. Yet as a "law", the *Decision* was abolished in 2009.[41] Under such circumstances, is the basis for the *Interim Regulation on Real Estate Tax* essentially absent? Meanwhile, what will be the legislative basis for further real estate tax legislation? These questions need to be answered.

It is worth noting that after less than one year from the release of such a *Decision*, on April 10 1985, the National People's Congress passed a *Decision on Authorizing the State Council to Formulate Interim Regulations Concerning*

126 *Legal protection of distribution rights*

Economic Institution Reform and Opening-up, which extended the authorization to the whole field of reform and opening-up, instead of limiting it to taxation. Meanwhile, in terms of the form and technique of legislation, it began to emphasize on formulating "interim regulations", instead of "publishing experimental regulations in the form of drafts", which are more progressive compared to the *Decision to Authorization* in 1984.

Considering the fact that the *Decision to Authorization* in 1984 has been "covered" by the *Decision to Authorization in 1985*, and relevant taxation legislation had been completed, in 2009 the Standing Committee of the National People's Congress abolished the *Decision to Authorization* of 1984. Since the *Decision to Authorization* of 1985 is still valid, it is reasonable to conclude that the current taxation legislation by the State Council should be based on the *Decision to Authorization* of 1985. It is because the scope of this Authorization is wider including the field of taxation law amendment or taxation system reform. In addition, the *Interim Regulation on Real Estate Tax* is not marked "draft" or "experimental", indicating that this Regulation is based on the 1985 *Decision to Authorization*.

However, given that the issues involved during the process of reform and opening-up are numerous and the field involved is broad, the 1985 Authorization is virtually a "blank authorization". According to such a decision, if the real estate tax legislation or amendment to real estate tax system is deemed as part of the reformation, and if various types of events relevant to the reform should be considered as "reform", then the State Council could continuously own the power to legislate with regard to relevant events that assist in deepening reform.

Real estate relates to the lives and basic rights of citizens. So, levying a tax on real estate directly impacts the property rights of citizens. For such taxation legislation, the long-term, general, and broad authorized legislation should be replaced by legal reservation, which is required by the strict principle of statutory taxation. The *Law on Legislation* does not only stipulate affairs in Article 8 that should only be governed by laws, but Article 11 also stipulates that "if the conditions are ripe for the enactment of national law, the National People's Congress or the Standing Committee thereof shall enact a national law in a timely manner. Upon enactment of the national law", the administration should "give in the power to legislation to the legislative body".

Therefore, China should focus on the reasonableness of authorized legislation, which is numerous, and also on the issues of "blank authorization" and "authorization transfer" which violate the requirement of authorized legislation. These do not only violate the stipulations of Article 10 of the *Law on Legislation*,[42] but also harm the stability of the foundation for taxation legislation, and which leads to the deficiency of the basis making it more obvious in the field of local taxation legislation. Though the *Interim Regulation on Real Estate Tax* reserves some space for the local governments to exercise the power to legislate on taxation in terms of the determination of taxation basis,[43] there are still problems including whether the local governments should be allowed to conduct real estate tax reform experiments and to make stipulations concerning taxation elements during the process of experiments; whether the local governments should be entitled to adjust the taxpaying agents and scope of tax levying (for example, whether to levy tax on owners of non-profit self-residing houses); and whether the local governments are entitled to adjust the taxation foundation and rate (which constitutes "transfer authorization"). To strictly abide by the principle of statutory taxation, without authorization, not even the central government should or could make stipulations concerning taxation elements, let alone local governments. Thus the legislative basis for real estate tax legislation is extremely important and directly relates to the legitimacy of the legislation. In China, there is a need to focus on the issue of the legitimacy of authorized legislation and local experiments in the field of real estate tax.

To explore the change of real estate tax legislation, China has conducted real estate tax system reform experiments in Shanghai and Chongqing. Scholars have paid much attention to the issue of the legislative basis for these experiments. In fact, the difference in experiments conducted in different areas, the difference between areas under and not under such experiment, and the difference between areas with different experiments have led to the unification of the legal application and are against the principle of fair taxation in practice. Meanwhile, from the perspective of the principle of statutory taxation, scholars have put forward doubts against the legality of the real estate tax experiments claiming that the legislative basis for the experiments is lacking and the State Council cannot transfer the authorization concerning real estate tax legislation. It is fair to say that these opinions are worthy of our attention for real estate relates to the fundamental rights of citizens and the experiments concerning real estate taxation should be extremely prudent. At the very least, continuous or frequent experiments should be avoided because of the maintenance of the stability and unification of fundamental rules.[44]

4.3.3 The legislative mode for real estate tax

The real estate tax involves a wide range of affairs and a different arrangement of elements, so the allocation of legislative power would constitute different legislative modes. For such purpose, the following part will discuss the issue of legislative mode of real estate tax, mainly from the perspectives of taxpaying agents, tax levying objects, the basis for the calculation of tax, and relevant legislative agents.

4.3.3.1 The choice on the mode of taxpaying agents: for-profit or non-profit

Does real estate tax target for-profit or non-profit agents? This is a crucial choice for the mode of legislation. From the current *Interim Regulation on Real Estate Tax* in China, both for-profit and non-profit agents are taxpaying agents. However, through the system of tax-exemption, the levying only targets for-profit agents.

Based on the "theory of taxability", the precondition for taxation is the nature of income and profit. Only for-profit or operational incomes are suitable for the levying of tax. Therefore, for real estate tax, it is appropriate to distinguish

128 *Legal protection of distribution rights*

business and non-business operational real estate. To levy tax on business operational real estate is normally done without question, and is a long-term system in China. While for governmental branches, the third sector, individual residential or non-business operational real estates, for which there is no direct economic earning, the tax is exempted according to current regulations. This fits the "theory of taxability" claiming that there is "no taxation without economic earnings".[45] Besides, the understanding of real estate earnings is another issue. For instance, does it refer to the economic gains (i.e. operational profits, rent profits) resulting from owning real estate, or to other types of gains (i.e. residing, reputation) resulting from owning such real estate? Is it the realized, substantial profit, or is it potential profit?[46] These questions would all affect the legislation on real estate tax. Although many states have already levied a tax on individual self-residing real estate, the theoretical foundation or basis for taxation may differ from one another.

In general, the *Interim Regulation on Real Estate Tax* in China targets agents owning business operational real estates, and the tax on agents owning self-residing real estate is exempted. In terms of defining the nature of business operation or for-profit, it is easy when determining business operations such as house renting, while different opinions exist concerning whether leaving real estate properties idle for a long period of time is a for-profit activity. In fact, if the goals to regulate and control are not considered, it may be more appropriate to levy tax when the earning is realized. Besides, contrary to the taxation on for-profit earnings, the reasons for multiple taxation preferential measures in the real estate tax system are usually based on considerations to "non-profit" contributions.

Whether the nature of the agent is for-profit or non-profit would affect the reasonableness of the levying of real estate tax. Yet, from the fundamental or original meaning, the levying of real estate tax by the state is because the state provides protection to the ownership of the real estate, thereby guaranteeing the right of survival of citizens. Meanwhile, because real estate is considered as "immovable property" and could be a steady source for taxation, it is common for different states to levy real estate tax for a long period of time.

However, the self-residing non-profit real estate is a basic necessity. Individual residents may possess, utilize, and benefit from the real estate, yet when such real estate is for self-residence, the realization of earning (profit) is different from "income", and therefore the rate for real estate tax should not be high. It should not constitute an important source for state fiscal revenue, but rather as a source for local fiscal revenue to a certain extent.

4.3.3.2 Choice of the mode of taxation object: simple or compound

From the perspective of taxation object, legislation on real estate taxation could be divided into the mode of simple object and the mode of compound object. The former indicates the legislative mode that only levies a tax to "real estate", while the latter levies compound tax toward "real estate", "land", and so on. Relevant to these two modes is the question as to whether China should establish a simple system of "real estate tax" by improving the current system, or should it integrate other types of systems, thereby forming a unified "real estate and land tax" system? Different opinions exist concerning this issue.[47] Based on the special land system in China, even when the ownership of the land remains unchanged, there is still a need for deeper research regarding whether and how to integrate the real estate tax system and land tax system.

The choice of the mode of the taxation object directly affects the foundation of taxation and involves the right and obligation of taxpayers and the interest of the state. Choosing the mode of compound object requires that the different values of estates in different periods and areas should be considered. For that, once the value of the land is contained (especially land with decades of history), the taxation foundation would be largely different compared with the mode of simple object. The simple object mode levies tax on the real estate and the land respectively, while when levying real estate tax, the factor of land is involved. This scenario may constitute a serious duplication of taxation. Currently, there are many types of tax in the field of real estate including business tax, income tax, property tax, etc. Under the system of "separation between real estate and land", levying real estate tax instead of real estate and land tax would be much simpler.

From the dimension of time, there is another simple mode option that consists in only levying tax on real estate that is bought after the legislation of the new law, namely the increment mode or the non-retrospective mode. Correspondingly, there is another type of compound mode – levying tax also on the real estate that was bought before the release of the new law. This is often referred to as the total mode or retrospective mode.[48] The choice among the abovementioned modes also has a significant impact on the interests of taxpaying agents and on the real estate tax legislation.

Thus, it could be concluded that applying the simple or compound mode not only involves the integration of types of tax, but also the adjustment to the taxation foundation, for the integration or separation of objects directly affects the taxation foundation. Since the object is directly related to both taxpaying agents and to the taxation foundation, it is also necessary to view the issue of legislative mode from the perspective of the basis for the calculation of tax.

4.3.3.3 The choice of the mode as the basis for the calculation of tax: quantity or price

From the perspective of the basis for the calculation of tax, the choice between quantity mode or price mode would directly influence the legislation and levying of the real estate tax. Though these two modes relate to the abovementioned modes or objects, they have independent values because even if the mode of simple object is applied, there are still problems associated with the choice between the two different modes or the basis for the calculation of tax.

Generally speaking, the quantity mode emphasizes that the levying of tax should be based on the quantity, i.e. the acreage of real estate. The price mode levies tax according to the value of the real estate. The quantity of the real estate

130 *Legal protection of distribution rights*

is relatively stable, while the price is constantly changing. The choice between these two modes (or simultaneously applying both modes) in future real estate tax legislation would affect the determination of the tax foundation and the market expectation of the public.

Relatively speaking, purely calculating the tax according to quantity (i.e. the acreage) would avoid complicated evaluation[49] and frequent dynamic adjustment, making it easier and lowering the cost for levying. Under the quantity mode, for the realization of fairness or other values, different areas could, according to their specific conditions, adjust the rate or amount of the taxation, instead of adjusting to both foundation and rate of taxation. This makes it easier for the administration and taxpayers to comply with the new law. Besides, under the price mode, the economic value of the object is more emphasized. It could better reflect the thought of "taxation according to capability" and it seems fairer. Yet, if the owner has not "realized" the value of the real estate or if the price of real estate rises when the owner could not or is not willing to sell such real estate, then within a certain period, the burden borne by the owner may rise. Therefore, it is more reasonable that the owners bear such tax burden when such real estate is sought given that this matches with the income that is actually "realized".

Based on the experiments on the reform of the real estate tax system, the Chongqing mode emphasizes the value and the levying of tax on the luxurious consumption of real estate. The Shanghai mode emphasizes the amount and the acreage, and the levying of taxes on the over-consumption of real estate, These modes fall under the quantity mode. Besides, relevant to the aforementioned dimension of time, the price mode of Chongqing levies tax also on past real estate in stock. The scope of taxation includes both past and newly bought real estate. The Shanghai mode only levies a tax on newly bought, excessive real estate. The Shanghai mode is easier because it does not affect the real estate that is bought before the implementation of the system. Meanwhile, it complies with the legal principle of non-retrospective and the application of taxation law.

4.3.3.4 Choice on the mode of legislative body: parliament or government

Should the legislation of real estate tax insist on the principle of "exclusive to parliament", should it be enacted by the National People's Congress, or should it be dominated by the government, therefore, enacted by the State Council? As discussed earlier, in previous cases, the State Council is the main agent enacting the taxation legislation in China, while the National People's Congress mainly authorizes the State Council to legislate, constituting a legislative mode that is essentially dominated by the government. For that, the government normally emphasizes the administrative goals and the local governments value more local interest, meanwhile, the governments are "captured" by interest groups. According to public choice theory, sometimes the public interest of the society cannot be guaranteed, especially when the interests of governments, at different levels, conflict with each other. In fact, it is partly because of this that the goals of macro-regulation and control against real estate in China cannot be effectively realized.

Legal protection of distribution rights   131

For this reason, the mode of "exclusive to parliament" is preferable. Yet further investigation is needed concerning whether such mode could avoid the problems that would emerge under the mode of "government dominance". Besides, to understand the principle of "the local laws shall apply concerning immovable properties", in a broader sense, it could be concluded that the place of immovable property, such as real estate, is significant in determining the relevant rules, especially in terms of the evaluation of houses and land. Because of the difference in the level of economic development, the difference in real estate prices is significant. Thus, it is necessary to preserve space for local governments to exercise the legislative power in terms of taxation when determining the amount or basis for the calculation of taxation so as to better protect substantial fairness.

4.3.3.5 The choice for modes and the timing and cost for legislation

Nevertheless, when choosing the legislative mode for real estate tax, the timing and cost of legislation should not be ignored.

In terms of the timing of real estate tax legislation, it should be understood that the taxation legislation involves the interests of various agents, and strongly affects the feelings of the individual residents. Therefore, the legislation should both comply with the principle of statutory taxation and consider the requirement of the principles of fairness and appropriate tax burden. When the market agents bear a relatively heavy tax burden and a high living cost, and the living pressure is high, it is not appropriate to increase the tax burden of taxpayers. Thus, when choosing the legislation mode, it is important to consider that the tax burden generated from the non-profitable self-owned properties of residents should not be increased; rather, the simple object mode and quantity mode may be more preferable. From the perspective of "structural tax reduction" and increasing the domestic demand, the tax exemption system concerning this type of real estate should be maintained. Given that considerable taxation relating to real estate already exists in China, taxation types and burdens concerning real estate should be limited and restrained, not blindly expanded.

The consideration of the timing of legislation actually relates to the cost of such legislation. The real estate tax legislation should focus on the total cost after the legislation, including economic, social, and political costs, instead of the narrow legislation cost. Therefore, for real estate tax legislation, a comprehensive cost-benefit analysis is necessary and the aforementioned purpose of legislation should be considered. It should be clear what kind of goals could be achieved through real estate tax legislation. In practice, the total amount of real estate tax income in China is not high and the percentage is minimal and far from supporting the local fiscal demands. Meanwhile, further estimation is required to figure out to what extent and how long it will take to realize the so-called, macro-regulation and control aims, including smoothing the real estate price and repressing opportunistic investments. Besides, the levying of the real estate tax would affect the evaluation of the legitimacy of the government and may involve issues as political and social cost, which all need significant attention. After all, "a sound taxation

132 *Legal protection of distribution rights*

system is characterized by the low cost for management and implementation" (Oates 2012).[50]

4.3.4 Summary

The previous part discussed three fundamental issues concerning real estate tax legislation that directly relate to the goals, directions, foundations, institutional structure of the legislation; the legality and reasonableness of the whole legislation; and the distribution of interests among relevant agents. It further outlined the necessity to reach consensus in terms of these issues during the legislation process for real estate tax.

Among the three fundamental issues, the purpose for real estate tax legislation, and the interrelations among the institutional functions, values, and principles of real estate tax need to initially be clarified in order to guide the entire legislation process. Meanwhile, real estate tax is only one type of property tax and the function of the real estate tax system could exercise in solving various social-economic problems is limited and should not be overestimated. Though real estate tax legislation is a significant component in the whole property tax legislation, it is insufficient to resolve the multiple complicated and realistic problems, including fair distribution or decreasing the distribution gap or problems related to the real estate tax system or even the whole taxation law system.

The legislation basis as the foundation of the legislation of real estate tax directly affects the legality of such legislation. Thorough comprehension of the issues existing in the field of authorized legislation is indispensable. Since the legislation of property tax (including real estate tax) directly involves the property right of citizens, the principles of legislative power exclusive to the parliament or statutory taxation should be maintained because it is better than conducting common authorized legislation for long periods, let alone "blank" authorization or transferring authorization. This will make the foundation or the basis of the whole taxation legislation more solid.

The legislation mode for real estate tax directly affects the agent structure of the legislation and is relevant to the reasonableness of the legislation. The choice of the relevant modes with regard to agent, object, and tax foundation would especially affect the scientific accuracy and taxpayers' compliance of such legislation. As for the choice for the mode of legislative agent, it will affect the precedence of the legislation and the protection of the interests of relevant agents. Whatever legislation mode is chosen, the timing and cost of legislation should be considered for the better construction of the entire real estate tax system.

In general, as an important property tax, real estate tax directly influences the property right of citizens and the distribution of income of relevant agents. The legislation must strictly comply with the three fundamental principles of legal compliance, fairness, and efficiency. Each issue, among the three fundamental issues that are most important, requires further investigation given that this would be valuable reference and universally applicable experience for real estate tax

Legal protection of distribution rights 133

legislation and even for the whole taxation law legislation, and further, for the systematic rule of law construction.

4.4 The issue of the binary system and the protection of local fiscal revenue

The binary system of taxation is the most important system through which the central and local governments distribute fiscal revenues. However, the current binary system is commonly considered deeply problematic. In other words, though it solves the past problem of "strong branches, week trunk",[51] the local fiscal revenue is seriously affected, and significant issues including land finance, local debt, etc., subsequently emerge. Therefore, the core issue to solve the problem between central and local governments is to solve the dominant problems existing in the current binary system and effectively guaranteeing the fiscal revenue of local governments.

4.4.1 Background and problem

In terms of the deepening and breakthrough of the whole reform of the state, the reform to finance and the taxation system has always been of far-reaching significance. At present "business tax to VAT" as a major reform in the taxation area, has attracted considerable attention from all groups and the relevant issues and influences of such system change have been thoroughly understood. Yet at the same time, the research and discussion on the significantly important reform on the binary system of taxation seem relatively silent. Therefore, there is a need for further analysis and discussion from different perspectives by academia.

The binary taxation system relates to the success or failure of the reform of the tax system in China, and of the whole fiscal institution. Scholars have conducted significant research and arrived at a consensus in terms of the advantages and disadvantages of such a system,[52] laying significant foundations for continuous research on the issue of binary taxation system. In recent years, due to the attention to "land finance" and local debt risks, less attention has been paid to the improvement of the binary taxation.[53] Yet the binary taxation system is linked to wide areas meaning that unlike the implementation of "business tax to VAT", reform in this area has been slow.

That notwithstanding, this issue should be viewed from a broader perspective. As a vital component in the whole distribution system, the binary taxation system connects the distribution of fiscal and taxation power of different levels of governments and involves the "primary distribution" and "secondary distribution" of the governmental system. It directly impacts the public economy and largely affects the private economy. Therefore, the reform requires more intense design at the macro level. Otherwise, the implementation of various taxation reforms including "business tax to VAT" will surely be hindered. Besides, the improvement of the binary taxation system also links with market

134 *Legal protection of distribution rights*

reform, shifts government functions, thereby strengthening the supervision of the legislative organ and promoting the reform of the judicial system which is actively promoted by the state. Without the effective and orderly implementation of the reform of the binary taxation system, other significantly important reforms would be affected to different degrees making it difficult to realize the benefits of such reforms.

Considering this, inherent difficulties must be overcome. Approaches to the improvement of the system should be researched from different perspectives and they should target significant problems relevant to the reform of the binary taxation system. Based on the nature of the "system", it is necessary to conduct discussions and research from alegal perspective. Meanwhile, considering the fact that the binary taxation system involves numerous legal issues, it is necessary, mindful of the fact that the status of sharing tax is gaining ground in China, to bring forward the special type of "sharing binary taxation system", and to discuss an approach for the legal improvement that targets existing issues.

As a result, the following part discusses the formation and actual performance of "sharing binary taxation system", and through the analysis of the structure of relevant taxation power, the legal causation and relevant legal issues will be revealed. Furthermore, it analyzes the important issues and relevant approaches for improving the "sharing binary taxation system", and highlights the interrelations between the construction of a local taxation system and the improvement of a binary taxation system.

4.4.2 *The formation of the system and the relevant taxation power structure*

4.4.2.1 *The formation of the "sharing binary taxation system"*

Under the structure of binary taxation system, types of taxation are normally categorized as central tax, local tax, as well as sharing tax (by the central and local governments). When the binary taxation system was first introduced, most of the taxes are central and local, while the sharing tax was relatively less common. Yet with the development of the practice of binary taxation system, many local taxes later became sharing taxes making the sharing tax more prominent from the perspective of the number of types of tax and the percentage of taxable income. Such a binary taxation system could be described as a "sharing binary taxation system".

Judging from the amount of types of taxes, in the field of commodity tax, VAT and business tax have long been considered as sharing taxes (at the beginning stage of the implementation of binary taxation system, it was stipulated that for business tax, the proportion that is collectively submitted by the headquarters of banks and insurance companies belongs to the central government, and the rest belong to the local governments). In recent years, with the implementation of "business tax to VAT", more items of business tax have become sharing taxes because they are transferred into VAT. In the field of income tax, the corporate income tax and individual income tax have both become sharing taxes (corporate income tax that is collectively submitted by headquarters of banks belongs to the central government, and the rest is "shared between central and local governments"). Besides, resource tax, security transaction stamp duty, city maintenance, and construction tax have already been considered as sharing taxes. Thus, it could be concluded that the most major taxes have been categorized as sharing tax.

Judging from the taxation income, the percentage being constituted by the abovementioned sharing taxes is significant. Many taxes are major taxes that provide revenue. The taxation income brought by VAT and corporate/individual income tax constitute over 60% of the overall taxation income. From both the importance and the proportion, the sharing tax has exceeded pure central tax (i.e. consumption tax and customs) and local tax (i.e. land tax, real estate tax, deed tax, and vehicle and vessel tax) transforming sharing tax into the main form in the framework of the binary taxation system, and thus making the "sharing" characteristic prominent.

The "sharing binary taxation system" in China is not distributed equally. The portion being acquired by the central government is normally higher. For example, apart from the types of tax which directly constitute the income of the central government,[54] the distribution of VAT income is 75% for the central and 25% for the local governments. For income tax, the distribution is 60% for the central and 40% for the local governments. As for security transaction stamp duty, it is 97% for the central and 3% for the local governments. These figures indicate that the obvious characteristic is that the central revenue constitutes a higher percentage within the shared income, or in other words, the central government gains more benefits. Thus, the so-called "sharing" does not mean co-ownership, but a type of "owned by shares". Strictly speaking, "sharing tax" should be called "dividend tax".

Meanwhile, the "sharing binary taxation system" in China emphasizes the sharing between central and local governments, but, in reality, it dost not totally integrate all levels of governments given that it succeeds in "dividing the income" between central and provincial governments. Lower governments are not included, therefore the income of these governments lacks protection from the system. For these obvious flaws, economic scholars have had numerous discourses,[55] while the research conducted by legal academia is relatively insufficient. Therefore, it is quite necessary to expand the investigation from the perspective of the taxation power structure.

4.4.2.2 The taxation power structure of "sharing binary taxation system"

The legal causation and prominent characteristics of the abovementioned "sharing binary taxation system" could be described from the perspective of taxation power structure or taxation power configuration. After all, the distribution of the taxation power to legislate, levy taxes, administer, benefit, etc., has always been the core issue of the binary taxation system. Appraising the realistic distribution of powers to taxation would contribute to clarifying the causation for the shift, with bias, of a binary taxation system in China to a "sharing" system.

136   *Legal protection of distribution rights*

From the configuration of power to taxation legislation which is fundamental, China employs a centralization mode which consists in legislating the central and local tax at the state level. Sharing taxes constitute a major proportion in the overall taxation revenue, but the relevant legislative power has never been distributed to local governments. The centralization of taxation legislation would indeed contribute to the realization of state reason and goals with regard to macro-regulation and control, it would guarantee stability, and it would increase the ability of the central government to gain fiscal revenue. However, it would impact the taxation power of the local government. For this reason, China has provided the local government with limited powers to legislation concerning some taxation elements through several hidden authorizations[56] that could contribute to objectively protecting the right, the interest, and the enthusiasm of local governments.

Directly relevant to the centralization of the legislative power to taxation is the fact that, in terms of the power to levy and administer taxes, apart from central taxes, sharing taxes including VAT are mainly levied and administered by state tax administrations even though China has two sets of taxation administrative institutions, namely the state and local. This situation biases the configuration of power to tax levying and administration. Such an arrangement may contribute to the acquisition of important taxation revenue, prevent local protectionism, and effectively handle the relationship between central and local governments. Yet, with the rising number of sharing taxes, it has become more complicated for the new sharing taxes (which are originally local taxes) to be levied. In this light, both the past history and future development should be considered.[57] In addition, with the increasing of sharing taxes, which should be levied and administered by state taxation administrations, and the decreasing of numbers and proportions of local taxes, at least from the perspective of legal economics, a cost-benefit analysis should be conducted to decide whether it is necessary to keep the independent local taxation administrations.

The abovementioned taxation legislative power and the power to tax levying and administration would directly impact the power to benefit of taxation, while the component that attracts the most attention from the current binary taxation system is the distribution of the benefit of taxation income. As previously mentioned, the central government owns a bigger proportion, therefore the bias and difference are obvious. It is an important characteristic of the binary taxation system in China, and it reflects a prominent problem of the current system.

The most obvious problem brought by the above configuration to the power to taxation is the asymmetry of power-obligation or imbalance of power-duty, especially the asymmetry of the benefit to taxable income and obligation for the local governments to spend. And the lower the level of government is, the more severe the issue of asymmetry becomes. According to the original systematic arrangement, the transfer payment system could offset such a problem. However, in reality, the transfer payment system is incomplete, which intensifies the imbalance of the power-duty of the local governments. Local governments are compelled to explore other sources of income, resulting in "land finance" and local debt issues, and the increasing of fiscal, legal and political risks. In fact,

Legal protection of distribution rights 137

without the change of governmental functions, and without the reduction of the unnecessary functions of the government, these issues would constantly increase. For this reason, when improving the binary taxation system, the distribution of the power to impose taxes regarding the rights and interests of agents that affect the relationship between central and local governments must be reasonably adjusted.

4.4.3 Prominent issues and approaches to improvement of current systems

The formation of "sharing binary taxation system" in China is closely linked with the political and economic factors in specific historical periods, and with the level of the development of the rule of law. From the perspective of the law, the factors that affect the formation of such a system are multi-dimensional, the most prominent of which include norms, ideas, and principles. To expand the analysis from these three interrelated levels would not only contribute to discovering and systematically listing the prominent issues of the current system, but also to clarify the relevant approaches for the improvement of such system.

4.4.3.1 Observation on the level of norms

The binary taxation system is a vital system arrangement of the state in the field of public economy, and the system construction and function to regulate are significant. Therefore, the classification of taxes and the ownership of income among central and local governments are specifically stipulated by laws in many countries. Some even make explicit stipulations in constitutional law bringing it to the level of "economic constitution".[58]

Currently, China has not yet comprehended the binary taxation system from the level of "economic constitution". Though the binary taxation system affects the income distribution of the whole country and the relationship between state and citizen, especially the relationship between central and local government, the Constitution of China has not yet made any stipulations concerning the binary taxation system. Since 1983, China has amended the Constitution many times, however, any contents with regard to the fiscal and taxation system have not been included in the Constitution. This is partly due to the fact that the constitutional norm in China is brief and prudent, while the immature and instability of binary taxation system are also reasons resulting in such a circumstance.

When the 1982 Constitution was first released, the taxation system in China had not been instituted. It was solely through the taxation system reform in 1984 that the industry and commerce taxation system was first established. Then the taxation law reform in 1994 further improved the overall taxation system. Since of ownership of taxation income for many taxes in binary taxation system was not adjusted, and the allocation of relevant power to taxation remained unchanged, the whole taxation system is unstable and it is difficult to manage. At the same time, the decisions at the political and the economic levels have hindered the legislation on the taxation system objectively resulting in the lack of completion

138 *Legal protection of distribution rights*

of the taxation system law in China. At present, in the field of taxation system law, there is not one single law, and even a decent administrative regulation is absent. It has been over 20 years since the State Council released the *Decision on Implementing the Reform of Binary Taxation Fiscal System*, and it still is the most important regulatory document with the highest effectiveness concerning the binary taxation system. The development of a binary taxation system has broken through many stipulations of the *Decision* and therefore generates conflict in the legal basis. It is therefore necessary to pay special attention to the legality of the "sharing binary taxation system".

Considering the characteristic of constitutional norms in China and the fact that the legislation on binary taxation system is slow and insufficient, it is not realistic to incorporate stipulations concerning the binary taxation system into the Constitution. The legislation regarding the binary taxation system is lacking in China, and the current stipulations are relatively ineffective and impracticable leading to the frequent occurrence the "conflict of norms" or violations against the norms in system adjustment. For example, based on the *Notice on Printing and Distributing the Scheme on Reform to Income Tax Revenue Sharing* (Guo Fa [2001] No. 37), corporate income tax and individual income tax completely become sharing tax, which makes the *Notice* in conflict with the *Decision*. Though the *Notice* is the new regulation, the previous *Decision* is more fundamental. Another example is that the security transaction stamp duty has become a sharing tax and the proportion of the distribution has constantly changed, a phenomenon that, to a certain extent, violates the current system.[59] Without formal legislation, some system adjustments seek to establish their legal foundation by stating that the publishing is "decided by the State Council" or "with the approval of the State Council",[60] yet strictly speaking, such behaviours lack legality.

To solve these issues, one of the most important approaches towards the improvement of the current binary taxation system is to strengthen the legislation, provide a solid legal basis, and ensure that the framework for the separation of powers is legal. Meanwhile, current regulations need to be clarified and integrated to guarantee their coordination or consistency. In terms of the level of legislation, based on formal and practical needs, higher levels of scientific and systematic rules should be established. At least, legislation by the National People's Congress and its Standing Committee are indispensable (Bifeng Ye 2007).[61] This is also the internal requirement of the economic constitution.

4.4.3.2 *Review on the level of idea*

It is quite easy to find the flaws of legislation at the level of norms. To further review such legislation from the level of idea, we will find out that the existence of such issues is directly related to the lack of ideas about the rule of law. In fact, from the initial establishment of the framework of the binary taxation system to the specific expansion of the practice, the idea of the rule of law has always been lacking.

Most people understand that, originally, the binary taxation system was gradually implemented through respective negotiation between the State Council and

Legal protection of distribution rights 139

each local government. Of course, it is not appropriate to judge such actions according to the current standard. However, with the development of the rule of law of this country, especially with the establishment of the strategy of "governing the country according to laws", the practice of a binary taxation system deserves to reflect the idea and thinking of rule of law, otherwise put, the stability and predictability of the system would be insufficient, and the opportunistic activities of relevant agents will increase. In recent years, the number of sharing taxes has been changing, and the proportion of the distribution between central and local government has been adjusted, dynamically reflecting that the uncertainty of the binary taxation system in China is prominent, and this is against the idea of the rule of law. Besides, the implementation of the binary taxation system in China (especially the change in the number and proportion of sharing taxes) seems to be a process with continuous trying and experiments. However, this type of experiments, to some extent, reflects that the idea of the rule of law is insufficient. In fact, in the field of finance and taxation, not all affairs need to be "experimented". From the perspective of the uniformity of the rule of law, unnecessary "experiments" should be avoided otherwise the seriousness and compliance to taxation law would be severely affected.[62]

Because of the lack of ideas about of rule of law, the systematic thinking and design for the future development of "sharing binary taxation system" in China are still absent resulting in the prominence of uncertainty or unpredictability of the system. In fact, during the game between central and local government, the public usually cannot know what types of taxes or what proportion will be changed into sharing taxes. Also, it is difficult for the local governments to guarantee their right to taxation incomes. All these are obviously against the spirit of the rule of law.

In order to solve these abovementioned issues, during the process to improve the "sharing binary taxation system", the idea of the rule of law must be practised and the rule of law thinking needs to be emphasized. For this purpose, the overall level of rule of law of the binary taxation system must be enhanced, and the distribution of power to taxation, of taxation income, and the separation of tax types must be effectively realized through raising the quality and level of legislation, by clarifying systems and rules. With regard to the substantial aspect of the distribution of power and duty, the issue of "asymmetric structure" between central and local government concerning the distribution of power to taxation and finance must be overcome, so that the "ambiguity" of the power to taxation of local agents could be solved. The status, power, and duty of local governments under provinces needs to be clarified making them genuine agents of the binary taxation system. Therefore, the stability and predictability of binary taxation system could be raised.

According to the idea of the rule of law, the focus should be on the reasonableness and legality of the "sharing binary taxation system", and the amount of taxation by the state should be decided by the legal stipulations and level of economic development. Also, the distribution of taxable income among different levels of governments should correspond to the demand for providing public goods while the right to taxation income should match the obligation to expenses. In past years,

140 *Legal protection of distribution rights*

the State emphasized the need to "accelerate the reform to finance and taxation system, completing the system where the fiscal ability and function of central and local government could be matched".[63] However, simply emphasizing the matching between fiscal ability and function might not be proper for these two concepts do not belong to the same level and without independent configuration to the power to taxation or finance stipulated by laws, the fiscal ability through which local governments could provide public goods cannot be effectively guaranteed.

Besides, under the guidance of the idea of rule of law, the overall income structure of the state and the relevant proportions should be investigated by analyzing the interrelations between the system of distribution and system of government incomes, as well as the interrelations among affiliated systems of the binary taxation system. This could constitute the fundamental basis for the improvement of the system based on which the reasonableness of binary taxation system could be continuously increased, for the better protection of macro-regulation and control and of local development. Meanwhile, since the change of the binary taxation system is still frequent and the transfer payment system lacks legislation,[64] the issues of violation of regulations and the lack of rules should be solved through specific legislative procedure. This means the legality of the current binary taxation system could be enhanced, both formally and substantially.

4.4.3.3 Investigation on the level of principle

The abovementioned idea of the rule of law will become basic principles that are followed by binary taxation systems of different countries. These principles include the principle of statutory tax, the principle of fairness, the principle of efficiency, etc. However, from the practice of the binary taxation system in China, the fulfilment to these principles is quite insufficient.[65]

In accordance with the principle of statutory taxation, the power, the obligation, the duty of various agents along with the changes that are relevant to binary taxation system should be explicitly stipulated by the law. However, from the initial establishment to the formation of "sharing binary taxation system", each system adjustment, especially when relevant local taxes are changed into sharing tax, and the proportion of distribution between central and local governments are changed, is not decided through complete legislative procedure, let alone formal laws or administrative regulations as its basis. The reasonableness and legality are problematic, violating the basic principle of statutory tax. From the broad sense of the principle of statutory taxation, not only the power to impose taxes between state and citizen should be governed by laws, but the power to impose taxes among different levels of governments should also be strictly stipulated by laws. Therefore, the levying of taxes by both central and local government, as well as the basis for the determination of the sharing of taxation income should be governed by the law given that this could contribute to solving the issues of leadership of the administrative branch and the lack of rule of law in the "sharing binary taxation system" in China thereby facilitating the fulfilment of "governing the country according to law".

Legal protection of distribution rights 141

According to the principle of fairness, the arrangement of the binary taxation system should be reasonable, especially the distribution of power to taxation. Such power should abide by the principles of moderation and proportion, ensuring that the central and local government both gain what they deserve. Meanwhile, the expenses of different levels of government for fulfilling their functions or duties should match their incomes and should ensure that their power corresponds to their duty. Yet, under the framework of the "sharing binary taxation system" in China, the proportion that one level of government could gain usually does not match the duties it bears. This issue is more significant for the governments at the lowest level. Thus, the reasonableness and fairness of this system would naturally be doubted, and the activeness and provision of public goods of the local government would be affected. The realization of social fairness would also be affected.

According to the principle of efficiency, the implementation of a binary taxation system should contribute to boosting the efficiency of the public economy and facilitate the development of the private economy. From the perspective of fiscal federalism, each level of government is of great value, and to enhance the activeness of both central and local government through effective distribution of power to taxation, taxation types, and taxation income would increase the efficiency for the provision of public goods. Yet, without proper distribution of power and income, in which the central government benefits more, the activeness and capability of the local government would be severely affected, and the efficiency of governance and service of local governments would be decreased.

The deficiency and various negative influences of the current binary taxation system in China are directly related to the failure to strictly comply with the abovementioned three principles. Therefore, it is necessary to improve the system according to these principles. For example, though "sharing binary taxation system" solves the issue of "strong branch, weak stem", it makes the finance of some local governments difficult to operate resulting in the issue of "land finance" and local debt problems and increases the local fiscal risks. Therefore, the principles of statutory taxation and fairness should fully be upheld. Furthermore, during the process to improve the binary taxation system, various taxation rights, including the right to taxation income, should be protected. Meanwhile, the solution to the binary taxation system should be considered comprehensively by combining the amendment and improvement of the budget system, the state debt system and the transfer payment system. Principles of statutory tax and efficiency should be strictly followed to ensure the efficiency and performance of transfer payment and the issue of state debt.

4.4.4 The current binary taxation system and local taxation system construction

Under the framework of the "sharing binary taxation system", because the adjustment to taxation types and distribution proportions may generate a huge impact on local revenues, to ensure the realization of functions of local government, it is urgent to improve the local taxation system by enhancing the construction of the

142 *Legal protection of distribution rights*

local taxation system. This involves the issue of improving current laws concerning current binary taxation system.

Academia has already conducted multiple research on the types of taxes that should be categorized as a central tax and as a local tax. Most of the research emphasizes the determination of tax ownership according to the nature of such a tax. However, different to such theoretical discussion, the practice of binary taxation system in China emphasizes the categorizing of types of tax based on various standards, i.e. the amount of revenue, the industry, and the affiliation relationship of agents, which are not unified, to label many taxes as sharing tax. Given the decrease of pure local tax and the percentage of the relevant revenue, the concepts of "to establish local tax system" and "to seek for the main type of tax of local tax" have dominated discussions regarding the construction of local tax system.[66]

One major goal to strengthen the construction of a local tax system is to raise the local revenue to ensure the effective provision of local public goods. For this purpose, the sharing taxation system has already been adjusted in railway industry taxation, resource tax, etc.,[67] yet it is still far from meeting the huge local demand. Therefore, to find and strengthen the major tax of local government tax has become a significant approach to establish a local tax system. Yet from current practice, one single tax, like real property tax, could hardly bear such a burden. The increase of local taxation revenue should not only rely on multiple types of tax, but also on the rise in the proportion of distribution of sharing tax. Therefore, apart from considering local taxes, sharing taxes should also be considered in terms of local tax system construction. Coordination between the legislations on various taxes should also be considered in addition to legislation on single taxes such as real property tax, land property, etc. It is also crucial to ensure coordination between legislation on one single tax and improvement to the binary taxation system in order to determine a proper distribution proportion that local government could gain in sharing tax.

Correspondingly, during the process of "business tax to VAT", the question of ensuring local revenue has received constant attention. With the constant "expansion" of VAT and the cancellation of business tax, the distribution of VAT between central and local government should not remain at 3:1. After all, the majority of the revenue of business tax originally belongs to the local government. Besides, though land tax, real property tax, deed, etc., cannot become the main tax for local taxation authorities, in the long run, and with the changing functions of the local government, the local government cannot bear the duty to lead the economic development. Consequently, it will cease to become a major "economic agent", and with the establishment of uncorrupted government, public government, government of the rule of law, the expenses of the local government could be reduced and naturally the fiscal pressure for local government would reduce. Till then, the local government may effectively solve the issue of income by levying various immovable property taxes, by raising the distribution proportion in sharing tax, or by utilizing the legislative power empowered by law to impose a local tax. The overall construction of the local tax system would also reach a new level.

Legal protection of distribution rights 143

4.4.5 Summary

In the binary taxation system practised in China, with the expansion of the sphere of sharing tax, there has been a decrease in pure central or local tax as well as the relevant revenue, thereby creating the "sharing binary taxation system", a situation during which the sharing tax is the main part. Yet, the so-called "sharing" is not co-ownership, rather, it is a distribution according to certain proportion with the central government owning a major part of the distribution. This has resulted in a situation where the proportion of revenue does not match the duty to expense for different levels of government. The consequence is "land finance" and a debt crisis of the local government. This issue can be resolved through legal improvements to the "sharing binary taxation system".

We have to admit that the "sharing binary taxation system" once helped to solve two issues of "low proportion" that had troubled the government finance in China and impacted the enhancement of the capacity of the central government to macro-regulation and control. Yet, to comprehensively guarantee that both the central and the local government could better exercise their duties and that the relevant separation of power is reasonable and legal, the current binary taxation system needs further improvement to achieve distribution justice.

The taxation power structure analysis of "sharing binary taxation system" may contribute to determining its legal cause. Meanwhile, it would facilitate the revealing of the existing issues of norm, idea, and principle levels. In other words, the insufficiency of legislation resulting from the lack of ideas about the rule of law, failure of strict compliance to principles of statutory taxation fairness, and efficiency. To solve these problems, legal improvements to the "sharing binary taxation system" are necessary under the guidance of the idea of the rule of law. In particular, legislation should be strengthened and the level of legislation raised in order to realize "separation of tax according to regulations" and "separation of tax orderly". Besides, the distribution of power to taxation should abide by the principle of statutory tax, enhancing its predictability and stability. The principle of fairness should also be met so as to reflect the correspondence of power and obligation of government and render the separation more moderate, fair and reasonable. Also, the principle of efficiency is indispensable to better exercise the activeness of central and local governments, to raise the performance of the utilization of fiscal fund, and to promote the comprehensive development of the economy and society.

To strengthen the construction of the local tax system is closely relevant to legal improvements to the current binary taxation system. How to classify central, local, and sharing tax is relevant to the improvement of the binary taxation system and to the construction of the local tax system and local taxation revenue. Currently, every single local tax alone can hardly guarantee the local revenue; therefore, raising the proportion of the local government in sharing tax appears to be a more plausible choice. Yet, for the long run, the government function must be changed and the revenue and expense of different levels of government should be reduced. Meanwhile, a systematic design for the overall binary taxation system

144 *Legal protection of distribution rights*

and local tax system is required. The relationship between the central and local governments regarding fiscal power should be adjusted according to the law so as to promote the coordinated development of the economy, society, and the rule of law of finance and taxation.

Notes

1 Discussions concerning distribution are important in development economics, development sociology, and development politics. See Peigang Zhang and Jianhua Zhang. (2009). *Development Economics*. Beijing: Peking University Press, pp. 63–93; Jirong Yan. (2010). *Development Politics*. The 2nd Edition. Beijing: Peking University Press, pp. 47–49.

2 With the emphasis on legal problems existing during the process of development, and the change of idea in legal research, "development law" would become a rising field, and correspondingly, the right to development would become an important area in "development law". In the area of jurisprudence, issues including the right to development, law and economic development have become the basic themes of "law and development research". See Jianzong Yao. (1998). *Introduction to Research to Law and Development*. Changchun: Jilin University Press, pp. 138–144.

3 This may contribute to understanding the categorization to the right to development from the perspectives of agents, behaviour, and results. Specifically, it may help us to understand why in economic law research, the right to development of the state and citizens, individuals and groups, and the right to encourage development and the right to self-development should be distinguished.

4 Both the UN Charter in 1945 and the Declaration of Human Rights in 1948 reflect the idea of the right to development. The Declaration on Social Progress and Development in 1969 also brought forward the principles, aims, methods, and measures for development, having laid a vital foundation for the refinement of the right to development.

5 In the early 1970s, Keba M'baye, who had acted as the Supreme Justice of the Supreme Court of Senegal, brought forward the concept of "right to development" for the first time, in his speech entitled "The Right to Development as a Human Right". In 1986, the UN Congress passed many significantly important documents including The Declaration on the Right to Development, repeating that the right to development is an important component of human rights.

6 For example, Xinhe Cheng. (2001). *Sustainable Development: Theoretical Evolution and Institutional Innovation of Economic Law in China*. Academic Research, (2), p. 67; Dahong Liu. (2005). *On the Idea of Development of Economic Law: Research Paradigm based on System Theory*. Legal Forum, 20(01), p. 53.

7 The promotion to development by economic law is through a series of important norms, constituting the "economic law with the function to promote development". See Shouwen Zhang. (2008). On Economic Law with the Function to Promote Development. *Journal of Chongqing University* (Social Science Edition), 14(05), p. 97; Haitao Jiao. (2009). On the Function and Structure of Economic Law with the Function to Promote Development. *Political Science and Law*, (8), p. 77.

8 Xigen Wang. (2008). *Research on the Global Rule of Law Institution of Right to Development*. Beijing: China Social Science Press, p. 123.

9 In the past "the right to economic development of developing countries" was emphasized more, yet after the 2008 economic crisis, the recession and debt crisis in Europe and the US remind us that the right to economic development is also important for developed countries. In the new historical era, it is also worth researching whether the right to economic development should expand.

10 In the past, the right to economic development is divided into the right to individual development and to collective development from the perspective of human rights. Some scholars believe that if the agent of right to economic development is the group, then the group is the nation; when the agent is an individual, then the group means every social member. See Xigen Wang. (2002). *Basic Human Rights in Rule of Law Society: Research on Legal Institution of the Right to Development.* Beijing: People's Public Security University of China Press, pp. 88–89.

11 Joseph Stiglitz. (2011). *Freefall: America, Free Markets, and the Sinking of the World Economy.* Translated by Junqing Li. Beijing: Mechanical Industry Press, pp. 164–166.

12 For the specific discussion on such power to structural adjustment, see Shouwen Zhang. (2011). Economic Law Thinking on "Dual Adjustment". *Law Science.* (1), p. 22.

13 IMF emphasizes that the most important factor maintaining the stability of the economy is to control inflation. Besides, to reduce the deficit of the government is also important. These two aspects are directly related to the right to economic development. See Joseph Stiglitz. (2009). *Development and Development Policy.* Translated by Mo Ji. Beijing: China Finance Press, pp. 111–112.

14 Department of Finance and State Administration of Taxation. (2011). Experiment Scheme to Change Business Tax to VAT, *Finance Taxation* No. 110.

15 Chapter 32 of the *Outline of the Twelfth Five-year Plan of Civil Economic and Social Development of the PRC.*

16 The UN Congress A/Res/41/128. (1986). Article 2, Clause 3 of the *Declaration on the Right to Development.*

17 The UN Congress A/Res/41/128. (1986). Article 8, Clause 1 of the *Declaration on the Right to Development.*

18 Shouwen Zhang. (2009). The Meridian that Runs through the Research of Economic Law in China: from the Perspective of Distribution. *Politics and Law Forum,* 27(06), pp. 122–135.

19 Shouwen Zhang. (2011). Fiscal and Taxation Law Adjustment to Distribution Structure. *China Legal Science,* (5), pp. 19–31.

20 The State Council amended the *Interim Regulation on VAT* on November 5, 2008 to explicitly declare that the VAT would be transformed from productive to consumptive, and the amended Regulation came into effect on January 1, 2009 across the whole nation.

21 Qicai Gao. (2006). Modern Legislation Ideas. *Nanjing Journal of Social Sciences,* (1), pp. 85–90.

22 The regulatory documents concerning VAT are as many as hundreds, which not only affects the unification of VAT system, but also increases the complicity of the system, affecting the compliance to taxation law.

23 Though the administration of regulation and control focuses on the huge tax reduction effect resulting from VAT transformation, as well as the regulation and control effect, it is not generated from the function to regulation and control intrinsic to VAT. See Fangchun Zhao. (2006). Primary Investigation to Strengthening the Function to Macro-regulation and Control of Turnover Tax. *Modern Finance and Economics – Journal of Tianjin University of Finance and Economics,* 26(11), pp. 24–28.

24 In recent years, China has frequently hoped that a certain tax legislation could achieve the goals of distribution, regulation, and control, and even environmental protection. For instance, the vehicle and vessel tax, the real property tax legislation, etc.

25 Tifu An. (2008). Thinkings on the Promotion of VAT Transformation Reform in the Whole Country. *Fiscal Supervision,* (10), p. 3.

26 In 2004, based on the legislation scheme of the 11th Standing Committee of the National People's Congress, to stipulate specific laws on specific type of tax such as VAT has been listed as the First-category legislation items. Therefore, the *Law on VAT* will come soon which is significantly important for raising the level of legislation of VAT.

146 *Legal protection of distribution rights*

27 The small-scale taxpayers in China constitutes a large proportion in all VAT taxpayers. The difference in agent status and level of tax burden would affect many aspects. Therefore, in improving the legislation, such difference should be addressed. The "business tax to VAT" already reflected such focus. Besides, the frequent change of the actual rate brings the difference between the formal and actual rate, affecting the applicability of taxation law.

28 The specific terms to describe "supply" in VAT laws are different. Some translate it as "payment". See Xiaoqiang Yang. (2008). *China Taxation Law: Principles, Practice and Integration*. Jinan: Shandong People's Press, p. 155. Besides, some translate it as "provision". See Victor Thuronyi. (2006). *Comparative Tax Law.* Translated by Yi Ding. Beijing: Peking University Press, pp. 321. Currently, China divides the "taxable behaviour" of VAT into selling goods and providing labour.

29 Some deem that after VAT transformation, VAT is still not completely consumptive VAT. See Peiyong Gao. (2009). VAT Transformation Reform: Analysis and Prospect. *Taxation Research*, (8), pp. 36–39.

30 Small-scale taxpayers are not entitled to direct deduction, instead it is only under certain conditions can they exercise the deduction with the assistant of the taxation administration. Therefore, the right to deduction is a type of "indirect right to deduction".

31 If the tax is exempted for one stage, the deduction in the following stage would be affected. Therefore, to maintain the integrity of the deduction chain is more important.

32 For example, in the *Law on Taxation Levying Management* and its *Implementation Regulations*, as well as *Interim Regulation on VAT* and its *Implementation Regulations*, the right to determination is stipulated.

33 From the perspective of fiscal revenue, the real property tax revenue constitutes only a minor proportion in the whole taxation income. However, if the levying is extended to the field of self-residence properties, it will then generate huge impact on the distribution of personal income.

34 The real estate industry is treated as the pillar of the national economy, and it has a huge impact on various groups, therefore the change to relevant taxation institution needs to consider various factors. See Guoqiang Ma and Jing Li. (2011). Aims and Phases of Real Estate Tax Reform. *Reform*. (2), pp. 130–132.

35 Many scholars have explained from different perspectives why real estate tax cannot become a major tax and cannot become the main source for local revenue. See Zhiyong Yang. (2012). Aims of Real Estate Tax Reform from the Public Perspective. *Taxation Research*, (3), pp. 3–8.

36 The real estate institution reform experiment in Shanghai and Chongqing indicates that the taxation income generated through these two modes is both very limited, therefore real estate tax can hardly become the main tax of local tax.

37 China once tried to affect the real estate market through adjusting business tax and land VAT, through which business tax and land VAT, which had been neglected in macro-regulation and control, began to take the responsibility to affect the development of industry and to stabilize the market.

38 Some scholars believe that real estate tax can hardly adjust the income distribution effectively, and can hardly control the real estate price. See Sheng Li. (2012). Positioning of the Function of Real Estate Tax. *Taxation Research*, (3), pp. 13–16.

39 According to this decision, the State Council published six taxation regulation drafts, namely, product tax, VAT, salt tax, business tax, resource tax, and state-owned enterprise income tax. In 1993, the State Council explicitly stated that such six drafts were abolished.

40 The Department of Finance has already formulated four regulations (draft) for city maintenance and construction tax, real estate tax, land usage tax, and vehicle and vessel tax. These taxes are temporarily maintained and will be levied in the future.

Legal protection of distribution rights 147

41 This Decision to Authorization has been abolished by the *Decision concerning Abolishing some Laws* on June 27, 2009 by the Standing Committee of the National People's Congress.

42 Article 10 of the Legislation Law in China stipulates that "an enabling decision shall specify the objective and scope of the authorization" which means blank authorization is forbidden. Meanwhile, "the enabled body may not re-delegate its authority to any other body".

43 Article 3 of the *Interim Regulation on Real Estate Tax* stipulates that the provincial government is entitled to determine the amount of deduction of the remaining value of real estate, therefore local governments own the substantial power to legislation in determining the tax foundation.

44 For a relevant analysis, see Shouwen Zhang. (2000). The "Experiment Mode" of Taxation Legislation in China: Taking VAT Legislation Experiment as Example. *Law Science*, (4), pp. 61–68.

45 For a relevant analysis, see Shouwen Zhang. (2000). On the Taxability in Taxation Law. *Jurists Review*, (5), pp. 12–19.

46 For discussions on whether such income should be taxable, see Richard Posner. (1997). *Economic Analysis of Law*. Beijing: China Encyclopedia Press, pp. 635–641.

47 In the "Decision to Reform" in 2013, it has already been put forward that "the real estate tax legislation should be accelerated, and the reform should be promoted. The reform to resource tax should be reformed, and the environmental protection fee should be changed to tax". It could be concluded that the next step of tax institution construction is changed from "real estate tax" to "real estate and land tax", which is a significant change.

48 The increment mode or the non-retrospective mode could gain more support compared with total mode and retrospective mode, in terms of legal principle and social psychology. In real estate tax reform experiments this is also proved.

49 The evaluation to the basis for the calculation of tax is difficult. See Hongri Ni. (2012). Process and Suggestions for the Real Estate and Land Tax Reform. *China Taxation*, (6), pp. 56–57.

50 Wallace Oates. (2012). *Fiscal Federalism*. Translated by Fujia Lu. Shanghai: Yilin Press, p. 118.

51 "Strong branches, week trunk" is a metaphor indicating that the capability of the central government to gain fiscal revenue is weak, while that of the local government is comparatively strong. Under such distribution system, the capability to conduct macro-regulation and control, to execute, and to establish legitimacy would be affected.

52 For instance, Shangxi Liu. (2012). Advantage and Disadvantage of Binary Taxation System. *Review of Economic Research*, (7), pp. 20–28; Feizhou Zhou. (2006). 10 Years' Binary Taxation System: Institution and Influence. *Social Sciences in China*, (5), pp. 100–115; Kang Jia and Kun Yan. (2005). Mid-term and Long-term Thinkings on Improving Fiscal Institution Reform under Provincial Level. *Management World*, 21(08), pp. 33–37.

53 For instance, Xiulin Sun and Feizhou Zhou. (2013). Land Finance and Binary Taxation System: An Empirical Explanation. *Social Sciences in China*, (4), pp. 40–59; Zenghua Han. (2011). Primary Discussion on the Relationship between Binary Taxation System Reform and Debt Risk of Local Government in China. *Modern Finance and Economics*, 31(04), pp. 23–29.

54 For example, the VAT in the import belongs to the central government. The corporate income tax paid by the headquarters of banks also belongs to the central government.

55 For discussions on the solutions to relevant issues, see Kang Jia and Jingming Bai. (2002). Solving the Difficulties in County and Village Finance, and the Innovation in Fiscal Institution. *Economic Research Journal*, 37(02), pp. 3–9.

148 *Legal protection of distribution rights*

56 In business tax, stamp duty, and land usage tax systems, there are stipulations providing that provincial government could determine the rate in the relevant jurisdiction within the legal scope.

57 For instance, *The Notice to Distribute the Reform Scheme of Income Tax Revenue Sharing* published by the State Council made such considerations with regard to the adjustment in the levying body.

58 For instance, in the Constitution of the Federative Republic of Brazil, Title VI "Taxation and Budget" makes specific stipulations on the power to tax levying of federal, state, special district, and city. In addition, in Section VI "Tax Revenue Sharing", specific stipulations are made concerning the distribution of various taxation incomes.

59 Some scholars believe that the security transaction stamp duty is a tax for security transaction, instead of the traditional stamp duty. However, if it is a new type of tax, then the State Council is not entitled to levy it. This involves the issue of basis for initiating new tax. If it is traditional stamp duty, then we have to face the issue of how to understand the adjustment to the items of stamp duty and whether the local stamp duty should be transformed to a sharing tax.

60 For example, the *Reform Scheme for the Sharing of Income Tax* which came into effect on January 1, 2002 stipulates that "the State Council decides to reform the current method that divides the income tax according to the affiliation of enterprises. Instead, the corporate income tax and individual tax is shared according to a fixed proportion between the central and the local government".

61 Bifeng Ye. (2007). Attempt of Economic Constitutional Law Research: Constitutional Interpretation to the Power to Decide Binary Taxation System. *Journal of Shanghai Jiaotong University* (Social Science Edition), 15(06), pp. 5–14.

62 For a relevant analysis, see Shouwen Zhang. (2013). The "Experiment Mode" of Taxation Legislation in China: Taking VAT Legislation Experiment as Example. *Law Science*, (4), pp. 59–66.

63 The "Decision to Reform" in 2013 does not mention the matching of fiscal capability and power. Instead, it states that "the institution where the power and responsibility to expense corresponds with each other should be established", which means power and responsibility to expenses of the central government should be enhanced. National defense, foreign affairs, and national security are central affairs, while social security, construction, and maintenance of major projects are common affairs. The relationship should be cleared. Regional public affairs are local affairs. The responsibility to expense should be distributed between central and local government according to the responsibilities.

64 To solve the problem that the transfer payment system lacks legal support, the Law on Budget, amended in 2014 added clauses concerning transfer payment. However, these clauses are mostly principles and specific laws on transfer payment are needed.

65 Some scholars, from the perspective of fiscal federalism theory, deem that the "sharing" distribution of taxation power is against the principles of fairness and efficiency. See Hongyou Lu and Feng Gong. (2007). Normal Analysis to the Distribution of Power to Taxation among Governments in China. *Economic Review,* (3), pp. 56–60.

66 For relevant research, see Xiaoping Kuang and Ying Liu. (2013). Institutional Change, Power to Taxation Configuration and the Reform to Local Tax System. *Research on Financial and Economic Issues*, (3), pp. 77–81; Kang Jia. (2013). The Distribution of Power after the Reform of Fiscal Institution in China. *Reform*, (2), pp. 5–10.

67 For instance, the *Notice concerning Adjusting the Distribution of Taxation Income from Railway Transportation Corporations* stipulates that business tax, city construction and maintenance tax, and education fees paid by railway transportation corporations became local revenue, instead of central revenue. The corporate income tax is shared between central and local governments by the proportion of 60:40.

5 Legal response to distribution crises

Distribution systems within various legal systems including economic law have a huge impact on preventing distribution crises, and only by strengthening the regulation by distribution systems can the distribution risk be better prevented and solved. Once a distribution crisis happens, the response to it should strictly follow the stipulations of the law. In fact, the problems in the legal response to distribution crises are all worth researching. Taking the distribution system in economic law as an example; the following part intends to illustrate prominent problems in the process to handle a crisis, and the importance to strengthen theoretical research and system construction. Based on such efforts, the chapter illustrates how to resolve distribution risks and crises by effectively regulating taxation under the framework of "binary structure" and taking the taxation regulation in the economic law field as an example.

5.1 The economic law response to distribution crises

5.1.1 The emergence of the issue

In the present age, development is the most important theme for all countries. The development of a country must follow objective laws constantly focusing on their comprehensiveness, coordination, and sustainability to prevent and resolve various crises including distribution crises.[1] This is how the benign operation and effective development of the economy and society could be realized. Meanwhile, the development of one country needs the quantitative provision of public goods, meaning that the support of the national public economy is indispensable and economic law regulation is necessary. The level of the rule of law of economic regulation directly affects the comprehensive and coordinated development between the economy and society, influencing the realization of the welfare of the people and their human rights. It could thus be concluded that, in terms of the development of one country, it is not only vital to focus on coordination and validity but also on the interrelation between the rule of law in economy and the welfare of the people.

From the coordination and validity of development, how to prevent and solve the economic and social crisis is undoubtedly a constantly important issue. As a

150 *Legal response to distribution crises*

type of distribution crisis, the international financial or economic crisis of 2008 was a burst of multiple problems accumulated during the process of economic operation. It severely affected the development of the economy and triggered crises in the political, social, and legal fields. In the face of a crisis, it is through brave and wise action as well as comprehensive measures geared towards specific problems that the perils can be eliminated and the crises solved.

To handle the economic crisis, many countries employed numerous economic policies, among which the fiscal policy and currency policy were prominent. For instance, the employment of fiscal policy tools including budget expense, taxation reduction, national bond increase, and government procurement, makes fiscal policy the most prominent contributor in dealing with crises. The implementation of these policies, however, cannot exist without effective protection from economic law, hence the interrelation between crisis handling, economic rule of law, and the welfare of the people, etc.

In fact, based on the principle of statutory taxation, in many fields including budget, taxation, and national bond, the laws should be strictly obeyed, even during severe crises. For this reason, in the process of dealing with crises in many countries, adjustment to economic law is emphasized and economic legislation has to be improved. At the same time, because of the urgency to deal with the crisis, violations against the spirit of rule of law may also occur, thereby laying potential dangers to the construction of an economic law system. Without a timely amendment, it may transform into a crisis for the development of economic law affecting the development of economic law.

Therefore, the following section analyzes the economic policies and economic measures that China used in dealing with the crisis including a discussion of the legal issues, the issue of effective development of economic law, and emphasizing that in dealing with crisis there is a need to focus on the effective development of the economy[2] on the reasonableness and on the legality of the system arrangement for solving the crisis (especially the economic policies and relevant legislation). All of these measures to resolve the crisis are required to abide by the spirit of the law. It is solely through this that the aim of economic law is better fulfilled. Besides, dealing with the crisis would facilitate the effective development of economic law and promote the deepening of economic law research. On the other hand, the deepening of economic law research would benefit the effective development of economic law, which would contribute to the prevention and resolution of the distribution crisis.

5.1.2 *Unlocking the main economic measures dealing with the crisis*

During the process of dealing with the distribution crisis, including financial crisis and fiscal crisis, many countries widely employed fiscal measures, taxation measures, and financial measures, especially the budget and tax reduction. In China's case, the main fiscal and taxation measures dealing with the economic crisis in 2008 mainly included the budget, taxation, national bonds, government procurement, transfer payment, etc. The following section further analyzes these measures.

Legal response to distribution crises 151

1 The budget. After the emergence of the crisis, China restarted positive financial policies by increasing the budget expenses in order to solve the shortage of effective demand through the investment of government public fund. China planned to invest four trillion within two years. This attracted wide attention both at home and abroad, given that it was a direct and vital measure to deal with the crisis akin to the 700 billion dollars economic stimulus plan in the US.

2 Taxation. The taxation measures employed to deal with the crisis were numerous. Examples include 1. Tax rate adjustment. To encourage the development of the capital market, the state decreased the security transaction stamp duty to 0.1%[3] while, in order to increase taxation revenue and guide the consumption, the consumption tax rate for liquor and cigarette was increased. Besides, the state also adjusted a series of "quasi tax rate", for example, in the field of VAT, the rate for small-scale taxpayers was decreased to 3%, and at the same time, the rate for export tax rebate was increased to encourage exportation.[4] 2. Adjustment to the tax base. Consumptive VAT was applied and the items or scope for deduction adjusted for corporate income tax. At the same time, a "fee to tax" was applied to reform the sector of refined oil.[5] 3. Taxation preferential measures. A large amount of tax reduction or exemption were applied, including the exemption to interest tax for personal bank deposit.[6]

3 National bond. The national bond has long been an important measure to deal with economic fluctuation.[7] In 2007, China decided to issue a special national bond worth 1.55 trillion yuan. Besides, in the 4 trillion investment plan, a significant proportion of the fund came from the issuing of the national bond. In the process to deal with the economic crisis, the national bond played a vital role to offset the deficit[8] and to increase domestic demand.

4 Government procurement. Public procurement by the government directly affects the interest of numerous market agents and the prosperity and revival of the market. Employing the procurement measure is relevant to the rights and interests of micro-agents, and to the national interest and national economy. To a certain extent, it could exercise the function of macro-regulation and control. In government procurement, whether domestic commodity has priority (including the scale, proportion, and quantity of domestic commodity) is not only an important issue in domestic law, it also involves the coordination between international economy and laws.[9]

5 Transfer payment. Government procurement and transfer payment are both important forms of budget expenses, yet the nature and field of each are different. With regard to dealing with a crisis, apart from the government procurement directly affecting market agents, transfer payments are indispensable because they have a significant impact on the survival of residents and consumer spending. Therefore, transfer payments in the field of social security and subsidies is an important measure in dealing with crisis and in stimulating consumption. The Chinese government has invested huge amounts in social security. For example, in the field of medicine alone, the government put forward a plan to invest 850 billion yuan. Besides, the rise of the level of

152   *Legal response to distribution crises*

coordination of pension and the expansion of the social security scope both require significant investment by the state.

These measures are all direct fiscal and taxation measures. In fact, many policy tools in economic law are directly or indirectly relevant to fiscal and taxation measures. For instance, to deal with the crisis, China put forward a scheme to adjust and revive ten industries.[10] The publishing of these schemes seemed to be policy or regulation measures, yet the support by fiscal and taxation measures is important. Even currency measures need to coordinate with fiscal measures. From the above, it can be concluded that both fiscal and taxation measures are extremely important in dealing with a crisis.

The section above briefly laid out the measures employed by China. The measures can be said to be multiple and they include basic measures, such as budgetary, taxation, and assistive measures. These measures include direct economic measures and indirect economic measures integrated within other economic policies. Therefore, they require comprehensive and objective analysis and evaluation for their specific employment and the effect to solve the crisis of various economic measures.

When the principle of statutory tax is emphasized, the implementation of these economic measures requires confirmation and protection by the law. The processes to employ these measures are the same processes to implement economic law. Therefore, through the determination and implementation of these measures, the achievement of economic law system construction is presented. Meanwhile, the issues existing in economic law regulation are exposed contributing to exploring the basic approach to the future improvement of economic law systems.

5.1.3 Existing problems in the construction of the economic law system in China exposed by the crisis

Through examining the economic measures employed in order to deal with the crisis, the prominent problems existing in the construction of an economic law system in China can be found. Currently, there are many problems in the field of constructing an economic law system in China, yet the following problems are especially prominent and are worthy of our attention.

5.1.3.1 The legislation institution

The problem of the institution of economic law legislation is a problem with a long history that has been discussed frequently over the years. Still, it is a significant topic, the core of which is the allocation of legislative power. According to the strict principle of statutory taxation and the requirement of exclusiveness of the law and parliament, legislative power should mainly be exercised by the legislative body, and the government can only exercise partial legislative power through the authorization of laws or the legislative body. At the same time, it should not be the most influential owner of legislative power. Even considering the requirement

Legal response to distribution crises   153

of realistic macro-regulation and control or in dealing with urgent crises, emphasizing a "dynamic" principle of statutory taxation, the limitation of the legislative power by the government still cannot be ignored.[11] It is solely through this power that the principle of statutory taxation in economic law can keep its core content while developing with the change of the circumstance. Furthermore, this is the sole approach through which such a principle could deal with urgent issues in economic life and meet the basic requirements of the spirit of the rule of law.

Judging from the various measures employed to deal with the crisis, the government is in a prominently advantaged position with regard to economic legislative power. This is relevant to the fact that, in history, the government has owned too much legislative power, and that, in reality, the need to immediately deal with the crisis is urgent. For instance, matters including taxation reduction or exemption, adjustment to the taxation basis or rate, and amendments to taxation elements should all be conducted in accordance with the principle of statutory taxation. However, because of the dual influence of historical and realistic factors, these issues, in practice, are normally handled by the State Council or even its functional departments.

Therefore, though it is, to some extent, economically reasonable to employ these measures to handle the crisis, some measures do not comply with the spirit of the rule of law and to the stipulations of the laws. Therefore, they should not be effective in the long term and should not become a common practice. Through resolving problems with regard to the institution, clearly identifying and allocating the legislative power of relevant agents, and ensuring that the exercising of power is in accordance with the law, the development of economic law itself can be better promoted.

5.1.3.2 The exercise of power

The economic measures employed during the process of handling the crisis involve the exercise of many types of power including the power to budget, the power to adjust the budget, the power to adjust the tax base and rate, the power to decide on taxation preferential measures, the power to issue the national bond, the power to regulate and control the government procurement, the power to transfer payment, the power to issue currency, and the power to industry adjustment. The allocation of these powers has been stipulated in legislation, however, in practice, there might exist issues including exceeding the powers and abuse which may result in the insufficient, incomplete, late, or untimely exercise of power by some agents.

For example, in the abovementioned 4 trillion-yuan investment plan, the central government should increase its expense by 1.18 trillion, which makes the originally balanced budget imbalanced resulting to the sharp increase of the deficit of the central government and requiring a huge amount in the form of adjustments to the budget. From the perspective of the major investment plan or the budget adjustment, the budget should be approved by the Standing Committee of the National People's Congress according to its power to adjust budgets due

154 *Legal response to distribution crises*

to the fact that the investment plan is massive and it involves budget adjustments amounting to 1.18 trillion within a period of two years. However, the reality is that the release of the investment plan and the adjustment to the budget is decided only by the regular meeting of the State Council and without the approval of the Standing Committee of the National Congress. The problem, in terms of the exercise of power, is obvious. It is also the reason why such a 4-trillion investment plan was seriously criticized immediately after its release. In fact, if the Standing Committee could exercise its power to approve budget adjustments sufficiently and in a timely manner, such a vital measure to deal with the serious crisis would be more legalistic and would be respected.

The 4-trillion investment plan is closely linked to the exercise of power over national bond issuance. After all, when the deficit sharply increases because of the expansion of budgetary expenses, the national bond inevitably becomes an important approach to offset the deficit. As early as 2007, China decided to issue a special bond worth 1.55 trillion. Because of the large scale and the long period (which covers many years), the Standing Committee of the National People's Congress specifically discussed and approved it,[12] thereby allowing it to meet the requirement of the exercise of power to national bond issuance. Normally, according to the statutory national bond principle, all the national bonds should be approved by the national legislative bond and the government should not exceed its authority to make the decision at its own discretion because it would be against the basic spirit of constitutionalism. This endeavour would guarantee better supervision regarding whether or not the country is dealing with a crisis situation.

The 4-trillion investment plan is also closely linked with the power to procurement regulation and control. The purpose of the massive investment plan was to increase the domestic demand, adjust the economic structure, and recover the economy. An important form to realize the investment plan is government procurement. The preference of government procurement and the priority of domestically manufactured commodity would influence the sales of products in different industries, different regions, and different countries. It will also affect the recovery of the economy. Therefore, the power to procurement regulation and control is also vitally important.

The 4 trillion investment plan was only one of the measures to deal with the crisis and relieve the distribution conflicts in China. It involved many economic law issues, especially the issue of the exercise of power, which requires deeper investigation. For example, in terms of the abovementioned power to approve the adjustment budget, stipulations by the Constitution and Law on Budget are extremely clear. Yet, in practice, the power owned by the agent may be void or such agent cannot fully exercise such power. Another example is that the power to approve the issuance of national bonds should be exercised by the legislative body, and it has been exercised by the legislative body in the past. However, in the event of a crisis, the exercise of this power seems to be hindered. As for the power to procurement regulation and control, it has not been treated as a relatively independent power, therefore a macro or comprehensive mechanism is still lacking.

All these deficits are likely to generate negative effects on the crisis relief or the development of the economy.

Besides, the taxation measures employed to deal with the crisis, including the so-called structural tax reduction, VAT transformation, adjustment to consumption tax, taxation arrangement in industry adjustment, and revival scheme involve important powers in economic law including the power to approve taxation preferential measures, the power to determine the tax basis, and the power to adjust the taxation item and rate. There have already been basic stipulations concerning the exercise of these powers in relevant taxation laws, yet in terms of implementation, there are still problems. These powers, as previously mentioned, are mainly exercised by the State Council and its functional departments. Though it facilitates the timely response to newly emerging problems in the economic field, this situation is far from the requirement of the spirit of the rule of law. In addition, the crisis brings factors that would contribute to the decrease of taxation, while the demand for taxation income rises, the problem of taxation levying and administration becomes increasingly prominent. Therefore, limitations to the exercise of power to taxation levying and administration should be made.

Various agents should actively exercise these powers of economic law as their statutory function. Such agents should neither abandon nor abuse such power. The basic goals of the rule of law in the economy can only be achieved through performing their duties, complying with stipulations, being subject to supervision, coordinating with each other, and exercising the powers according to the laws.

5.1.3.3 Transparency

The degree of transparency directly influences the right to information of relevant agents. For instance, fiscal transparency affects the right of citizens and taxpayers. The transparency of economic legislation and execution has always been followed closely by the public because it is directly connected to the basic rights of relevant agents. The basic transparency in the economic field needs to be kept, both in times of crisis and non-crisis times.[13]

In reality, the transparency of economic legislation in China urgently needs to be improved. The fiscal and taxation legislation involves the basic property rights of citizens and directly affects the interest of the state, society, and individuals, which means prudence must be exercised when handling it. Fiscal and taxation legislation should reflect the coordination and balance of the interest between the state and citizens. If the fiscal and taxation legislation is understood as an "agreement", in the broad sense, between the state and citizens, then such "agreement" would be of profound influence. Therefore, it must be transparent. Specifically, the public should acquire the reason and background for such legislation. Meanwhile, the formation of the basic contents of fiscal and taxation legislation should acquire opinions widely and thoroughly coordinate the interests of different parties. It is by so doing that legislation can better reflect the will of the people and the state, and be equipped with stronger execution and operability.

156 *Legal response to distribution crises*

During the process to deal with the crisis, China also paid attention to the transparency of economic legislation. The opinions of the public were collected during the process of refined oil "fee to tax" reform. The period of opinion collection was short and it was deemed as formalism. However, even such "formalism" is vague in legislation. The amendment to interim regulations for VAT, consumption tax, and business tax was conducted without opinion collection. In other taxation legislation fields, such cryptic behaviour is also very common.[14]

The weakness in the degree of transparency for economic legislation would affect the execution of relevant laws, making the basis and performance of such execution doubtful. Meanwhile, the transparency of economic law execution is also a problem. The lack of transparency in the amount, direction, and performance of transfer payments, and the issue of overtaxing due to the crisis attracted public attention. As for some of the long-standing problems, such as the lack of transparency in budget expenses, they have been basically solved after many years' efforts.[15] Increasing the transparency of economic execution and the strength of supervision by various parties would subsequently solve many problems in the execution of economic law.

China has already implemented *The Regulation on Government Information Disclosure* which, to some extent, encourages the transparency of legislation and execution. According to this regulation, a large amount of information should be disclosed in accordance to the laws,[16] and "disclosure should be the norm and confidentiality should be the exception", which would, without any doubt, facilitate the further development of the level of rule of law.

5.1.3.4 Procedural protection

Procedural protection is indispensable to the separation of the power to legislation and the exercise of power, and also to the increase in the degree of transparency and expansion of public participation. The importance and modernity of economic law require the integration of substantial law norms and procedural law norms. Therefore, economic legislation would involve significant procedural law norms. Nonetheless, the issue of procedural protection is still prominent.

For instance, during urgent circumstances such as economic crises, there should be emergency procedures for the government to conduct regulation and control. These procedures should spell out under what circumstance such procedure should be initiated, by which agent, and which agents should be responsible for bringing forward the urgent budget expense scheme, approving, executing, scrutinizing, etc. Also, how the committee should be formed and how discussions and decision making should be conducted are issues that need procedural protection. The release of the abovementioned 4 trillion investment plan also involves the issue of procedural protection.[17] Without a clear procedure to conduct the investment, the degree of corruption would rise, seriously affecting the performance of the investment of these funds.

Besides, the exercise of power to regulation and control by various agents also requires the protection of the procedure. It is necessary for the regulation and

Legal response to distribution crises   157

control of the issuance of national bonds, the adjustment to tax foundation and rate, the determination of taxation preferential measures, and the implementation of transfer payment. Yet the implementation of macro-regulation and control still lacks open and specific procedural arrangements, resulting in the absence of legally backed comprehensive regulation and control. The economic rule of law can hardly be realized when the discretion of people instead of laws is common.

The abovementioned procedural protection directly affects economic legislation and execution, and the exercise of power to regulate and control. That means it would further affect the transparency of regulation and control. If every stage in the construction of an economic law system could be in accordance with open and specific procedures, the transparency of finance and taxation would be naturally increased. Meanwhile, relevant arrangements have to be made in terms of procedural protection due to the fact that the transparency of regulation and control directly involves the right to information, to participation and scrutiny by the public, to the protection of the constitution, and to the rights of fiscal and taxation law.

It is perceptible that procedural protection is vital for better economic legislation and execution, for the effective exercising of power to regulation and control by various agents, for increasing the transparency of regulation and control, and for protecting the rights of the public. Only through substantially increasing the level of procedural protection can the development of economic law be better promoted.

5.1.3.5 The issue of legal awareness and rule of law ideas

With the gradual improvement of the state rule of law system, the legal awareness and rule of law ideas have continued to witness significant and vital progress. However, it is also necessary to review the deficits with regard to legal awareness and rule of law ideas by combining the existing problems in the process to deal with crises.

For example, during the process to exercise various powers to regulation and control, the public should be equipped with relatively strong legal awareness. It is especially important that the staff of state institutions have a strong awareness of legal issues. Correct legal awareness is vital for the formation of the rule of law ideas. In order to realize the goals of regulation and control, it is essential to guarantee that all the actions are taken in accordance with the law and all the regulation and control are integrated into the routines of the rule of law. If the interest of the departments, regions, and the state could be unified when exercising power to regulation and control, the rights and interests of various agents could be balanced, and the overall effect of economic law regulation and control would be improved.

In conclusion, the problems concerning the construction of an economic law system also existed before the occurrence of crises. Some problems became more prominent during the process of dealing with the crises.

The distribution and law crisis could be avoided if the economic legislation system could be constantly improved, if the issue of allocation and exercise of

158 *Legal response to distribution crises*

power to regulation and control could be solved, if the degree of transparency could be constantly enhanced, if the procedural protection could be strengthened, and if the legal awareness and rule of law ideas could be increased. To sum up, the distribution crisis could be effectively solved through the strengthening of economic law regulations.

5.2 Crisis response and the development of economic law

5.2.1 *The crisis response requires the promotion to the "effective development" of economic law*

The "effective development" of economic law is a vital topic worthy of our attention.[18] As an indispensable department in the legal system of a state, economic law should gain effective development for the overall construction of the rule of law and for the response to distribution problems and crises. The previous section discussed specific problems affecting the development of economic law by combining economic measures employed to deal with crises. On such foundation, it is necessary to further clarify the internal requirement and important value of the "effective development" of economic law with a view to achieving better promotion to economic law regulation, better solutions to distribution problems with higher efficiency, and preventing and resolving distribution crises.

In terms of "effective development", the "effectiveness" on one hand emphasizes that economic law has to comply with objective regulations, the will of the people, and the spirit of the rule of law for it to be legal and valid. On the other hand, it emphasizes that the development of economic law has to focus on the entirety of economic law, considering the internal coordination within the economic law system, valuing the sustainability of economic law, and thus making the development of economic law more efficient and fruitful.

With regard to the aspect of "effective development", the "development" emphasizes not only the increase in quantity but also the rise of quality. Therefore, it is not simply that the more economic law legislation, the better; instead, the abovementioned problems should be solved, including first, the coordination of legislation institutions. The allocation of power to legislate should be coordinated and the various legislative agents should exercise their power to legislate according to the laws that would contribute to the internal harmony and unity of the economic law system. Second, the allocation of power should be harmonious and appropriate. Only when various powers, especially the power to macro-regulation and control, are allocated appropriately and the relevant agents exercise their power thoroughly and promptly can the goals of economic law be achieved. Third, the degree of transparency of economic law should be increased. Transparency reflects the communication among relevant agents and it is only through effective output and feedback, and the strengthening of systematic input, that the sustainable operation of economic law system can be realized. Fourth, procedural protection should be reinforced. Without procedural protection, the formulation and implementation of economic law would be out of order and in conflict with the norms. Meanwhile, under procedural protection, the operation of economic law

Legal response to distribution crises   159

would be more efficient and produce more beneficial results. Fifth, legal awareness should be increased and the idea of the rule of law should be strengthened. The legal awareness and the idea of the rule of law are vital to the solution to these problems, which directly affect the effective development of economic law.

Based on the internal requirements of "effective development", the achievements and deficits of the construction of economic rule of law in many aspects could be analyzed. For example, in recent years, the State Council and its functional departments have formulated a significant number of economic laws. Meanwhile, economic law norms also exist in other laws. The economic legislation is voluminous. However, the quantity of legislation does not necessarily indicate the development of economic law or the "effective development" of economic law. The legislation is not sufficiently systematic, and structure, hierarchy, function, and coordination are lacking. Legislation in high precedence is not common and some important pieces of legislation are still absent. Coordination among laws, on different levels or the same level, is not enough, and the intersection, overlapping, contradiction, and conflict among them are common. There is still ample space for the economic law system to exercise its overall function. The existence of these problems indicates that the effective development of economic law still needs to be undertaken.

Promoting the effective development of economic law is of great value in many fields including the economy and law. The effective development of economic law would contribute to the effective development of the economy, especially the publishing of macro-regulation and control measures according to the law. The effective exercise of the power to macro-regulation and control would facilitate solving distribution problems, preventing and resolving economic crises. During the process to deal with economic crisis (especially financial crisis and fiscal crisis), economic law itself would gain further development. On the other hand, the effective development of economic law itself promotes the completion and improvement of the economic law system, making the operation of economic law fit the fundamental spirit of the rule of law. Therefore, it would contribute to solving the potential crisis and realizing the goals of the rule of law.

To promote the effective development of economic law, it is crucial to highlight the relationship between the quality and quantity, and the form and essence. In terms of the relationship between quality and quantity, the quality of legislation should be increased, instead of partially emphasizing on the quantity of legislation. In terms of the form and essence, legislation should reflect the spirit of the rule of law, ensuring that economic law is legal and valid, instead of merely equipping economic legislation with the appearance of laws. If the legislation is against the spirit of the rule of law, the rise in the quantity of such legislation would only increase the negative effects.

To promote the effective development of economic law, there is a need to constantly increase the quality of legislation and the level of execution of economic law as well as its "entirety, coordination, sustainability".[19] The whole picture of economic law should be considered regarding its development. It is only based on the entirety of the economic law system that the issue of coordination could

160   *Legal response to distribution crises*

be better handled. Also, it is the sole approach likely to achieve the completion of main laws. Under such circumstances, different legislations would be mutually complementary instead of being in conflict with each other, thereby forming a joint force. Meanwhile, it is by reflecting the spirit of the rule of law, the demand of the people, and objective economic regulations that economic law can be sustainable and can gain effective development.

5.2.2 Crisis response calls for the deepening of economic law theories

As mentioned earlier, it is only through continuously solving distribution problems, and preventing and resolving distribution crisis that the coordinated and effective development of the economy and society can be better promoted, thereby making sure that all the economic measures employed during the process to deal with the crisis are protected under economic law. In fact, the effective development of economic law and the increase of the level of economic rule of law would contribute to preventing and resolving economic crisis as well as further deepen research in economic law theory. Meanwhile, the deepening of economic law theory research would further facilitate the effective development of economic law, raise the level of economic rule of law, and help to better prevent and resolve economic crises. Given their relevance to crisis response, it is necessary to strengthen the following theoretical research:

5.2.2.1 Risk prevention and control theory

From the perspective of risk prevention and control, economic law is an important law to prevent and control risks. The reason why economic law could prevent and control the risks in the functioning of the economy and society is that it has specific functions, and the department laws in economic law are all capable of preventing and controlling risks. For example, in the economic law system, finance and taxation law could properly distribute wealth among states, corporations, and individuals by ensuring the effective distribution of income, thus protecting the economy and promoting social justice. Through the effective allocation of resources and through effective macro-regulation and control, the benign operation of the economy and society would be encouraged. By balancing fairness and efficiency, basic human rights could be protected, the development of various agents including corporations could be enhanced, and the coordinated and stable development of the economy and society would be realized. This would also prevent and resolve risks including economic and social risks.

Besides, not only the entirety of finance and taxation law has the function to prevent and control the relevant risks during the operation process of economy; specific finance and taxation law systems could also prevent finance and taxation risks, including budget risk, taxation risk, state bond risk, procurement risk, and transfer payment risk.

In fact, just as private economy agents, the state, as the agent of the public economy, also needs to prevent risks and crises. The financial risk of the state is

Legal response to distribution crises 161

directly connected with an oversized budget expense, debt burden, tax burden, or insufficiency of taxation income. Therefore, it is vitally important to resolve the issues including the deficit, the reliance on debt, the unfairness of the tax burden, and the unsustainability of tax levying. Regarding system construction, transfer payment and the scale of government procurement, along with the scale of taxation and bond issuance should especially be considered. Through the optimization to taxation law, state bond law, charging law, etc., a benign "give and take" or "obtain and use" relationship can be established.

Based on the abovementioned theoretical understanding and realistic requirements, combining the amendment to the *Law on Budget* and the formulation of the *Law on National Bond*, and combining the release of many taxation laws, it is necessary to further strengthen systems, including budget balancing, budget adjustment, deficit and scale of debt control, etc., so that the drafting, reviewing, and execution of the budget and the issuance and collection of national bonds could be more complete. Besides, due to the fact that the endeavour to levy tax and the fairness of tax affect tax levying by the state, the compliance of citizens, and the taxation risks that may be incurred, it is necessary to further emphasize the reasonableness and the legality of the taxation law system while focusing on the theory of taxability in taxation law.

5.2.2.2 Information revealing theory

As it is widely known, the current risk to society is directly relevant to the insufficiency and uncertainty of information. To resolve the risks brought by the uncertainty of information, the system of information revealing or information publication needs to be established in many legal fields in order to protect the right to information of various agents, including the right to information of taxpayers, investors, consumers, and administrators. Therefore, the information revealing theory should be studied for crisis response and relevant economic law regulatory issues.[20]

Information revealing in economic law includes the release of information by the state to citizens and information reporting by citizens to the state. The core is the issue of the right to information of the state or citizens. Normally, it is the right of citizens that is emphasized. For instance, in the field of budgetary law, the right to information concerning the budget has always been discussed. Besides, in terms of the right of taxpayers, normally the right to information by taxpayers is treated as a fundamental right.[21] The right to information concerning the issuance and use of national bonds, transfer payment, government procurement, and government charge is equally worthy of our attention.

Apart from the abovementioned rights, to enhance the administration, the state also needs to acquire relevant information. That is why in many systems, the right to information of the state is also stipulated. Agents specifically, including enterprises and individuals, should report their economic activities, income, and other relevant conditions so that the state may make judgements concerning taxation, fee-charging, bond issuance, etc. At the same time, there is a need to make arrangements regarding fiscal expenses.

162   *Legal response to distribution crises*

It is worth noting that the stipulations to the right to information of citizens are usually made from the perspective of rights, while the right to information of the state is, in many cases, stipulated from the perspective of the obligation to provide information to the citizens. For example, the right to information of taxpayers in current taxation law in China mainly includes the right to know the taxation laws and regulations and taxpaying procedures. Specifically, it includes the length of time, approach, stages and required documents, the determination of the taxable amount and the legal basis, facts and calculation methods for taxation administration decisions, ways of relief when a dispute arises and the relevant requirements, etc.

Corresponding to the right to information is the obligation to provide information of taxpayers, including the obligation to provide information in a timely manner. In other words, apart from providing information through taxation registration and taxpaying reports, the taxpayers should also provide other information including the change of business operation status, disasters, etc. Besides, taxpayers should also report other taxation-related information, including the information concerning transfer pricing, illustrations about the conditions of taxation arrears to mortgagees and pledge holders, reports about the merging or separation of enterprises, statements about all bank accounts, reports about the disposal of property, etc.

In fact, the right to information of all agents cannot be realized without complete information revealing. For this reason, it is necessary to strengthen the study to the substantial system and procedural system concerning information revealing in economic law as a way of comparatively refining systematic information revealing theory.

5.2.2.3 Change of circumstances theory

The financial crisis or economic crisis resulted in major changes of circumstances which not only severely affected the performance of private contracts, but also made the originally balanced income and expense imbalanced. This means the crisis had an impact on the implementation of the state budget. Therefore, the practice of legal theory concerning a change of circumstances is not limited in private law areas. Efforts should be made to clarify the employment of such theory in public law areas including economic law and to refine the change of circumstances theory in economic law fields.

The economic law problems brought forward by the change of circumstances are, in many aspects including the budget adjustment, a change of budget expense priority, minor adjustments to the taxation system, the issuance of special national bonds, the improvement of regulation and control procedures, etc. These problems are relevant to many important fields of economic law and form essential content to economic law system construction that requires further and extensive research.

To research the change of circumstances theory and system in the economic law field, many factors need to be considered. These factors include the scale

Legal response to distribution crises   163

of the circumstances, the unpredictability of the change, and the scope of comprehensive circumstances. They also include the elements of change of circumstances that should be listed based on the self-sufficient nature of economic law that the substantial law is closely linked with procedural law, and the problems such as the changing procedures, adjustment to rights and obligations, and the distribution of duties, so that the economic law theory can be further completed.

5.2.3 Summary

During the process of crisis response, the economic measures indeed have special importance. However, protection by economic law is indispensable for the exercise of its function. For such purpose, the issues of legislative institution, exercise of power, transparency, procedural protection, legal awareness, and the idea of the rule of law should be handled well and the reasonableness and legality of the economic law system should be constantly improved. It is by so doing that the effective development of economic law can be promoted and the relevant problems in economic, social, political, and legal areas solved, and various crises, both existing and potential, prevented and resolved.

Crisis response is closely connected with the effective development of economic law. On the one hand, the crisis provides a vital opportunity for the effective development of economic law, while on the other hand, the effective development of economic law provides significant legal protection for the effective development of the economy and society, contributing to the prevention and resolution of crises including distribution crisis.

Both crisis response and effective development of economic law require the deepening of economic law theories. Meanwhile, the deepening of research to economic law theory would further promote the level of economic rule of law, facilitating the effective development of economic law and the resolution of distribution problems. Therefore, it would contribute to the prevention and resolution of distribution risk and crisis. From the interrelation between the effective development of economic law and economic law theory research, there is a need to reinforce research in risk prevention and control theory, information revealing theory, and changes of circumstance theory, given that these have dire consequences vis-à-vis the promotion of comprehensive development of economic law theory.

In general, by analyzing the economic measures and legal problems aimed at solving the economic crisis, we can deeply understand the necessity of strengthening economic rule of law and promoting the effective development of economic law to better solve distribution problems and encourage the benign operation of the economy and society. Meanwhile, the effective development of crisis response and economic law demands the deepening of economic law theory research, which would facilitate the guidance capability of economic law theory and result in better solutions to the crisis through economic law regulations.

164   *Legal response to distribution crises*

5.3 The distribution regulation to "binary differentiation"

As is mentioned before, in terms of crisis response, China, as well as many other states, employs measures of macro-regulation and control to prevent and solve distribution crises by formulating the regulation and control in the field of distribution ("distribution regulation and control" in short). Theoretically, such regulation and control are also regulatory, meaning, in the broad sense, they constitute regulations. It is especially important to emphasize distribution regulation and control as a way to effectively solve the problem of "binary differentiation", which is the only way to better prevent and solve distribution crises.

From the past experience of relevant states, the development of the economy and society in China has reached a fundamentally important historical period, and the conflicts in economic and social life have become increasingly prominent. Macro-regulation and control and market regulation have been increasingly important. In such circumstances, issues that are worth discussing include how to reveal the prominent distribution problems existing in economic and social areas and to solve such problems through distribution regulation and control; how to prevent and solve distribution risks and crises; and what problems should be solved in terms of distribution regulation and control.

Academia and the industry have had a serious debate over fiscal, taxation, and financial regulation and control, and many opinions have already been shared widely. Yet, regarding the distribution problems that various regulations and control measures aim to solve, new perspectives should be taken. In particular, new problems in terms of distribution regulation and control call for our attention.[22] For such purpose, the following part intends to bring forward and discuss the issue of "binary differentiation" existing in the field of distribution, and to further reveal relevant differentiation in distribution, thereby laying the foundations for the solving of distribution regulation and control problems.

5.3.1 "Binary differentiation" is a prominent problem in the economic field in China

There are many difficult problems existing in the process of the development of a market economy in China, among which "binary differentiation" is without any doubt an extremely prominent problem. "Binary differentiation" results in the formation of a series of binary structures and it further intensifies the "non-balance" in China's economy.

The so-called "binary differentiation" emphasizes that during the development process of the economy and society, in some economic areas there exist two poles that are distinctly opposite to each other and they gradually move apart from each other. The extreme presence of "binary differentiation" is "polarization", which is the most serious problem in the non-balance structure and which has the tendency to damage harmony. For instance, in the field of social distribution, there exists a polarization between two groups, with high and low income respectively. The polarization of income is an issue that attracts the attention of the public. If such a problem cannot be properly solved, higher distribution risks or crises will emerge. Another example is that in terms of the economic scale, there exists polarization between large and medium-small size enterprises, for the income and capability of distribution vary enormously.[23] Among these polarizations, in general, people comparatively focus more on the polarization between advantaged and disadvantaged agents in terms of the economy, the developed areas and left-behind areas in terms of space, and the sunrise and sunset industries. The issues resulting from these "polarizations" are exactly the most difficult issues during the development process of the market economy in China. Meanwhile, they are also the problems that affect the benign operation and coordinated development of the economy and society in China.

The "binary differentiation" reflects the distinct in the economic capability of the relevant economic agent which causes the gap in distribution. Such differentiation is not only an economic issue but also, to some extent, a social and even political problem, directly affecting the realization of basic human rights and the stability of the state. Therefore, the issue of binary differentiation emerging from the developing process of the market economy in China must be seriously addressed.

Various "binary differentiations" in economic areas would form all kinds of binary structures, for example, urban and rural areas, developed and underdeveloped areas, public and private sectors, groups with high and low income, etc. These issues are all related to distribution issues. The binary structure of the urban and rural areas attracted the interest of Arthur Lewis, the representative of development economics, as early as in the 1960s.[24] Today, the binary structure of urban and rural areas and the related distribution problems are widely known, and the state is focusing on the solution to such problems.

Besides, similar to the binary structure of urban and rural areas, there also exists the binary structure of developed and underdeveloped areas, resulting from the imbalance of local economic development, which creates a series of economic, societal, and constitutional problems.

Furthermore, the issue of the gap between the rich and poor, which is within the binary structure of people with high and low income, and the relevant economic and social fairness are fiercely discussed topics. These problems reflect the imbalance and incoordination in the development of the market economy in China and constitute a direct reflection of distribution imbalance. In general, the binary structures resulting from various "binary differentiation" are all related to distribution problems. The relevant problems reflect the non-harmonious factors in the development of the market economy in China, and the lack of coordination in the operation of economy and society, where distribution risks and crises exist, thereby affecting the sustainability of the development of the economy and society. Therefore, from the perspective of preventing and solving distribution crises, promoting the stable development of economy, and establishing harmonious society, the issue of "binary differentiation" has to be solved, especially the distribution differentiation or distribution gap as well as the problem of unfair distribution.

166 *Legal response to distribution crises*

5.3.2 *Distribution regulation and control are indispensable in resolving "binary differentiation"*

The "binary differentiation" problems in the economic area are the reflection of the imbalance of economic development. To solve the issue of imbalance, the effective distribution regulation and control is indispensable, while within the distribution regulation and control, the taxation regulation and control is, without any doubt, crucially important. For that, the taxation regulation and control could be applied to a wide sphere and, because it is direct and effective, it is indispensable in solving various binary differentiation issues. These factors make it significantly representative of comprehensive distribution regulation and control.[25] The following section will illustrate this through several examples.

First, in terms of the binary structure of economic space, during the process to solve the binary structure between urban and rural areas, how to promote the development of agriculture, the rise of farmer income, and the construction of villages are the vital tasks for taxation regulation and control. Considering these elements, as early as in 2006, the state decided to abolish the agricultural tax which had some effects on increasing the income of farmers. Yet it was far from enough. There are many factors hindering the ability to increase the income of farmers many of which cannot be resolved through taxation. At least, the coordination of other systems is required. Therefore, taxation regulation and control should combine with other types of regulations and control measures, and only through such coordination and joint efforts could the relevant problems be better solved.

Besides, in terms of promoting the development of agriculture and the construction of villages, with regard to distribution regulation and control, the system construction is insufficient though there are already some laws and regulations. In fact, the following relevant questions are all worthy of research:how the development of agriculture should coordinate with other industries, how the industry could repay agriculture, how to effectively solve the "binary differentiation" between traditional and new-emerging industries, how to prevent the decline of the fundamental status of agriculture, and what distribution regulation and control could do in terms of these aspects, etc. It is only through the strengthening of relevant institution construction that the issue of binary structure between urban and rural area can be better solved.[26]

Second, consistent to the issue of binary structure between urban and rural areas, the solution to the binary structure between economically developed and left-behind areas (or "binary structure between the east and west") also requires taxation regulation and control. To some extent, the taxation preferential measures contributed to the current status of the developed areas, while the backwardness of some regions, apart from the differences in natural resource, is partly due to the lack of taxation preferential measures, etc. Therefore, in order to achieve coordinated development among regional economies, China implemented many strategies including the "West Development Program", the "Northeast Revitalization",

Legal response to distribution crises 167

and the "Rise of Central China". Taxation regulation and control and taxation preferential measures are both indispensable during the implementation process of each strategy.

Third, in terms of social distribution, economic development brings to light the problem of unfairness in social distribution caused mainly by primary distribution of the market. It was once expected that secondary distribution by taxation regulation and control could achieve distribution justice. This caused a serious debate regarding the amendment of the *Law on Individual Income Tax*. Though this law has been amended many times it is still far from the expectations of the people in terms of the strength of regulation and control and the function. Therefore, since the issue of unfairness in social distribution still exists, the voices advocating for taxation law reform and other reforms to strengthen the capability to regulation and control of the taxation law would not cease.[27]

Fourth, in terms of regulation and control in specific industry or market, taxation regulation and control are definitely indispensable. Without the development of certain industries such as real estate and energy, economic problems or even economic crisis may emerge. Similarly, the security market, insurance market, and land market are all vital areas that may bring prominent economic problems. Appropriate and effective taxation regulation and control should be conducted according to the specific conditions of these industries and markets.

It could be concluded that taxation regulation and control is vital both from the perspective of economic agents and regions as well as the relevant market and industry. It is an important measure that could be widely applied and could have direct effects. Therefore, when the state tries to solve various "binary differentiations", especially in solving distribution problems or responding to distribution crises, based on the functions and analyses of benefit and loss of various regulation and control measures, the taxation regulation and control usually is directly chosen.

5.3.3 Positioning to taxation regulation and control should be appropriate

In recent years, when facing prominent problems in economic life, taxation is usually the first measure that is employed. The state utilizes the leverage of taxation to solve the "mountain of problems" when the economy is either over-heated or over-cooling and requires macro-regulation and control. Taxation is also useful during the implementation process of the "West Development Program" or "Northeast Revitalization", and either in the capital market, real estate market, or other important markets to eliminate obstacles that block the development of the economy and society.

Such an approach has existed for a long time and it is sometimes strengthened. For instance, in order to solve the various "binary differentiation" problems emerging during the development process of the economy and society in China and to eliminate the unfairness in social distribution in an attempt to create a "harmonious society", the *Law on Individual Income Tax* was amended.[28] When faced with the unfair treatment of domestic and foreign-invested enterprises, the

168 *Legal response to distribution crises*

people expressed the hope to unify the laws of corporate income tax on domestic and foreign enterprises.[29] When faced with problems of imbalance in the regional economic development, people hoped to solve such problem through tax reform, therefore the VAT transformation experiment, which was later expanded, emerged.[30] Even regarding the regulation and control of the real estate market, it is the taxation measure that was applied.[31] As for the capital market that is directly related to the distribution of wealth, the adjustment through taxation is indispensable. Taxation and taxation law play a fundamental role in the development of the economy and society in China today. "To adjust the taxation" has already been a consensus and "prohibition through levying taxation" and "promoting through tax reduction or exemption" have been widely used. Under such circumstances, it is necessary to deeply investigate taxation regulation and control, and the appropriate positioning to it.

Based on such thoughts, the government and the public sometimes expect that taxation measures will always bring positive results;[32] this makes taxation and taxation law bear heavy expectations and hope. The significance of taxation and taxation law to the state and citizens is increasingly known by the people who believe that their implementation could resolve any problem in real life including the tricky distribution issues. However, is this really the case? Judging from taxation adjustments, in order to promote the development of the capital market in China, the number of taxation adjustments that are beneficial to the capital market is high. They include the adjustment to security transaction stamp duty and the taxation reductions and exemptions to equity exchanges. Unfortunately, all these measures have failed to bring the capital market out of the low valley.

In fact, just the same with other types of distribution regulation and control measures, taxation regulation and control is just an external force, an external factor that could only exercise limited influence. Its limitations are noteworthy, meaning that an appropriate positioning to taxation regulation and control should be done. On one hand, the positive functions of taxation regulation and control should be admitted, and on the other hand, performance should not be exaggerated. Taxation and taxation law regulation and control, as external factors and forces, usually cannot solve the fundamental problems in each area.[33] Based on the current situation where the function of taxation law is overestimated, an appropriate positioning to the taxation regulation and control targeting on "binary differentiation" should also be done as a means of providing a better solution to distribution issues and a better response to distribution crisis.

5.3.4 Basis for distribution regulation and control

There should be a legal basis for any distribution regulation and control measure, which is the only way to promote the solution to distribution problems. Taking taxation regulation and control as a highly representative example, the specific taxation regulation and control measure in order to solve distribution problems is varied. However, the basis is mainly taxation policies and laws. Generally speaking, taxation policies are more flexible, are distinct from each other, and are easy to change, while taxation laws are principles, are more universally applicable and stable, meaning that only the stable and effective taxation policies and policy tools can be absorbed by the taxation laws and become vital elements of taxation law. In this sense, taxation policies and taxation laws are both internally consistent and different.

Taxation policy is a vital precondition for taxation legislation, while taxation legislation is vital in protecting the effective implementation of taxation policy. Taxation policy targets emergencies. It could be applied in order to solve the prominent issue of "binary differentiation" in economic and social life and the response to distribution crisis. Taxation law should be long term and it should be made to establish a long-term institution, which is fundamental for the constant solving of "binary differentiation" problems and preventing the occurrence of distribution crisis. In accordance with the principle of statutory taxation, many taxation policies, especially the policies that are relevant to the substantial rights and obligations of taxpayers, should be promoted to law. Therefore, taxation regulation and control must be based on taxation laws, both in terms of substantial content of taxation regulation and control and of the relevant procedure. It is very important to clarify such relationships to guarantee the effects of taxation regulation and control.

Whether taxation regulation and control could achieve actual effects relies on the legality of the basis for taxation regulation and control and the reasonableness of taxation policy and laws. Therefore, only taxation regulation and control with reasonableness and legality can gain effectiveness and the support of citizens and acquire higher legality and effective compliance by the people.

However, despite all these factors, based on the consideration to maximize the interest, market agents who are specific taxpayers may conduct various games including evading taxes. As a consequence, when emphasizing the legality and effectiveness of the basis for taxation regulation and control, the non-cooperative game of market agents should also be considered.

Judging from reality, in some areas, "binary differentiation" problems such as the expansion of the distribution gap are still worsening, sometimes even distribution regulation and control is applied and relevant problems are not solved fully. For this reason, it is necessary to consider whether such problems could be solved through distribution regulation and control, identifying the factors or reasons that hinder the resolution of these problems, and which limitations of regulation and control are worthy of note.

5.4 The actual performance and legitimacy of distribution regulation and control

5.4.1 Reasons affecting the performance of distribution regulation and control

The limitations of distribution regulation and control affect actual performance. The reasons could be divided into internal and external factors. The limitations of the various distribution regulation and control measures themselves are the internal factors, while the deficit of the distribution system of the state, the lack

170 *Legal response to distribution crises*

of legal awareness, and games among various agents also largely affect the actual performance of distribution regulation and control. These constitute the external factors affecting the performance of distribution regulation and control. Both types of reasons should be researched profoundly.

The following part takes taxation regulation and control as an example to illustrate that for the limitations of taxation regulation and control measures, increasing consensus has been achieved through previous research, and if the external factors affecting the actual performance of taxation regulation and control are integrated, then the reasons affecting the actual performance of taxation regulation and control could be concluded as the following aspects.

First, from the function of taxation, the function to distribute income may sometimes conflict with the function to macro-regulation and control. To gain income is, after all, the most fundamental and primary function and the government always raises the level of the legal compliance as it attempts to gain more income in order to realize its economic and social functions. While in terms of taxation regulation and control, the common practice of using taxation preferential measures may generate taxation expenditure of the state while decreasing taxation income. Therefore, when the state is facing fiscal pressure and the government expects higher income, some taxation regulation and control measures that may affect the income of the government would be limited.

Second, from the scope of taxation regulation and control, the agents directly affected by taxation regulation and control generally are limited to specific taxpayers, namely agents bearing specific taxpaying duties within a certain period. As for agents without such obligation, since they are the fish that escape the net of taxation, such regulation and control would not generate a direct outcome for them and this will limit the performance of taxation regulation and control.

Third, from the principle of taxation regulation and control, the principle of fair taxation is equally important. When conducting specific taxation regulation and control activities, the following issues have to be considered: how to balance horizontal and vertical fairness; and how to balance formal and substantial justice and genuinely achieve the taxation according to capacity. Taxation regulation and control should directly reflect the relevant taxation policies, and while "there would be no policy without discrimination", taxation regulation and control through discrimination, leading people to chase the interest and avoid the harm. During the process of discrimination, it is not easy to correctly acknowledge the condition, avoid the actual unfairness of the tax burden, and ensure fair competition among market agents. Therefore, inappropriate taxation regulation and control may have a negative impact on the operation of the economy.

Fourth, from the perspective of taxation game, numerous and complicated games exist between the agents charged with regulation and control and agents being regulated, i.e. the tax levying agent and taxpaying agent.[34] On one hand, the agents being regulated may conduct the games or reactions, and their behaviour might be cooperative or non-cooperative. They may comply or refuse to comply with taxation regulation and control. If the agents being regulated ignore taxation regulation and control, especially when such agents choose to avoid paying tax through illegal methods, the actual performance of taxation regulation and control would be compromised.

Fifth, from the perspective of the agents who regulate and control, there also exists huge limitations. Especially under the current circumstances where the problem of lack of information is deteriorating, the agents who regulate and control usually cannot promptly and comprehensively acquire the information concerning market agents. The limitation of the rationale of the government is more prominent and the capability of perception concerning taxation regulation and control is affected further influencing the actual performance of taxation regulation and control. Therefore, it is a big challenge for the agents to regulate and control, given that it is hard to conduct such regulation and control at the appropriate time and space in order to better promote the stable growth of the economy and the benign and coordinated development of the economy and society.

Because of the limitations of taxation regulation and control, actual performance is affected. Consequently, in terms of the ability of taxation regulation and control, appropriate positioning is required in solving distribution issues. It is not reasonable to deny the function of taxation, while the tendency to believe that taxation could solve any problems should also be avoided.

5.4.2 The legitimacy of distribution regulation and control

As discussed above, during the process to deal with "binary differentiation" problems including the distribution gap, there is no distribution regulation and control measure that is workable for all circumstances, and the actual performance relies on factors from various aspects. The legitimacy of distribution regulation and control is also an important factor affecting the performance of distribution. That explains why it is necessary to discuss the issue of legitimacy.

Normally, the legitimacy of distribution regulation and control[35] includes the legitimacy from legal, economic, social, and political aspects. The legal legitimacy is the one which is the most direct and which attracts the most attention. If a certain distribution regulation and control behaviour lacks legitimacy, its effectiveness would be doubted and decreased under the current circumstance where the rule of law is emphasized. Therefore, from the perspective of legitimacy, the distribution regulation and control could be divided into regulation and control that is with and without legitimacy.

Legally speaking, legitimate distribution regulation and control should be conducted by the agents with the power to regulate and control and according to the law. Therefore, if an agent does not possess the power to regulate and control, the regulation and control conducted by such agents would be illegitimate. It could be concluded that the power to regulation and control is vital in ensuring legitimacy.

Formally, since distribution involves the basic rights of various agents, the power to distribution regulation and control comes from explicit authorization stipulated by the law. When the definition of the law is limited to written laws, the

172 *Legal response to distribution crises*

establishment, allocation, and exercising of power to regulate and control should be reflected by written laws of the state.

With the development of the economy and society, the economic and social functions of the state are increasingly expanding, and its powers are also increasing.[36] This situation has an effect on the emergence and development of the relevant power to regulation and control. As a vital function of the modern state, distribution regulation and control is a typical public good that cannot be provided by individual agents. From the perspective of meeting the need for the public good of citizens, distribution regulation and control is an obligation, instead of power, of the state.

According to the public good theory, the power to distribution regulation and control should be exclusive to the state. Though within a given period and space, human reason is limited and the problem of "government failure" should not be ignored, the function of the state, especially in terms of solving distribution problems and dealing with distribution crisis, should not be underestimated. After all, the solution to distribution problems and the distribution crisis response are the results of market failure, and, compared with other agents, the state possesses more legitimacy in exercising distribution regulation and control at the economic and social levels. This is also partly due to the monopoly of the state to the legislative power concerning distribution regulation and control.

In fact, since the initiation of reform and opening-up, especially since the decision to establish a market economy system, China has always focused on distribution regulation and control and on relevant legislation. The macro-regulation and control legislation have been raised to the constitutional level.[37] Meanwhile, goals or contents of macro-regulation and control are also added in some important laws that involve distribution to ensure that distribution regulation and control is legitimate.

Relevant to legitimacy, distribution regulation and control can also be divided as effective and ineffective. The legally ineffective distribution regulation and control might be effective economically. This highlights the issue of choice especially in times of conflict. Many would argue, especially from a legal perspective, ineffective distribution regulation and control should be abandoned despite the fact that it is economical. Yet, from a pragmatic point of view, some may believe that economically effective regulation and control, despite its legal ineffectiveness, is necessary and beneficial. This leads us to the main question of economic legitimacy.

The economic legitimacy of distribution regulation and control relies on its economic reasonableness, and it is essentially the "compliance to objective economic regulations". To a certain extent, the direct goal of distribution regulation and control is to solve the significant problems emerging in the distribution area. If a certain distribution regulation and control behaviour complies to economic regulation and achieves positive performance, relieving or solving the issue of imbalance in distribution, then such regulation and control behaviour is reasonable and has the tendency to further acquire the support of market agents or the social public, thereby gaining its legitimacy. Therefore, even when some

Legal response to distribution crises   173

regulation and control behaviours are against the realistic legal stipulations, they are deemed reasonable and would gain understanding and support. For example, China once raised the rate of export tax rebate in order to deal with the financial crisis and the policy reduced the burden of exporting enterprises. Though such policy lacked a legal basis, it achieved positive results in terms of the economy and gained support from the public.[38]

The reason is that the laws made by the state are always behind realistic economic activities, which are constantly changing and developing. Whether the laws can meet the requirement of real economic and social life is important in judging the vitality and effectiveness of such laws. Most of the economic reforms or distribution regulation and control conducted by different countries violate the framework of current legal stipulations and sometimes they are even against constitutional laws. However, due to its reasonableness in the economic aspect, such violations against the constitution are called "benign violation against the constitution". Different conceptions to such "benign violation against the constitution" or "benign violation against the laws" exist. Nevertheless, such phenomena should be as limited as possible in the field of distribution regulation and control. With the increasing of the level of rule of law and the deepening of people's recognition, the improvement of relevant laws could gradually solve such problems. Amendments to constitutional law and the frequent amendments to relevant legal norms in China all reflect the conception and efforts in this area.

Distribution regulation and control that is economically reasonable and legitimate would contribute to the solving of distribution problems and would prevent and resolve distribution crises, thereby promoting the benign operation and the coordinated development of the economy and society, thereby achieving legitimacy in the social and political fields. Therefore, institutional protection of distribution regulation and control, with economic reasonableness or compliance with economic regulations, should be provided in order to legitimize such regulation and control. The compliance of such regulation and control would increase and the expected goals of distribution regulation and control would be realized.

The brief discussion on the issue of the legitimacy of distribution regulation and control indicates that the legitimacy of distribution regulation and control does not only mean that it should formally meet the stipulations of relevant laws, but also that it should reflect the legitimacy in economic and social areas. Legal legitimacy itself is not enough for distribution regulation and control. Only regulation and control that meets economic regulations, fits the condition of the state and citizens, and aims at protecting social public interest and basic human rights is genuinely legal with valid regulation and control and therefore is of higher legitimacy.

5.4.3 Summary

The previous discussion mainly highlights the following opinions: "binary differentiation" is the prominent problem in the economic field in China, and it is a vital reason for the prominent distribution problems, and distribution regulation

174 *Legal response to distribution crises*

and control is indispensable as a response to "binary differentiation". Though taxation regulation and control is important in distribution regulation and control, appropriate positioning to it is necessary. The basis for various distribution regulations and controls is mainly policies and laws, and legitimacy would directly affect the actual performance of distribution regulation and control. The reasons for the performance of distribution regulation and control include internal and external reasons, and the limitations of distribution regulation and control itself are the internal reasons that are often closely connected to the external reasons. The legitimacy of distribution regulation and control involves legitimacy in various aspects including the law, economy, and society, and is a vital element affecting the actual performance of such regulation and control. Ensuring the legitimacy of distribution and control is also a vital task for distribution law system construction that contributes to the promotion of the benign operation and coordinated development of the economy and society under the framework of the rule of law.

Notes

1 Habermas believes that the present social science provides a systematic concept for crisis, identifying crisis as the continuous disorder of system integration. See Jürgen Habermas. (2000). *Legitimation Crisis*. Translated by Beicheng Liu and Weidong Cao. Shanghai: Shanghai People's Press, p. 4.
2 Crisis, after all, only exists within a limited period of time. Therefore, the response to crisis must consider long-term issues. The long-term, consistent, continuous, and effective development cannot be sacrificed for solving crisis. A popular consensus has been reached that crisis shall act as an opportunity for the way of economic growth to change and as a way for economic structure to be optimized.
3 On September 18, 2008, the Department of Finance and State Administration of Taxation announced that from the next day the way to levy security (stock) transaction stamp duty will be changed. Originally both parties were levied 1% for the purchase, in heritage or Hansel of the share (both Type A and Type B). After that, the levying would be imposed only on one party, and the buyer is not subject to such tax.
4 On October 21, 2008, the Department of Finance and State Administration of Taxation published the *Notice concerning Raising the Rate of Export Tax Rebate for Certain Commodities*, declaring that the rate of export tax rebate for 3,486 types of commodities including textures, cloth, and toys will be raised, constituting around 25.8% of all commodities.
5 In December 2008, the National Development and Reform Commission and Department of Finance jointly promoted the reform to the tax/fees for refined oil. Six items of fees including the road maintenance fee were changed into refined oil consumption tax. Such reform has been implemented on January 1, 2009. In November 2014, the State raised the rate of such tax and cancelled the consumption tax on vehicle tyres, etc.
6 The State Council announced that from October 9, 2008, the individual income tax on deposit interests was eliminated.
7 Especially in 1998, when the deficit raised sharply due to the financial crisis and the flood, China started to increase the issuance of national bonds to deal with the economic fluctuation and to raise the domestic demand.
8 To deal with the economic crisis in 2008, the planned deficit for 2009 reached 950 billion, among which the deficit of the central government was 750 billion, an unprecedented amount. The scale of deficit resulted to the pressure to the issuance of

Legal response to distribution crises 175

the national bonds. Meanwhile, problems such as the reasonable scale for national bond issuance and the issuance of local bonds attracted wide attention.

9 The government procurement involves many industries and fields, therefore the law on government procurement is closely related to many industry laws and there is coordination with many laws including law on railway, law on road, law on construction, law on national defense, etc. Meanwhile, in the context of economic globalization, international coordination concerning government procurement among WTO members is also crucial.

10 The implementation of the "Scheme for Adjustment and Revitalization" of ten industries, namely steel, vehicle, electronic products, textures, logistics, non-ferrous metal, equipment manufacture, petrochemical, light industry, shipbuilding, is directly or indirectly relevant to fiscal and taxation policies. Fiscal and taxation policies played a vital role in the industry structure adjustment in the abovementioned ten industries as well as related industries.

11 As discussed above, on June 27, 2009, the Standing Committee of the National People's Congress passed the *Decision to Abolish Certain Laws*, having abolished the *Decision to Authorize the State Council to Reform the Industry and Commerce Taxation System and to Publish and Experiment Relevant Taxation Regulations and Drafts*, despite the fact that *Decision on Authorizing the State Council to Formulate Interim Regulations Concerning Economic Institution Reform and Opening-up* was still valid. This expanded the power of State Council to Taxation legislation and lacks necessary limitation on the power to legislation concerning finance and taxation.

12 According to the *Decision to Approve the Department of Finance to Issue Special National Bond to Purchase Foreign Exchange and to Adjust the Limitation on the Balance of National Bond of the End of 2007* of the Standing Committee of the National People's Congress, the Department of Finance issued a special RMB national bond worth 1.55 trillion. This was the largest special national bond since 1949 and it aimed to solve the excess of liquidity in the financial field.

13 OCED states and international organizations such as IMF pay huge attention to fiscal transparency and emphasize on regulating transparency through many types of legislation. See International Monetary Fund. (2001). *Fiscal Transparency*. Beijing: The People's Press, pp. 6–10.

14 Correspondingly, the *Decision on Several Major Issues concerning Comprehensively Promoting the Rule of Law* ("Rule of Law Decision") of the Central Committee of the CPC in 2014 especially emphasized the phases of public participation and expert discussion which contributed to making the legislation more scientific and democratic, thereby making the legislation reflect more the requirement of the reality.

15 In recent years, China has been improving the transparency of public expenditures and has achieved positive results. Besides, the Law on Budget amended in 2014 especially emphasizes the transparency of budget. The *Decision of Rule of Law* in 2014 provides more requirement on transparency. All these factors lay vital foundations for the transparency of economic law regulations.

16 On January 7, 2009, attorney Yan Yiming in Shanghai submitted applications to the Department of Finance and Development and the Reform Commission for information disclosure, including the application for disclosing fiscal budget and final account, and the progress of the 4 trillion economic stimulus scheme, which reflects the attention to fiscal and taxation transparency.

17 In recent years, China has formulated the regulation on governmental investment management, in which the decision-making procedure is the vital component.

18 The effective development of economic law is directly related to the effective regulation of economic law to the field of distribution, while the effective development of the economic law system also requires the effective development of economic law theories. For relevant discussion, see Shouwen Zhang. (2005). On the "Effective Development" of Economic Law Theory. *Studies in Law and Business*, 22(01), pp. 10–14.

176   *Legal response to distribution crises*

19 From the perspective of systematic analysis, "effective development" and "scientific development" are internally consistent. To be "comprehensive, consistent and sustainable" is vital to scientific development in every field. Only through scientific development can development be effective. This is also the basic requirement for the construction of future economic rule of law institution.

20 From that viewpoint, the information level is also an important level for economic law research. Meanwhile, enhancing research on information theory and institution would also contribute to the development of information law. In fact, in information law theory, there are many factors consistent with economic law theory. See Shouwen Zhang and Qingshan Zhou. (1995). *Information Law*. Beijing: China Law Press, pp. 56–70.

21 Both China and some other countries value the right to information of taxpayers, which is the foundation for taxpayers to exercise their rights. For this purpose, the State Administration of Taxation has declared that the right to information is the first right in the *Announcement concerning the Right and Obligation of Taxpayers* published on November 6, 2009.

22 Distribution regulation and control is the prominent nature of policy and law. When combined with specific fields or objects, particular problems would emerge regarding the positioning, direction, and degree of regulation and control. This makes it a persistent problem.

23 The expansion of the income distribution gap is a vital problem for the public, given that it affects the harmony and stability of society. The voice for reducing the distribution conflicts through relevant policies and laws has been increasing and, because of that, the distribution gap has become huge. Similarly, to solve the gap between large enterprises and medium and small-scale enterprises, China has published important laws including *Law on Promoting Medium and Small-scale Enterprises* and *Antitrust Law*, which is necessary for promoting fair and effective competition between large enterprises and medium and small-scale enterprises.

24 Correspondingly, the issue of distribution is not only an issue of "development economics", but also an issue of "development law".

25 In terms of taxation regulation and control to fair distribution, particular problems including the accumulation and burden of taxation need to be solved. See Qingwang Guo. (2012). Several Deep-level Problems concerning the Fair Income Distribution of Taxation. *Finance & Trade Economics*, 33(08), pp. 20–27.

26 Binary structures such as urban and rural areas, the east and west regions, and the domestic and foreign will lead to the formation of a series of binary structures in the institution, while the binary structure at the level of economy-institution is the foundation and precondition to conduct distribution regulation and control. For a relevant discussion, see Shouwen Zhang. (2004). *Reconstruction of Economic Law Theory*. Beijing: The People's Press, pp. 37–47.

27 From this sense, compared with traditional regulatory laws, the taxation law norms with prominent nature of regulation and control would be easy to change, which would generate new problems in the field of taxation. For relevant analysis, see Shouwen Zhang. (2002). The Periodical Change of Macro-regulation and Control Law. *Peking University Law Journal*, 14(06), pp. 695–705.

28 The fierce discussion on the amendment to the *Law on Individual Income Tax* reflects the expectations of the people. Yet the issue of unfair distribution is complicated and taxation measures alone cannot solve this problem. The limitations of taxation law, and even the whole legal system, should be admitted.

29 The unification of two sets of taxation systems had been postponed, indicating that the participation of parties of interest would make things more complicated. After the implementation of the unified *Law on Corporate Income Tax*, the actual performance and new emerging problems have been seen. See Haiyong Wang. (2009). Effect, Problems and Suggestions to the Implementation of Law on Corporate Income Tax. *Taxation Research*, (02), p. 31.

Legal response to distribution crises 177

30 It is not difficult to find out in the discussion on the merits and faults in the experiments of taxation reform in the northeast region regarding regional economic development that taxation regulation and control also has multiple limitations.

31 From 2005 to the present, how to regulate and control the real estate market through taxation measures has always been a hot topic and it is closely connected with the regulation and control to relevant markets including the capital market.

32 Many years ago, scholars discussed this issue. See Qiren Zhou. (2005). Experts' Reasons for their Preference for Taxation. *The Economic Observer*, August 1. In fact, the general public may also have a preference for taxation, constituting the unreasonable expectation to taxation regulation and control.

33 In fact, both taxation regulation and control and taxation law adjustment are limited by subjective and objective conditions. See Shouwen Zhang. (2016). *Treatises on Fiscal and Taxation Law*. The 2nd Edition. Beijing: Peking University Press, pp. 107–109.

34 In macro-regulation and control, two types of agents are involved, the agent to regulate and the agent to be regulated, constituting the subject-object binary structure in the regulation and control relationship. In specific taxation levying, a binary structure of the levying agent and the taxpaying agent is formed. The game and relevant legal regulations are mainly conducted between these binary agents.

35 Legitimacy is a concept with complicated meaning. In this article, the meaning of the concept is mainly limited to the meaning of compliance to legal norms or regulations and of being supported and admitted by the social public.

36 Wagner's law and other scholars' research have constantly proven this point. The rise of the percentage of governmental fiscal expenditure in the GDP also proves this issue.

37 For example, Article 15 of the Constitution of PRC stipulates that "the state practices a socialist market economy. The state shall enhance economic legislation and improve macro-regulation and control". Therefore, macro-regulation and control is lifted up to the level of constitutional law, and the issue of the relationship among market economy, economic legislation, and macro-regulation and control is brought forward.

38 The adjustment to the rate of export tax rebate as a taxation regulation and control behaviour has to be based on laws, and the illegal regulation and control without a sufficient legal basis should be prohibited. The frequent change of the rate would, to some extent, be against current laws, and would generate negative influence on the right to request for tax rebate, affecting the stability and predictability of taxation law.

6 Conclusion

The distribution problem is complicated, and we must pay attention to potential distribution risks that prevent the emergence of distribution crises. To solve complicated distribution problems, different distribution systems need to be employed, especially the important distribution system within economic law. For this purpose, this book observes distribution systems from the perspective of economic law and emphasizes on analyzing existing problems in the distribution systems within economic law field based on the discussion of the relationship between distribution systems within economic law and distribution systems within other fields of law, and reflects on the approach to its improvement.

6.1 Basic understanding of this book

This book treats the whole distribution system as one system and believes that to solve distribution problems based on a systematic distribution system would contribute to the development of the economy and society. Therefore, this book brings forward the analytical framework of "institution-distribution-development". Based on such a framework, this book focuses on the internal and external relationship among distribution systems within the economic law field and on relevant distribution differences from the perspective of economic law. It emphasizes the fact that distribution rights and interests of relevant agents should be effectively protected in order to substantially solve the distribution problems, effectively prevent distribution risks, and respond to distribution crises. Thus, the logical line of "internal and external relationship-distribution difference-distribution right and interest-crisis response" throughout the whole book is formed.

Based on the above framework and following the above logical line, the following basic understandings are formed:

1 Distribution systems in economic law are vital to the solution to distribution issues, while distribution systems in economic law alone are far from being sufficient in solving distribution problems. Therefore, comprehensive regulation through various laws should be addressed and, at least within the legal system, coordinated regulation between economic law and other departmental law should be strengthened. This would contribute to promoting the

Conclusion 179

coordination among distribution systems of different types (including differences in precedence and nature), thus achieving an effective distribution regulation. Besides, even among distribution systems of the same type, mutual coordination is also important, given that it is through this means that the comprehensive function of the distribution system can be better exercised.

2 Emphasizing the coordination among distribution systems is also due to the fact that there exists a contradiction between unity and difference among distribution systems. On one hand, from the perspective of the rule of law, distribution systems, as a type of "system", should be unified. Yet, on the other hand, distribution systems, as a system of "distribution", should consider the differences existing among distribution agents and subjects, thereby reflecting different treatment and substantial justice. Both the difference outside the unified distribution system and the unity of the differentiated system arrangement should be considered in order to ensure the realization of the spirit of fairness and the rule of law. Meanwhile, the unity and differences within distribution systems should be viewed dialectically under the framework of the rule of law.

3 If the coordination among distribution systems is lacking, or if the allocation of power concerning distribution is not reasonable, various problems, in terms of economic law regulation, would emerge. This would result in a situation where practical distribution problems would be difficult to solve, and distribution risks would occur leading to distribution crises. Therefore, the distribution right and interest of relevant agents – distribution agents and distribution subjects – should be protected according to the law.

4 The rule of law should also be emphasized during the process of crisis response and the target should be the emerging distribution crisis. Specific measures and specific system arrangements should both comply to the statutory principle including the principles of fairness and efficiency in order to avoid the emergence of new crises, especially the "rule of law crisis", during the process of dealing with crises.

The formation of such basic understanding is closely relevant to various distribution systems in the economic law area. However, based on the special importance of fiscal and taxation law in dealing with distribution problems, including preventing and solving distribution crises, this book illustrates the importance of distribution systems and important issues in economic law, taking fiscal and taxation law as the vital representative of economic law. It emphasizes that distribution problems should be better solved, distribution risks should be prevented, and distribution crises should be dealt with by improving relevant distribution systems.

6.2 Thinking beyond the distribution system

This book, mainly from the perspective of economic law, discusses relevant problems concerning distribution systems. Though distribution systems in economic law are vital to solving distribution problems and preventing and solving

180 *Conclusion*

distribution risks and crises, the distribution system does not only exists in economic law. In fact, large numbers of distribution systems also exist in constitutional law and other types of laws. For this reason, this book conducts extended research to distribution systems relevant to economic law, focusing on the issue of coordinated regulation of distribution systems of economic law and constitutional, civil, and commercial law, and emphasizes that the goals of distribution regulation and control should be achieved through constant improvement to relevant systems, even within the economic law system itself.

Based on distribution orientation, the distribution system in the economic law area would contribute to solving resource allocation, especially the distribution of income and wealth. When distribution crises occur, the crisis should be effectively solved through self-adjustment. Therefore, various distribution systems in the economic law area should be able to effectively solve distribution crises and prevent economic fluctuation, thereby weakening the periodicity of the economy through constant regulation and control to distribution, equipping economic law with the prominent function of distribution regulation and control.

The distribution regulation and control function of economic law is based on the internal structure of economic law originating from economic measures that have been legalized. Various regulation and control measures within economic law are vital tools affecting distribution at the macro and micro levels, thereby providing the possibility to realize the distribution of regulation and control function of economic law. Therefore, the issue of market failures, such as the distribution gap, the unfairness in distribution, and distribution imbalance should be solved through economic law. Also, it is not only secondary distribution that economic law should influence; primary or "third" distribution should also be regulated. It is solely through exercising direct influence on the abovementioned distribution that the function of economic law to distribution regulation and control be better exercised. Correspondingly, the focus of the improvement of the economic law system is not only the area of secondary distribution but also other distribution stages which are also important problems that should be focused on in improving the distribution system.

From an economic law system improvement perspective, the distribution crisis is not only an economic crisis. To some extent, it is also a legal or rule of law crisis. If the allocation of rights by the laws fails to effectively solve the issue of fair distribution, then unfairness and injustice would inevitably cause an imbalance in distribution, and further result in social and political crises. Different disciplines of social sciences could discuss this phenomenon from different perspectives given that the distribution crisis resulted from the unreasonableness of the distribution system. Yet, from the perspective of economic law, a framework should be laid for the smooth functioning of the economy that would guarantee fairness and reasonableness of distribution through the distribution system in economic law. It should be an economy that showcases justice in distribution that is capable of preventing the occurrence of distribution crises and economic fluctuation – something that should be emphasized by every state.

Bibliography

1. Chinese treatises

Angang Hu, Shaoguang Wang, *et al.* (2003). *The Second Transformation: National Institutional Construction*. Beijing: Tsinghua University Press.

Baoshu Wang, ed. (2004). *The Theory of Economic Law*. Beijing: China Social Sciences Publishing House.

Bifeng Ye. (2007). Attempt of Economic Constitutional Law Research: Constitutional Interpretation to the Power to Decide Binary Taxation System. *Journal of Shanghai Jiaotong University* (Social Science Edition), 15(06).

Changbin Wang. (2004). *Comparative Studies on Corporate Group Laws*. Beijing: Peking University Press.

Changqi Li. (1995). *Economic Law – the Basic Legal Form of National Intervention*. Cheng Du: Sichuan People's Publishing House.

Chongen Bai and Zhenjie Qian. (2009). Who Are Taking Residents' Income? An Analysis of China's National Income Distribution Pattern. *Chinese Social Science*, (5).

Chongtai Tan. (1999). *New Developments in Development Economics*. Wu Han: Wuhan University Press.

Dachun Liu. (1998). Philosophy of Science. Beijing: The People's Press.

Dahong Liu. (2005). On the Idea of Development of Economic Law: Research Paradigm Based on System Theory. *Legal Forum*, 20(01).

Daiguang Hu. (1998). *The Shift and Influence of Western Economics Thoughts*. Beijing: Peking University Press.

Dazhi Yao. (2011). Distributive Justice: From the Standpoints of Social Vulnerable Groups. *Philosophical Researches*, (3).

Deming Chen, *et al.* (2014). *Economic Crisis and Reconstruction of Rules*. Beijing: Commercial Press.

Dingqi Wang. (2000). The Yumin Thoughts in the Shang Shu. *Social Science Research*, (4).

Dongqi Chen. (2000). *New Theory on Government Intervention*. Beijing: Capital University of Economics and Business Press.

Dongsheng Zhang, ed. (2013). *Annual Report of Income Distribution of Chinese Residents*. Beijing: Economic Science Press.

Fan He. (1998). *Constitution of Market Economy: Fiscal Problems in China*. Beijing: Today's China Publishing House.

Fang Cai. (2012). How to Understand the Reality of China's Income Distribution Reform: an Analytical Framework for Seeking Common Ground while Reserving Differences. In: Jinglian Wu, ed., *Comparison*, Vol. 59. Beijing: CITIC Press.

182 Bibliography

Fangchun Zhao. (2006). Primary Investigation to Strengthening the Function to Macro-regulation and Control of Turnover Tax. *Modern Finance and Economics – Journal of Tianjin University of Finance and Economics*, 26(11).

Feirong Peng and Quanxing Wang. (2011). On the Government Accountability in the Distributive Justice: From the Perspective of Risk and Law. *Journal of Social Sciences*, 1.

Feizhou Zhou. (2006). 10 Years' Binary Taxation System: Institution and Influence. *Social Sciences in China*, 5.

Guoqiang Ma and Jing Li. (2011). Aims and Phases of Real Estate Tax Reform. *Reform*, 2.

Haitao Jiao. (2009). On the Function and Structure of Economic Law with the Function to Promote Development. *Political Science and Law*, 8.

Haixin Yao. (2001). *Game Theory Analysis on Economic Policies*. Beijing: Economic Management Press.

Haiyong Wang. (2009). Effect, Problems and Suggestions to the Implementation of Law on Corporate Income Tax. *Taxation Research*, 2.

Hongli Zhang. (1998). *Theory on Scientific Methods*. Xi'an: Shaanxi People's Press.

Hongri Ni. (2012). Process and Suggestions for the Real Estate and Land Tax Reform. *China Taxation*, 6.

Hongyou Lu and Feng Gong. (2007). Normal Analysis to the Distribution of Power to Taxation among Governments in China. *Economic Review*, 3.

Hui Huang. (2009). The Application of Economic Institution Clauses in the Constitution: The Dispute Concerning German Economic Constitution. *Peking University Law Journal*, 21(4).

Hui Wang. (2010). Root, Influence and Reflection on the European Sovereign Debt Crisis. *Public Finance Research*, 5.

International Monetary Fund. (2001). *Fiscal Transparency*. Beijing: The People's Press.

Jia Kang. (2012). *Income Distribution and System Optimization and Change*. Beijing: Economic Science Press.

Jianbai Yang and Dongqi Chen. (2000). *Macro-Economic Regulation and Control and Policies*. Beijing: Economic Science Press.

Jiangping Xiao. (2002). *History of China Economic Law Theory*. Beijing: People's Court Press.

Jianmin Wang. (2010). *Economic Periodicity and Constitutional Order*. Hangzhou: Zhejiang University Press.

Jianwen Luo and Mingjun Deng. (2007). Ethical Analysis from GDP Worship to GNH Care. *Studies in Ethics*, 28(2).

Jianzong Yao. (1998). *Introduction to Research to Law and Development*. Changchun: Jilin University Press.

Jinjun Xue. (2013). *Growth with Inequality*. Beijing: China Social Sciences Publishing House.

Jirong Yan. (2010). *Development Politics*, 2nd Edition. Beijing: Peking University Press.

Jun Cui. (2011). *Fiscal System Arrangement to Adjust the Resident Income Distribution*. Beijing: Economic Science Press.

Jun Wang. (2009). *The Institutional Change and Thinking Evolution of Fiscal Institution in China* (Vol. 1, Part 2). Beijing: China Fiscal Economy Press.

Junpei Wu. (1992). *Thoughts Generate from Deficit*. Beijing: China Social Science Press.

Junpei Wu. (1993). *Thoughts on Deficit Economy*. Beijing: China Social Science Press.

Kang Jia. (2013). The Distribution of Power after the Reform of Fiscal Institution in China. *Reform*, 2.

Bibliography   183

Kang Jia and Jingming Bai. (2002). Solving the Difficulties in County and Village Finance, and the Innovation in Fiscal Institution. *Economic Research Journal*, 37(02).

Kang Jia and Kun Yan. (2005). Mid-term and Long-term Thinkings on Improving Fiscal Institution Reform under Provincial Level. *Management World*, 21(08).

Kechang Ge. (2004). *Basic Issues in Tax Law (Fiscal Constitution)*. Beijing: Peking University Press.

Kechang Ge. (2005). *Basic Topics of Taxation Law-On Fiscal Constitution*. Taipei: Taiwan Angle Publishing.

Keli Fang. (2003). "Harmony between Man and Nature" and Ecological in Ancient China. *Social Science Front*, 5.

Kepeng Xue. (2013). Investigation to the Origin of Economic Administrative Law Theory: Economic Administrative Law in the Context of Economic Law. *Contemporary Law*, 27(05).

Keqiang Li. (2010). Few Issues Regarding Economic Restructuring and Sustainable Development. *Qiushi Journal*, (11).

Lei Liu. (2006). On the Formation of Modern Enterprises and Income Tax. *Chinese Economic Studies*, 2.

Lianbin Qing. (2004). *Distribution System Reform and Common Richness*. Nanjing: Jiangsu People's Press.

Liansheng Zheng. (2010). Evolution, Influence, Reason and Reflection of EU Debt Issue. *International Economic Review*, 3.

Liping Sun. (2009). The Logic of the Financial Crisis and Its Social Consequences. *Chinese Journal of Sociology*, 29(2).

Ming Li. (2011). *Public Risk and Local Governance Crisis*. Beijing: Peking University Press.

Ming Li. (2011). *The Financial Crisis and Local Management*. Beijing: Peking University Press.

Mingsheng Yuan. (2008). The Crazy Stock Market, Stamp Duty and Rule of Law of the Government: Thinking on the Adjustment to the Rate of Security Exchange Stamp Duty from the Perspective of Jurisprudence. *Law Science*, 8.

Peigang Zhang and Jianhua Zhang. (2009). *Development Economics*. Beijing: Peking University Press.

Peixin Luo. (2009). Improvement of Legal Liability of Credit Rating Agencies in the Post-Financial Crisis Age. *Law Science Magazine*, 7.

Peiyong Gao. (2009). VAT Transformation Reform: Analysis and Prospect. *Taxation Research*, 8.

Pengcheng Gao. (2009). *Crisisology*. Beijing: China Social Sciences Publishing House.

Pengcheng Gao. (2009). *Study on Crisis*. Beijing: Social Sciences Academic Press.

Ping Zhang. (2010). The Current Status, Gap and Improvement of China's Public Financial Transparency Based on International Perspective. *Research on Economics and Management*, (09).

Pingxue Zhou. (1995). Attentions Shall Be Paid to the Research to the Economic Attributes of the Constitutional Law. *Law Science*, (12).

Pusheng Liu. (1999). Responsiveness of Economic Law. *Studies in Law and Business*, 2.

Qianfan Zhang. (2001). Regulation and Control to Interstate Trades by the Federal Government of USA. *Journal of Nanjing University (Philosophy, Humanities and Social Sciences)*, 38(02).

Qianfan Zhang. (2011). *The US Federal Constitution*. Beijing: China Law Press.

Qicai Gao. (2006). Modern Legislation Ideas. *Nanjing Journal of Social Sciences*, 1.

184   *Bibliography*

Qingwang Guo. (2012). Several Deep-level Problems Concerning the Fair Income Distribution of Taxation. *Finance & Trade Economics*, 33(08).

Qiren Zhou. (2005). Experts' Reasons for Their Preference for Taxation. *The Economic Observer*, August 1.

Qizai Zhang. (2001). *New Economic Sociology*. Beijing: China Social Science Press.

Quanxing Wang and Ping He. (2008). A Brief Discussion on the Structural Research Method in Economic Law Research. *Journal of Chongqing University* (Social Science Edition), 14(5).

Renwei Zhao. (1999). *Research on Resident Income Distribution in China – the Income Distribution in the Economic Reform and Development*. Beijing: China Fiscal Economy Press.

Renyu Huang. (1997). *Chinese Big History*. Beijing: Sanlian Book Store.

Ruifu Liu. (2000). *The Theory of Economic Law*. Beijing: Peking University Press.

Shanguang Sun. (2007). Research on the Asymmetry of Local Government's Financial Power and the Change of Constraint and Incentive Mechanism after the Tax Sharing System. *Comparative Economic and Social Systems*, 1.

Shangxi Liu. (2006). *Macro Financial Risks and Government Fiscal Responsibilities*. Beijing: China Financial and Economic Publishing House.

Shangxi Liu. (2012). Advantage and Disadvantage of Binary Taxation System. *Review of Economic Research*, 7.

Shaoguang Wang. (1999). *Diversity and Unity: Global Comparative Study on the Third Sector*. Hangzhou: Zhejiang University Press.

Shaoguang Wang. (2007). From Tax State to Budget State. *Readings*, (10).

Shaoguang Wang and Anguang Hu. (1993). *A Study of China's Capacity*. Shenyang: Liaoning People's Publishing House.

Sheng Li. (2012). Positioning of the Function of Real Estate Tax. *Taxation Research*, 3.

Shiyi Zhao. (2001). Basic Questions on Economic Constitutionalism, *Chinese Journal of Law*, 23(04).

Shouwen Zhang. (1994). On the Purposes of Economic Law. *Peking University Law Journal*, 31(1).

Shouwen Zhang. (1996). On Statutory Taxation. *Chinese Journal of Law*, 18(06).

Shouwen Zhang. (2000). On the Taxability in Taxation Law. *Jurists Review*, 5.

Shouwen Zhang. (2000). On the Modernity of Economic Law. *Chinese Legal Science*.

Shouwen Zhang. (2000). The "Experiment Mode" of Taxation Legislation in China: Taking VAT Legislation Experiment as Example. *Law Science*, 4.

Shouwen Zhang. (2001). Basic Hypothesis of Economic Law. *Modern Law Science*, 23(6).

Shouwen Zhang. (2001). The Universal Applicability of Taxation Law and its Limitations. *Peking University Law Journal*, 13(05).

Shouwen Zhang. (2002). Periodic Change of Macro Control Law. *Peking University Law Journal*, 14(5).

Shouwen Zhang. (2003). A Discussion on Establishing Fundamental Principle of Economic Law. *Journal of Peking University* (*Philosophy of the Social Sciences*), 40(2).

Shouwen Zhang. (2003). Policy Analysis on Economic Law. *Studies in Law and Business*, 5.

Shouwen Zhang. (2003). The Abstract and Value of the Category of Taxation Behavior. *Taxation Research*, 7.

Shouwen Zhang. (2004). *The Reconstruction of Economic Law Theory*. Beijing: People's Press.

Shouwen Zhang. (2005). On the "Effective Development" of Economic Law Theory. *Studies in Law and Business*, 22(01).

Shouwen Zhang. (2005). The Development Law Science and Development of Law Science. *Law Science Magazine*, 3.

Shouwen Zhang. (2005). *Treatise on Fiscal and Taxation Law*. Beijing: Peking University Press.

Shouwen Zhang. (2007). Legal Analysis to the Collective Taxpaying by Corporate Groups. *Law Science*, 5.

Shouwen Zhang. (2008). *Economic Law*. Beijing: Renmin University of China Press.

Shouwen Zhang. (2008). On Economic Law with the Function to Promote Development. *Journal of Chongqing University* (Social Science Edition), 14(05).

Shouwen Zhang. (2008). The Integration and Limitations of the Corporate Income Tax Law. *Taxation Research*, 2.

Shouwen Zhang. (2009). Analysis to the Financial Crisis from the Perspective of Economic Law. *Legal Forum*, 24(3).

Shouwen Zhang. (2009). *General Economic Law*. Beijing: Renmin University of China Press.

Shouwen Zhang. (2009). *General Introduction to Economic Law*. Beijing: Renmin University Press.

Shouwen Zhang. (2009). The Meridian that Runs through the Research of Economic Law in China: From the Perspective of Distribution. *Tribune of Political Science and Law*, 27(6).

Shouwen Zhang. (2009). On Promotion-Type Economic Law. *Journal of Chongqing University* (Social Science Edition), 14(6).

Shouwen Zhang. (2011). Distribution Difference and Regulation of Fiscal Law. *Tax Research*, 2.

Shouwen Zhang. (2011). Economic Law Thinking on "Dual Adjustment". *Law Science*, 1.

Shouwen Zhang. (2011). Excavation and Expansion of Theories on Economic Law in Post-crisis Era. *Journal of Chongqing University* (Social Science Edition), 3.

Shouwen Zhang. (2011). Fiscal and Taxation Law Adjustment to Distribution Structure. *China Legal Science*, 5.

Shouwen Zhang. (2012). *Economic Law*, 2nd Edition. Beijing: Renmin University of China Press.

Shouwen Zhang. (2012). Economic Law Thinking on the Right to Economic Development. *Modern Law Science*, 34(2).

Shouwen Zhang. (2012). *Principles of Taxation Law*, 6th Edition. Beijing: Peking University Press.

Shouwen Zhang. (2012). The Right to Economic Development: From the Perspective of Economic Law. *Modern Law Science*, 17(03).

Shouwen Zhang. (2012). Three Basic Problems of Real Estate Tax Legislation. *Taxation Research*, (11).

Shouwen Zhang. (2013). *General Theory of Economic Law*. Beijing: Peking University Press.

Shouwen Zhang. (2013). The "Experiment Mode" of Taxation Legislation in China: Taking VAT Legislation Experiment as Example. *Law Science*, 4.

Shouwen Zhang. (2014). "Decision to Reform" and the Consensus for Economic Law. *Legal Commentary*, 32(2).

Shouwen Zhang. (2014). Legal Adjustment to the Relationship between the Government and Market. *China Legal Science*, 5.

186 *Bibliography*

Shouwen Zhang. (2014). Statutory Principle of Taxation Should Be a Priority in Rule of Law. *Global Law Review*, 36(01).

Shouwen Zhang. (2016). *Treatises on Fiscal and Taxation Law*, 2nd Edition. Beijing: Peking University Press.

Shouwen Zhang and Qingshan Zhou. (1995). *Information Law*. Beijing: China Law Press.

Shuang Li. (2007). *Choices on System and Policy That Could Realize Fair Distribution*. Beijing: Economic Science Press.

Shuguang Zhang. (2010). Challenges Brought by the International Financial Crisis Facing Microeconomics. In: Jianming Wang, ed., *Business Cycle and Constitutional Order*. Hangzhou: Zhejiang University Press.

Tan Chongtai. (1999). *New Developments in Development Economics*. Wuhan: Wuhan University Press.

The *Decision on Several Major Issues Concerning Comprehensively Promoting the Rule of Law* ("Rule of Law Decision") of the Central Committee of the CPC (2014).

Tiankui Jing. (2000). *Social Development and Development Sociology in China*. Beijing: Xuexi Press.

Tiechuan Hao. (1996). On Benign Violation Against the Constitution. *Chinese Journal of Law*, 18(04).

Tifu An. (2004). Structural Tax Reduction: Choice for Taxation Policy under the Limitation of Macro-economy. *International Taxation in China*, (11).

Tifu An. (2008). Thinkings on the Promotion of VAT Transformation Reform in the Whole Country. *Fiscal Supervision*, (10).

Tifu An. (2012). On Several Issues Concerning Structural Tax Reduction. *Taxation Research*, 5.

Wanjun Jin. (2007). Primary Thinking on the Issue of Deviation between Regional Taxation and Tax Resource. *Taxation Research*, 1.

Wei Zhao. (1999). *Intervention in the Market*. Beijing: Economic Science Press.

Weidong Ji. (1999). *Construction of Rule of Law Order*. Beijing: China University of Political Science and Law Press.

Weidong Ji. (2009). Judicial Responsibility in the Economic Crisis. *Caijing Magazine*, 229(1).

Wenchuan Xia. (2007). Thinkings on Collective Taxpaying of Corporate Income Tax. *Taxation Research*, 1.

Wenxian Zhang. (1994). View of the Spirits of Market Economy and Contemporary Law. *China Legal Science*, 6.

Xiangcai Zhong. (2008). China's Unified Economic Thoughts in the 1930s and 1940s. *Historical Review*, 2.

Xianguo Yao and Jiqiang Guo. (1996). On Labour Rights. *Academic Monthly*, No. 6.

Xiaolu Wang. (2013). *Strategic Distribution on National Income*. Beijing: Xuexi Press, and Haikou: Hainan Press.

Xiaomin Chen. (2000). *The Banking Law in the United States*. Beijing: China Law Press.

Xiaoping Kuang and Ying Liu. (2013). Institutional Change, Power to Taxation Configuration and the Reform to Local Tax System. *Research on Financial and Economic Issues*, 3.

Xiaoqiang Yang. (2008). *China Taxation Law: Principles, Practice and Integration*. Jinan: Shandong People's Press.

Xie Di. (2003). *Government Regulation Economics*. Beijing: Higher Education Press.

Bibliography 187

Xigen Wang. (2002). *Basic Human Rights in Rule of Law Society: Research on Legal Institution of the Right to Development*. Beijing: People's Public Security University of China Press.

Xigen Wang. (2008). *Research on the Global Rule of Law Mechanism Concerning the Right to Development*. Beijing: China Social Science Press.

Xigen Wang and Kangmin Wang. (2009). On Regional Development Rights and the Concept of Law Update. *Political Science and Law*, (11).

Xingyun Peng and Jie Wu. (2009). From the Subprime Mortgage Crisis to the Evolution and Diffusion of the Global Financial Crisis. *Economic Perspectives*, 2.

Xinhe Cheng. (2001). Sustainable Development: Theoretical Evolution and Institutional Innovation of Economic Law in China. *Academic Research*, 2.

Xinhe Cheng. (2008). Research to the 30-years Development of the Economic Law in China. *Journal of Chongqing University (Social Science Edition)*, 14(04).

Xinqiao Ping. (1996). *Fiscal Principles and Comparative Fiscal System*. Beijing: SDX Joint Publishing Company.

Xiulin Sun and Feizhou Zhou. (2013). Land Finance and Binary Taxation System: An Empirical Explanation. *Social Sciences in China*, 4.

Yifeng Wu. (1998). *Government Intervention and Market Economy*. Beijing: Commercial Press.

Yinchu Ma. (2001). *Finance Study and Chinese Finance: Theory and Practice*. Beijing: Commercial Press.

Yining Li. (1994). Rationality and Coordination of Income Distribution. *Social Science Front*, 6.

Yining Li. (1994). *Shareholding Systems and Market Economy*. Nanjing: Jiangsu People's Press.

Yongjun Liu, *et al.* (2009). *Research on the Income Distribution Gap of Chinese Residents*. Beijing: Economic Science Press.

Yue Wu. (2007). *An Introduction to Economic Constitutional Law: The Game between Economic Right and Power in China During Transformation*. Beijing: Law Press.

Yunliang Chen. (2007). The Power of the State to Regulate: The Fourth Form of Power. *Contemporary Law*, 29(06).

Yushi Gui. (2005). *Economic Institution in Chinese Constitutional Law*. Wuhan: Wuhan University Press.

Zenghua Han. (2011). Primary Discussion on the Relationship between Binary Taxation System Reform and Debt Risk of Local Government in China. *Modern Finance and Economics*, 31(04).

Zhengwen Shi. (2007). Discussion on the Issue of "Income not Subject to Taxation" in Law on Corporate Income Tax. *Taxation Research*, 9.

Zhihui Gu and Fang Cai. (2005). The Financial Pressure upon China and the Economic Transition Therein from 1978 to 2002: the Theory and a Case Study. *Management World*, 7.

Zhiwei Tong. (1996). "Benign Violation Against the Constitution" Should not be Recognized. *Chinese Journal of Law*, 18(06).

Zhiyong Yang. (2012). Aims of Real Estate Tax Reform from the Public Perspective. *Taxation Research*, 3.

Zhongqiao Duan. (2013). Distributive Justice, Equality and Deserve: Answering Prof. Yao Dazhi. *Jilin University Journal* (Social Sciences Edition), 53(4).

Zixuan Yang. (2009). *Theory of the State Coordinating*. Beijing: Peking University Press.

188　*Bibliography*

2. Foreign treatises and translations

A. Jacques and G. Schrams. (1997). *Economics & Law.* Translated by Yuquan. Beijing: Commercial Press.

Aaron Wildavsky. (2009). *Budgeting: A Comparative Theory of Budgetary Processes.* Translated by Yannan Gou. Shanghai: Shanghai University of Finance and Economics Press.

Adam Smith. (2003). *The Nature and Causes of the Wealth of Nations.* Translated by Guo Dali and Wang Yanan. Beijing: Commercial Press.

Albert Hyde. (2006). *Government Budgeting: Theory, Process and Politics*, 3rd Edition. Translated by Yannan Gou. Shanghai: Shanghai University of Finance and Economics Press.

Alfred Marshall. (1983). *Principles of Economics.* Translated by Zhu Zhitai. Beijing: Commercial Press.

Allan Schmid. (2011). *Property, Power, and Public Choice.* Translated by Huang Zuhui. Beijing: SDX Joint Publishing Company, and Shanghai: Shanghai People's Press.

Anne Robert Jacques Turgot. (2007). *Reflections on the Formation and Distribution of Wealth.* Translated by Tang Risong. Beijing: Huaxia Press.

Anthony I. Ogus. (2008). *Regulation: Legal Form and Economic Theory.* Translated by Luo Meiying. Beijing: Renmin University Press.

Aoki Masahiro. (2001). *Comparative System Analysis.* Translated by Li'an Zhou. Shang Hai: Shanghai Far East Publishing House.

Aristotle. (2003). *Nicomachean Ethics.* Translated by Shenbai Liao. Beijing: Commercial Press.

Arjen Boin, Bengt Sundelius, and Eric Stern. (2010). *The Politics of Crisis Management: Public Leadership Under Pressure.* Translated by Zhao Fengping. Zhengzhou: Henan People's Press.

Arjen Boin, Paul 't Hart, Eric Stern and Bengt Sundelius. (2010). *The Politics of Crisis Management: Public Leadership under Pressure.* Translated by Fengping Zhao. Zhengzhou: Henan People's Publishing House.

Arye L. Hillman. (2006). *Public Finance and Public Policy: Responsibilities and Limitations of Government.* Translated by Wang Guohua. Beijing: China Social Science Press.

B. Fennebrunner. (2009). *The Theory of Income Distribution.* Translated by Min Fant. Beijing: Huaxia Press.

Cass R. Sunstein. (2002). *Risk and Reason: Safety, Law, and the Environment.* Cambridge: Cambridge University Press.

Charles A. Beard. (2011). *An Economic Interpretation of the Constitution of the United States.* Translated by He Xiqi. Beijing: Commercial Press.

Charles Kindleberger. (1989). *Economic Laws and Economic History.* Cambridge: Cambridge University Press.

Clive Schmitthoff. (1993). *Selected Works on International Trade.* Translated by Zhao Xiuwen. Beijing: China Encyclopedia Press.

David Denney. (2009). *Risk and Society.* Translated by Ma Ying. Beijing: Beijing Publishing Group Company, Beijing Press.

David Easton. (1999). *A Systems Analysis of Political Life.* Translated by Wang Puju. Beijing: Huaxia Press.

David Ricardo. (2005). *On the Principles of Political Economy and Taxation.* Translated by Zhou Jie. Beijing: Huaxia Press.

Bibliography 189

Dennis Meadows, Donella Meadows, Jørgen Randers and William W. Behrens III. (2006). *Limits to Growth*. Translated by Li Tao. Beijing: Mechanical Industry Press.

Dieter Grimms. (2010). *Ursprung, Wandel und Zukunft der Verfassung*. Translated by Gang Liu. Beijing: China Law Press.

Donella Meadows, Jørgen Randers and William W. Behrens III. (2006). *Limits to Growth: The 30 Year Update*. Translated by Tao Li. Beijing: China Machine Press.

Douglass North. (1994). *Structure and Change in Economic History*. Translated by Yu Chen and Huaping Luo. Shanghai: SDX Joint Publishing Company and Shanghai People's Press.

Douglass North. (1999). *The Rise of The Western World: A New Economic History*. Translated by Yining Li. Beijing: Huaxia Publishing House.

Émile Durkheim. (2000). *De la Division du Travail Social*. Translated by Dong Qu. Beijing: SDX Joint Publishing Company.

Étienne-Gabriel Morelly. (1996). *Code of Nature*. Translated by Jianhua Huang and Yazhou Jiang. Shanghai: Commercial Press.

Frank H. Knight. (2010). *Risk, Uncertainty and Profit*. Translated by Jia An. Beijing: Commercial Press.

Friedrich August von Hayek. (2000). *Law, Legislation and Freedom*. Vol. I. Beijing: Encyclopedia of China Publishing House.

Friedrich Hayek. (1997). *The Constitution of Liberty*. Translated by Deng Zhenglai. Beijing: SDX Joint Publishing Company.

Friedrich Hayek. (2000). *Law, Legislation and Liberty*. Vols. II, III. Beijing: China Encyclopedia Press.

Geoffrey Brennan and James M. Buchanan. (1985). *The Reason of Rules: Constitutional Political Economy*. Cambridge: Cambridge University Press.

Geoffrey Brennan and James M. Buchanan. (2004). *Constitutional Economics*. Translated by Keli Feng, et al. Beijing: China Social Science Press.

George Garvey and Gerald Garvey. (1990). *Economic Law and Economic Growth: Antitrust, Regulation, and the American Growth System*. Westport: Greenwood Publishing Group.

Gordon Tullock. (2008). *Economics of Income Redistribution*. Translated by Fan Fei Liu Kun. Shanghai: Shanghai People's Press.

Gunter Gabisch. (1993). *Business Cycle Theory – A Survey of Methods and Concepts*. Translated by Xue Yuwei. Beijing: SDX Joint Publishing Company.

Gustav Radbruch. (1997). *Einführung in die Rechtswissenschaft*. Translated by Mi Jian. Beijing: China Encyclopedia Press.

Harold R. Kerbo. (2012). *Social Stratification and Inequality: Class Conflict in Historical, Comparative, and Global Perspective*. Translated by Jiang Chao. Shanghai: Shanghai People's Press.

Hartmut Maurer. (2000). *Allgemeines Verwaltungsrecht*. Translated by Gao Jiawei. Beijing: China Law Press.

He Mengbi. (2000). *Collections on the Theory and Practice Concerning Order Policy in Germany*. Translated by Pang Jian. Shanghai: Shanghai People's Press.

Henc van Maarseveen. (2007). *Written Constitutions: A Computerized Comparative Study*. Translated by Yunshen Chen. Beijing: Peking University Press.

Henry George. (2006). *Progress and Poverty*. New York: Cosmo Inc.

Hiroshi Kaneko. (2004). *Tax Law*. Translated by Xianbin Zhan. Beijing: China Law Press.

Ikumi Io Daneon Akbane. (2010). 経済法総論 (*Pandect on Economic Law*). Translated by Keiko Yoshida. Beijing: China Legal Publishing House.

190 Bibliography

James M. Buchanan. (1991). *Public Finance*. Translated by Zhao Xijun. Beijing: China Financial & Economic Publishing House.

James M. Buchanan. (2012). *Explorations into Constitutional Economics*. Translated by Jia Wenhua. Beijing: China Social Science Press.

James M. Buchanan and G. Tullock. (2000). *The Calculus of Consent: Logical Foundations of Constitutional Democracy*. Translated by Guangjin Chen. Beijing: China Social Science Press.

James M. Buchanan and Richard A. Musgrave. (2000). *Public Finance and Public Choice: Two Contrasting Visions of the State*. Translated by Chengzhao Lei. Beijing: China Finance and Economic Press.

Janos Kornai. (1986). *Economics of Shortage*. Translated by Xiaoguang Zhang, Zhenning Li and Weiping Huang. Beijing: Economic Science Press.

János Kornai. (1986). *Growth, Shortage and Efficiency: A Macrodynamic Model of the Socialist Economy*. Translated by Zhiyuan Cui and Mingjin Qian. Cheng Du: Sichuan People's Press.

Jody S. Krause and Steven D. Walt. (2005). *The Jurisprudential Foundations of Corporate and Commercial Law*. Translated by Haijun Jin. Beijing: Peking University Press.

John B. Clark. (2008). *The Distribution of Wealth*. Translated by Wang Yilong. Beijing: Huaxia Press.

John Fei and Gustav Ranis. (2014). *Growth and Development from an Evolutionary Perspective*. Translated by Hong Yinxing. Beijing: Commercial Press.

John Rawls. (1988). *A Theory of Justice*. Translated by Huaihong He, *et al*. Beijing: China Social Sciences Publishing House.

John Rawls. (2002). *Justice as Fairness: Political not Metaphysical*. Beijing: SDX Joint Publishing Company.

Jonathan Hughes and Louis Cain. (2011). *American Economic History*. Translated by Di Xiaoyan. Beijing: Peking University Press.

Joseph E. Stiglitz. (1998). *The Economic Role of the State*. Translated by Bingwen Zheng. Beijing: China Materials Press.

Joseph E. Stiglitz. (2009). *Development and Development Policy*. Translated by Ji Mo. Beijing: China Finance Press.

Joseph E. Stiglitz. (2009). *Why Does the Government Intervene the Economy: the Role of the Government in Market Economy*. Translated by Zheng Bingwen. Beijing: China Goods Press.

Joseph E. Stiglitz. (2011). *Freefall: America, Free Markets, and the Sinking of the World Economy*. Translated by Li Junqing. Beijing: Mechanical Industry Press.

Joseph E. Stiglitz. (2013). *The Price of Inequality*. Translated by Ziyuan Zhang. Beijing: China Machine Press.

Joseph Schumpeter. (2007). *The Theory of Economic Development*. Translated by Li Mo. Xi'an: Shaanxi Normal University Press.

Jürgen Habermas. (2000). *Crisis of Legitimacy*. Translated by Weidong Cao. Shanghai: Shanghai People's Publishing House.

Jürgen Habermas. (2000). *Legitimations Probleme im Spat Kapitalismus*. Translated by Liu Beicheng. Shanghai: Shanghai People's Press.

Jürgen Habermas and Strukturwandel der Öffentlichkeit. (1999). *Untersuchungen zu einer Kategorie der bürgerlichen Gesellschaft*. Translated by Cao Weidong. Shanghai: Xuelin Press.

Karl Pearson. (1999). *The Grammar of Science*. Translated by Li Xingmin. Beijing: Huaxia Press.

Bibliography 191

Kevin Dowd and Mervyn K. Lewis. (2000). *Current Issues in Financial and Monetary Economics*. Translated by Yulu Chen. Beijing: China Tax Publishing House.

Kimsawa Ryu. (2005). *An Introduction to Economic Law*. Translated by Man Daren. Beijing: China Legal Publishing House.

Lawrence M. Friedman. (1977). *Law and Society: An Introduction*. New Jersey: Prentice-Hall Inc.

Lawrence M. Friedman. (1994). *The Legal System: A Social Science Perspective*. Translated by Li Qiongying. Beijing: China University of Political Science and Law Press.

Lin Yifu. (2012). *New Structural Economics – Reflecting the Theoretical Framework on Economic Development and Policy*. Translated by Su Jian. Beijing: Peking University Press.

Malcolm Rutherford. (1999). *Institutions in Economics*. Translated by Chen Jianbo. Beijing: China Social Science Press.

Mancur Olsen. (1995). *The Logic of Collective Action*. Translated by Chen Yu. Beijing: SDX Joint Publishing Company.

Mancur Olsen. (1999). *The Rise and Decline of Nations: Economic Growth, Stagflation, and Social Rigidities*. Translated by Lv Yingzhong. Beijing: Commercial Press.

Manfred E. Streit and Wolfgang Kasper. (2000). *Institutional Economics: Social Order and Public Policy*. Translated by Chaohua Han. Beijing: Business Press.

Martin Bronfenbrenner. (2009). *Income Distribution Theory*. Translated by Ming Fang. Beijing: Huaxia Press.

Masahiko Aoki. (2001). *Toward a Comparative Institutional Analysis*. Translated by Zhou Lian. Shanghai: Shanghai Far East Press.

Mauro Cappelletti. (2000). *Access to Justice and the Welfare State: An Introduction*. Translated by Liu Junxiang. Beijing: China Law Press.

Max Weber. (1998). *On Law in Economy and Society*. Translated by Zhang Naigen. Beijing: China Encyclopedia Press.

Max Weber. (2009). *Gesammelte Aufsätze Zur Wissensehastflehre*. Translated by Han Shuifa. Beijing: Central Compilation & Translation Bureau.

Michael E. Porter. (2002). *The Comparative Advantage of Nations*. Translated by Li Mingxuan. Beijing: Huaxia Press.

Neil MacCormick and Ota Weinberger. (1994). *An Institutional Theory of Law: New Approaches to Legal Positivism*. Translated by Zhou Yeqian. Beijing: China University of Political Science and Law Press.

Nicola Acocella. (2001). *The Foundations of Economic Policy: Values and Techniques*. Translated by Guo Qingwang. Beijing: Renmin University Press.

Paul Krugman. (1999). *The Return of Depression Economics and the Crisis of 2008*. Translated by Zhu Wenhui. Beijing: Renmin University Press.

Peter McLeod Jackson , ed. (2000). *Current Issues in Public Sector Economics*. Translated by Guo Qingwang. Beijing: China Taxation Press.

Peter S. Stein and John Shand. (2004). *Legal Values in Western Society*. Translated by Wang Xianping. Beijing: China Legal Publishing House.

Philip T. Hoffman and K. Norberg. (2008). *Fiscal Crises, Liberty, and Representative Government 1450–1789*. Translated by Chu Jianguo. Shanghai: Gezhi Publishing House and Shanghai: Shanghai People's Publishing House.

Phillip Cagan, ed. (1988). *The Economy in Deficit*. Translated by Tan Benyuan. Beijing: China Economy Press.

Ray Huang. (1997). *China: A Macro History*. Beijing: SDX Joint Publishing Company.

Richard A. Musgrave. (1959). *The Theory of Public Finance*. New York: McGraw-Hill.

192 Bibliography

Richard A. Musgrave. (1996). *Fiscal System*. Translated by Dong Qinfa. Shanghai: Shanghai People's Press, and Beijing: SDX Joint Publishing Company.

Richard Jones. (1994). *An Essay on the Distribution of Wealth and on the Sources of Taxation*. Translated by Yu Shusheng. Beijing: Commercial Press.

Richard Posner. (1997). *Economic Analysis of Law*. Beijing: China Encyclopedia Press.

Roberto Mangabeira Unger. (2001). *Law in Modern Society: Toward a Criticism of Social Theory*. Translated by Wu Yuzhang. Nanjing: Yilin Press.

Rolf Stober. (2008). *Allgemeines Wirtschaftsverwaltungsrecht: Grundlagen des Wirtschaftsverfassungs- und Wirtschaftsverwaltungsrechts, des Weltwirtschafts- und Binnenmarktrechts*. Translated by Libin Xie. Beijing: Commercial Press.

Ronald Coase, Armen Alchian and Douglass North. (1994). *Property Rights and Institutional Change: Collections of Translations of Property School and New Institutionalism School*. Translated by Liu Shouying. Beijing: SDX Joint Publishing House, and Shanghai: Shanghai People's Press.

Samuel Fleischacker. (2010). *A Short History of Distributive Justice*. Translated by Wanwei Wu. Nanjing: Yilin Translation Publishing House.

Simon Kuznets. (1955). Economic Growth and Income Inequality. *American Economic Review*, 45(1).

Stephen Breyer. (2008). *Regulation and its Reform*. Translated by Li Honglei. Beijing: Peking University Press.

Talcott Parsons. (1989). *Economy and Society*. Translated by Liu Jin. Beijing: Huaxia Press.

Tansou Akinobu and Atutanizyou Zin, ed. (1985). *Introduction to Modern Economic Law*. Translated by Cichang Xie. Beijing: Mass Press.

Tansou Akinobu and Hiroshi Iyori. (2010). *Economic Law*. Translated by Yoshida Keiko. Beijing: China Legal Press.

Theodore Dezamy. (2009). *Code de la communauté*. Translated by Huang Jianhua. Beijing: Commercial Press.

Thomas Kuhn. (2003). *The Structure of Scientific Revolutions*. Translated by Jin Wulun. Beijing: Peking University Press.

Thomas Piketty. (2014). *Capitalism in the Twenty-First Century*. Translated by Ba Shusong. Beijing: CITIC Press.

Uekusa Masu. (1992). 公的規制の経済学 (*Public Regulation on Economics*). Translated by Zhu Shaowen. Beijing: China Development Press.

Ulrich Beck. (2004). *Risk Society: Towards a New Modernity*. Translated by Bowen He. Nanjing: Yilin Press.

US Congress. (1986). *Tax Reform Act*. (100 Stat. 2085, 26 U.S.C.A. §§ 47, 1042).

Utz Schliesky. (2006). *Öffentliches Wettbewerbsrecht*. Translated by Wenguang Yu. Beijing: China Law Press.

Victor Thuronyi. (2006). *Comparative Tax Law*. Translated by Yi Ding. Beijing: Peking University Press.

Wallace E. Oates. (2012). *Fiscal Federalism*. Translated by Lu Fujia. Nanjing: Yilin Press.

Walt Whitman Rostow. (2010). *The Stages of Economic Growth: A Non-Communist Manifesto*. Translated by Xibao Guo and Songmao Wang. Beijing: China Social Sciences Publishing House.

William Thompson. (1997). *An Inquiry into the Principles of the Distribution of Wealth Most Conducive to Human Happiness*. Translated by He Muli. Beijing: Commercial Press.

Wolfgang Feikenje. (2010). *Economic Law*. Translated by Shiming Zhang. Beijing: China Democracy and Legal Press.

Wolfgang Fikentscher. (2010). *Wirtschaftsrecht*. Translated by Zhang Shiming. Beijing: China Democracy Legislative Publishing House.

Yoshio Kanazawa. (2005). 経済法序論 (*Introduction to Economic Law*). Translated by Man Daren. Beijing: China Legal Publishing House.

Index

4-trillion investment plan 153–4
2008 financial crisis 47n49, 105, 150

abolition of taxes 38–41
agent binary structure 13–14
agricultural tax 38
allocation of taxation power, collective
 taxpaying 86–8
asymmetric structure 139
authorized legislation 25

Beard, Charles A. 13
benign law 116
benign violations 26
binary differentiation 164–9
binary structure 14
binary system of taxation 133–4, 143;
 improvement of current systems 137–
 40; local taxation system and 141–2;
 sharing binary taxation system 134–5
budgets, distribution crises 151
business tax to VAT 41–2, 69, 71–3, 108,
 133, 142

change of circumstances theory 162–3
changes, in taxation law 33–5
Charter of the United Nations 101
choice for modes and cost of legislation,
 real estate tax legislation 131–2
choice of mode as basis for calculation of
 tax, real estate tax legislation 129–30
choice of mode of legislative body, real
 estate tax legislation 130–1
choice of mode of taxation object, real
 estate tax legislation 128–9
Chongqing, calculating real estate tax 130
civil right bills 14
collective taxpaying 82–4, 90–1; aims of
 85–6; allocation of taxation power 86–8;

exception to principle of independent
 taxation 88–9; transfer pricing and loss
 transfer 91–2
collective-sharing systems 98n72
competition 10–11; fair competition
 109, 111
complex branches 84
compound object, real estate tax legislation
 128–129
configuration to the power to
 administration of taxation levying
 bodies 120
consistency 18
consistency of distribution systems 6–7;
 economic dimensions 9–12; internal
 consistency 8–9
Constitution of the People's Republic of
 China (PRC): Article 3 Clause 1 64;
 Article 15 22, 97n48, 177n37; Article
 15 Clause 1 10, 22; Article 15 Clause
 2 10, 23; Article 15 Clause 3 10, 23;
 Article 56 64
constitutional foundation, for economic
 law 21–24
constitutional law 28; coordinated
 development of 20–21; coordination
 with economic law in development
 process 26–28; economic dimensions
 9–12; influence on economic law
 12–16; promotion of development
 through development of economic
 law 24–26; relationship to economic
 law 8–9
constitutional law economics 7
constitutional law violation 19
constitutionalism 19
consumptive VAT 42
coordinated development of distribution
 systems 19–29

Index 195

coordination: between economic law and constitutional law in development process 26–8; institutional coordination 33–5; internal coordination *see* internal consistency; of taxation law system 38–43
cost of legislation, real estate tax legislation 131–2
crisis 174n2
crisis response and, development of economic law 158–63
currency 107

Decision on Authorizing the State Council to Formulate Interim Regulations Concerning Economic Institution Reform and Opening-up 125–6
Decision on Implementing the Reform of Binary Taxation Fiscal System 138
Decision to Authorization 1984 53, 66–7, 125, 126
Decision to Authorization 1985 53–5, 59, 61, 66, 71, 72, 126
Decision to Authorize the State Council to Reform the Industry and Commerce Taxation System and to Publish and Experiment Relevant Taxation Regulations and Drafts 125
Decision to Reform (2013) 147n47, 148n63
Declaration of Human Rights in 1948 144n4
Declaration on Social Progress and Development in 1969 144n4
Declaration on the Right to Development 102, 108, 110
deduction 82
determination, power of 121–122
development 102
development law 101, 111–112
development of economic law, crisis response and 158–163
deviation 97n61
differences outside, unified distribution system 49–61
differentiated distribution, unified regulation to 61–74
differentiated treatment 67
discriminated distribution 67
distribution 1; protection of the right of economic development 101–112
distribution crises: economic law development 158–63; economic law response to 149–58

distribution law 1
distribution of interest 100–1
distribution regulation, binary differentiation 164–9
distribution regulation and control 168–73
distribution risks 1
distribution systems 1–2; coordinated development of 19–29; economic dimensions 9–12; internal consistency 7–9; internal coordination 36–43; internal differences in 74–81; mutual completion 29–36
duty of tonnage 65

economic constitution 9, 14, 19, 22
economic constitutional law 7–8
economic constitutional norms 7
economic development, right to 101–12
economic dimensions 7–12, 26
economic law 1–3, 28, 102, 105, 110; constitutional foundation for 21–4; coordinated development of 20–1; coordination with constitutional law in development process 26–8; crisis response and 158–63; economic dimensions 9–12; influence of constitutional law 12–16; promotion of constitutional law development through the development of economic law 24–6; relationship to constitutional law 8–9; response to distribution crises 149–58; right to economic development 103–4; risk prevention and control theory 160–1
economic law agents 106
economic legislation 50
economic measures, unlocking to deal with crisis 150–2
economic norms 17
economic structure, 105
economic system reformation and opening up 54
effective development of economic law 158–9
efficiency of: legislative experimentation 57–8; taxation law 59–60
exercise of power, distribution crises 153–5
expansion of tax collection powers 68; VAT 142
experiment models, VAT 52–3
experimentation 49–51; future of 60; legislative experimentation 53–5; taxation legislation 58–60; VAT 51–3

196 *Index*

extension experiment 57–8
external effects, of changes to taxation law and institutional coordination 33–5

fair competition 109, 111
fairness 68, 90; binary system of taxation 141; legislation experiment 59–60; legislative experimentation 55–7
Federal Commerce Commission 24
fiscal revenue 110
flexible methods 18
for-profit, real estate tax legislation 127–8
fourth type of power 11

GDP (gross domestic product) 110
Gini coefficient 111
good governance 37, 113, 116
government, choice of mode of legislative body 130–1
government procurement 175n9; distribution crises 151

Human Rights Committee 109

improvement of current systems, binary system of taxation 137–40
income tax 30
income tax legislation 50
inconsistency 18
independent taxation 88–9
influence of constitutional law and economic law 12–16
information revealing theory 161–2
institutional construction 82
institutional coordination, external effects of the change of taxation law 33–5
institutional law 24; stipulations 18
Interim Regulation on Corporate Income Tax 82
Interim Regulation on Real Estate Tax 123, 125, 126, 128
Interim Regulation on Taxation 118
Interim Regulation on VAT 51–2, 113, 121–2
Interim Regulations 54
internal consistency, economic nature of distribution 8–9
internal coordination, among identical distribution systems 36–43
internal differences in, distribution systems 74–81
internal limitations, Law on Corporate Income Tax 79–81

Interstate Commerce Act 1887 24–5
Interstate Commerce Commission 24

judicial verdict 27
jurisdiction: collective taxpaying 89–90; power of 120–1

land finance 124, 136
Law for Individual Income Tax 42
law of distribution 110
Law on Budget 161
Law on Corporate Income Tax 74–81, 86
The Law on Facilitating Medium and Small-scale Enterprises 104–5
Law on Individual Income Tax 167
Law on Legislation 59, 66, 71, 116, 118, 126
Law on National Bond 161
Law on Personal Income Tax 67
Law on Tax Collection 62, 64
Law on Taxation Collection Management 72
Law on Taxation Regulation 34
Law on VAT 117
laws of the economy 10
legal awareness, distribution crises 157–8
legal precedency theory 22
legal protection, right to economic development 106–8
legal systems, consistency in distribution systems 6–7; economic dimensions 9–12; internal consistency 8–9
legality of legislation experiment 53–5, 58–9
legislation, taxation 50
legislation experiment, fairness 59–60
legislation idea, VAT 113–14
legislation institutions, distribution crises 152–3
legislative experimentation: efficiency of 57–8; fairness 55–7; legality of 53–5, 58–9
legislative precedency, VAT 116
legislative technique 117–18
legislative value-orientation 115–16
legitimacy, distribution regulation and control 172–3
level of idea 138–9
level of principle, binary system of taxation 140–1
Lewis, Arthur 165
limitations: of Law on Corporate Income Tax 79–81; to quantification of duty

Index 197

78–9; of subjective quantification 77–8; of unification of Law on Corporate Income Tax 75–7
local fiscal revenue 133–4
local taxation system, binary taxation system and 141–2
loss transfer, collective taxpaying 91–2
low-lying land effect 56

macro-regulation and control 10–11, 25, 28, 106–7, 115; binary differentiation 164; real estate tax 124
Magna Carta 13, 15
market agents 106
market economy 10, 14
market economy system 22, 25
market failure 19
M'baye, Keba 144n5
merging taxes 39–40
micro-economy 25
moderation 68–9
mutual completion among distribution systems 29–36

national bond, distribution crises 151
national factors 81; collective taxpaying 82–4
National People's Congress 55, 66, 125, 130
neutrality of taxation 34
neutrality of VAT 114
non-judicial verdicts 27
non-profit, real estate tax legislation 127–8
normative dimension 27
Notice on Printing and Distributing the Scheme on Reform to Income Tax Revenue Sharing (Guo Fa [2001] No. 37) 138

over-cooling the economy 115
overheating of the economy 114
ownership 31

parliament, choice of mode of legislative body 130–1
performance of, distribution regulation and control 169–73
personal income tax 67
Planning Outline for the Twelfth Five-years 108
power, distribution crises 153–5
power of determination 121–2

power of jurisdiction 120–1
power of tax reduction 62–3
power to administration of taxation levying bodies 120
power to regulate 105
price of real estate 129–30
price transfer, collective taxpaying 91–2
principle of difference 75, 83
principle of differentiation 110
principle of independent taxation 88–9
principle of moderation 68
principle of proportion 96n39
principle of taxation efficiency, Law on Corporate Income Tax 80
private law 30
private ownership 14
private property rights 32–4
private-owned enterprises 109
procedural protection, distribution crises 156–7
productive VAT 42
promoting development of economic law 159–60
property 124
property protection rights 13
property rights 30–1; public versus private 32–3
proposal for taxation reduction 36–7
Proposal for Authorizing the State Council to Reform the Industry and Commerce Taxation System and to Publish and Experiment Relevant Taxation Regulations (Draft) [(84) State Council Letter No126] 125
protection: of local fiscal revenue 133–44; of property rights 31; of right to distribution, VAT transformation 112–22; of the right to economic development 101–12
public ownership 14
public procurement 151
public property rights 32–4

quantification of duty, limitations to 78–9
quantity of real estate 129–30

rate differences, Law on Corporate Income Tax 78
rate of security exchange stamp duty 96n38
real estate 100
real estate tax legislation 122–3; basis for 125–7; choice for modes and cost

198 *Index*

of legislation 131–2; choice of mode as basis for calculation of tax 129–30; choice of mode of legislative body 130–1; choice of the mode of taxation object 128–9; for-profit or non-profit 127–8; purpose of 123–4
reducing taxes: exercising tax reduction power in accordance with the laws 65–9; statutory power to reduce taxes 63–5; structural taxation reduction 61–2
regulation 10, 22, 25; distribution regulation and control 168–73; macro-regulation and control *see* macro regulation and control; taxation regulation and control 167–8
Regulation on Agriculture Taxation 38, 66
Regulation on Government Information Disclosure 156
Regulation on VAT (draft) 53
Regulations for VAT 51
relationships, constitutional law and economic law 8–9
right constitution 14
right to decision making 105
right to deduction 118–20
right to development 144n5
right to development-promotion 112
right to direct deduction 119
right to distribution, VAT transformation 112–22
right to economic development 100, 145n10; protection 101–12
right to indirect deduction 119
right to promote development 104
right to self-development 104, 112
right-obligation structure 10
risk prevention and control theory, economic law 160–1
rule of law 18, 139–40

separation of "two kinds of right" 32–3
Several Instructions concerning Encouraging and Guiding the Healthy Development of Private Investment 109
Several Instructions concerning Encouraging, Supporting and Guiding the Development of Non-public Economy Including Self-employed Business and Private Business 109
Shanghai mode, calculating real estate tax 130

sharing binary taxation system 134–5, 143; level of idea 138–40; level of principle 140–1; taxation power structure 135–7
Sherman Anti-trust Act 1890 24
simple object, real estate tax legislation 128–9
social distribution 167
special receipt (*Fapiao*) 116, 118
special taxation measures 62
Standing Committee of the National People's Congress, 18, 38, 51, 53, 66
State Administration of Taxation 82, 87–8
State Council 18, 39, 66
state-citizen property rights 13
state-citizens 104
statutory power to reduce taxes 63–5
statutory taxation 65, 90
Stiglitz, Joseph 105
stipulations, taxation 65
structural taxation reduction 37, 39–41, 43, 61–2, 66, 68–9, 72–4; VAT *see* VAT
subjective quantification, limitations of 77–8
systematic duplicate taxation 41
system-distribution-development 1–3

tax expense 87
tax preferential measures 79
tax reduction elements 65, 67
tax reduction power 62–3; exercising in accordance with the law 65–9; VAT 69–72
taxation 14–15; distribution crises 151; real estate tax legislation *see* real estate tax legislation; special taxation measures 62; statutory power to reduce taxes 63–5; structural taxation reduction *see* structural taxation reduction
taxation according to capability 130
taxation adjustment, coordination of taxation law system 38–41
taxation law 30, 60–1; collective taxpaying 82; external effects 33–5; external effects of change and institutional coordination 33–5; fairness 59–60; treatment differences in regard to corporate groups 84
taxation law adjustment 30–1
taxation law system, coordination 38–43
taxation legislation 50; experimentation 58–60

Index 199

taxation levying bodies 120
taxation management 81
taxation offset 82
taxation policy 169
taxation power, collective taxpaying 86–8
taxation power structure, sharing binary
  taxation system 135–7
taxation preferential measures 151, 166–7
taxation reduction 42; proposal for 36–7
taxation regulation and control 166–8, 170
taxes, merging 39–40
taxpayers' rights to deduction 118–20
theory of taxability 127–8
theory of taxation power 123
Three Determination Program 18
timing for legislation, real estate tax
  legislation 131–2
transfer payment 151
transitional experiments 57–8
transparency, distribution crises 155–6
trans-territory 84
treatment differences in regard to corporate
  groups, taxation law 84
trial legislation pattern 25
triangle-relationship 21
types of distribution systems, coordinated
  development of 19–29

unification of Law on Corporate Income
  Tax 74–5
unified distribution system, differences
  outside 49–61
unified regulation to differentiated
  distribution 61–74
United Nations: Declaration of Human
  Rights in 1948 144n4; Declaration on
  the Right to Development 108, 110,
  144n4; UN Charter in 1945 144n4
US Constitution 13; Article 1 Clause 8
  94n11, 96n45; Article 1 Clause 10
  95n32
usurious loans 109

value-orientation of VAT legislation
  115–16
VAT 42, 51–5, 57–8, 151; business tax to
  VAT 69, 71–2, 108, 133, 142; legislation
  idea 113–14; sharing binary taxation
  system 134–5; tax reduction power
  69–72; VAT transformation 112–22
VAT legislation 117–18
VAT Specific Receipt (*Fapiao*) 56,
  117, 119
VAT transformation 69–70, 72–3; right to
  distribution 112–22

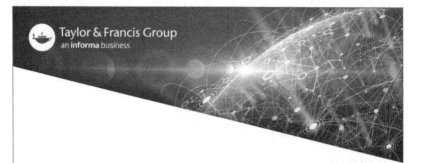